THE WEB OF

LAWFUL INJUSTICE

THE WEB OF
LAWFUL INJUSTICE

by

RALPH K. ATCHISON, JR.

with

CHARLES L. SOBER

as collaborator

Published by
RALPH K. ATCHISON, JR.
and CHARLES L. SOBER

This book is dedicated

to the little people

who believe in the principle

of Liberty and Justice

for all.

Acknowledgements

Gratefully acknowledged is the assistance and aid of the following people, without whom many features of this story would have been lacking:

Don M. Wolfe, Ph.D., of Princeton, Professor of English, Brooklyn College, New York.

William A. Dobkin of Pittsburgh, banker and merchant.

Marcus T. Allias, Ph.D., Lecturer in English, University of Pittsburgh, Pittsburgh, Pa.

Christopher J. Dattola, president of Ches-A-Rena, Inc., Cheswick, Pa.

Ira L. Sober of Vandergrift, accountant.

Paul Dunmire, chain banker and merchant of West Kittenning.

Other persons, too numerous to mention, who gave of time and effort to provide material which formed the basis and documentary proof of this story.

"*These written laws are just like spiders' webs; the small and feeble may be caught and entangled in them, but the rich and mighty force through and despise them.*"

— *Anacharsis*

Contents

xiii

Documentation

Foreword

THERE IS A GENERAL tendency to pass over numerous of life's tragedies, when problems of seemingly greater importance occupy the mind of the individual. In so doing the very core of the strength, not of an individual alone, but of the nation is infested with a blight which spreads like a cancer to eventually sap the life of a nation. In the story to follow, *The Web of Lawful Injustice*, which deals primarily with a criminal court trial in which a small town banker is involved, a greater truth is presented. The truth and the accompanying danger is revealed when the "small person" is caught in the toils of massive government, with every material resource at hand to threaten and condemn, and yet will make no effort to correct a wrong.

Because of the enormous growth in our Civil Government, because of the efforts to protect the entrenched bureaucratic officeholders, because of the interplay of forces in these bureaus, the story points out the difficulty of placing responsibility on either a bureau or an individual. The massive weight of a massive government and massive business seems to engulf any helpless individual who becomes enmeshed in a controversy.

Since the case originated in my area of Pennsylvania, I followed it closely. From a study of the story, the author makes no effort, no attempt to condone or uphold wrong-doing or an unlawful act. He not only attempts but does show the inconsistency of the modern era approach of law and rule. This is accomplished by taking the facts in the case as revealed through court transcripts and other data and showing that what is considered a crime for one, is practiced by those who readily turned informers. Thus, does law and justice become a mockery.

I found this story thought-provoking, interesting, compelling and at the same time disturbing. It is thought-provoking because it highlights the question of Government influence becoming entwined with so-called private enterprise. It is interesting because it reveals the myriad feelings of an individual, never before arrested and convicted, who undergoes the experience of a trial, days on the witness stand, subsequent conviction and imprisonment. It is compelling because deep within the heart and mind of all is the desire to see right triumph and justice done — yet there is no justice in this case. It is disturbing because it reveals how any individual who dares to try something different from the practices of the entrenched "bigs" is stripped not only of his resources, but is deprived of the "right of livelihood."

This is not some whimsy dreamed up in the mind to startle a complacent citizenry, who say "it could never happen to me." The characters, most of whom are unknown outside their own bailiwicks, are real, living people who had either a small or large part in the drama. The story shows the varied emotions that confront them when for the first time they fall under the limelight of publicity. It reveals, in some cases, the mental torture when they make efforts to correct the damage done by partial truths. It reveals how words spoken by government agents lead people to believe that material gain is at hand. When such gain is not forthcoming, they find they have helped to destroy the very people who might have possibly been in a position to help and aid.

This is a story that is vitally important to the thinking man or woman who is interested in the welfare not only of the nation but of that dynamic middle-class of citizens from whom have sprung the leaders and innovators in years past. If the bureaucracies, impervious to any corrective measures, continue to cut an ever widening swath through the rights of the people, it will be the death-knell, not only of the little banker, but of every enterprising individual who does not make obeisance to the faceless, unknown beings sitting in the seats of the mighty.

Introduction

THIS BOOK IS TIMELY and carries a definite message to those of us who are interested in this generation's America. It appears to me that it started out to first point up the case of Charles L. Sober, the principal character in the account.

However, it appears that research and the message collocated in activities that led to the Sober case, turns the book into what could be termed an historical document, cataloging and pinpointing the great problems that arise for the individual citizen when Government bureaucracy and Government influence become intertwined with so-called private enterprise.

I found it interesting and compelling. I found it thought-provoking and disturbing. I found also that in talking about the Sober case, the author was led into the question of the public press, the influence of private backing with public bureaus and vice versa.

All in all, it is a document of grave importance, and a timely catalogue for those who are looking for an answer to an enigma of big government, big business, and the relative worth of the rights of little people.

Without judging the right or wrong of the decision, or the justice that prevailed in the Sober case, one cannot help but note the book's attention to the dangers as they involve the average citizen in a faceless bureaucracy.

For the most part, the principal characters in the story are little people. There is no doubt, of course, that the book was written mainly for the purpose of showing Mr. Sober's side of the controversy. However, this does not detract from the great message contained throughout the relating testimony, the news accounts, the ultimate decision, and the present status of the case.

The case originated in my area of Pennsylvania, and I have followed it closely. I am sure the author makes no attempt to condone, or uphold wrong-doing or an unlawful act. What he attempts to do I am sure, is to show the inconsistency of the modern era approach of law and rule and order by pointing out the wrong and injustice of an era where the actions of one are not judged on the same basis as the actions of another.

If nothing else, it points out our road to big, big business, and perhaps the death knell of the little banker can be marked by the tolling of the bells for the end of the middle class American enterprise.

I might sum it up by saying that this book tends to show that in this day and age, what is sauce for the goose, is not always sauce for the gander.

CONGRESSMAN JOHN H. DENT
21st District, Pennsylvania

Preface

THIS STORY HAD ITS INCEPTION in the late summer of 1961, when the author, a long-time friend of C. L. Sober, now a resident of Pittsburgh, was approached by him. Sober, the principal character in a trial involving technicalities of a Federal Banking Law, felt that at the time of the case only one side of the story had been given any publicity, and that publicity was definitely in favor of the government's position. It was his desire that a booklet or pamphlet be written which would reveal many facets of the case, heretofore never brought before the public.

Briefly, his story was this: He had gained control of this small town bank, The Old Freeport Bank, in the face of stiff and bitter opposition. As executive officer of the bank he initiated many practices, which for kindness' sake will be labeled "unorthodox." His opponents termed these practices "unethical." However, the public, except for a few, showed its approval of the methods by patronizing The Old Freeport Bank. One of the practices initiated by him was a "no charge for checking accounts — regardless of balance." While the small depositors liked this service, Sober was approached by other bankers, who using the charge system for checking accounts, wanted him to follow their methods. Sober took the stand that stifled competition was in reality a violation of price fixing laws.

His stand resulted in remarkable growth for the bank, since the assets climbed from a little over a million dollars in 1952 to more than $8,000,000 in 1958. (See chart in documentation pages 2 and 3.)

During this period opposition to Sober and his methods continued to mount. His arrest was brought about in August of 1958, the principal charges being that he, involved with two of the bank's directors, received kickbacks (customers paying to individuals and bank officials — a fee for getting a loan), for aiding and abetting (helping the involved directors get money for securing the loans), and for conspiracy (entering into unlawful agreements with the directors in these loans). The same charges were leveled against the directors involved, while charges of embezzlement and falsification of records were placed against Ira Sober, son of Charles Sober. Jack Reese, cashier at the time, was charged with falsification of records.

The arrests and the removals of the principal officers of the bank came at a time when The Old Freeport Bank had applied for a charter to open a branch bank in Lower Burrell Township, adjacent to New Kensington. The Pennsylvania State Banking Department had granted the request, but it was held up by the Federal Deposit Insurance Corporation in Washington, D. C. A hearing regarding the granting of a charter was held in Washington, only the officials of the Old Freeport Bank, a state chartered bank, were never notified. Instead, representatives of two National Banks, who were direct competitors of the Old Freeport Bank, were said to have been present and to have testified in opposition to the granting of a charter. This hearing was followed by an examination of the Old Freeport Bank which lasted approximately four months and resulted in the removal of the officers.

While opinions vary, there are those even in banking circles who are of the opinion that a deliberate effort was being made at the time to close this small unorthodox institution. Yet, with all of the searching, no evidence was ever turned up that there was any shortage. To this day the bank has remained steady on the basis of the business instituted and built by Sober.

When the trial got under way, the question of law involved was the one relative to receiving money for getting loans for people. While the term "secure" in the story is used, it can be defined in two ways. For clarity, to "secure" a loan in banking terms means that the borrower or someone else puts up collateral (money, property, stocks, bonds or something of value) to back the loan in event the borrower defaults or fails to pay off the loan. The directors involved did not get money for getting these loans through, except in one instance. Both Dr. Heineman and Mr. Cypher placed their own money in the bank on Certificates of Deposit as additional backing, security, and collateral for the loans involved. During the trial it was pointed out that these men were getting a "kickback" on the loans since they received interest on the Certificates of Deposit. However, it has been revealed that banks often loan more than the borrower requires, with this additional money being placed in a savings or checking account, from which the borrower cannot draw. Sober's part in the "conspiracy" was the fact that the bank made money from such loans, and since he was a large stockholder, he in turn made money.

The trial was long, inflammatory and bitter. The daily papers in the area had a field day and the charges once expressed in print were repeated with an unnecessary frequency.

As the trial continued, items were revealed which in the minds of some, who followed the trial's progress, led to the theory that the case was being used to rid banking of an unorthodox banker who was making a success of his bank with unorthodox methods, and to promote certain individuals who were making a name for themselves by using the event as a stepping-stone to other fields.

After the trial and the defendants were found guilty on most counts, a new trial was sought on the basis of the testimony of two of the government's principal witnesses. At a hearing for a new trial, one of the witnesses declared that he told the "truth," but the way it was worded, it made it bad for the defendants. His wife who had not been called during the trial, testified that the government agents had stated that they would have their property returned to them. This allegation, of course, was denied by the accused government agents. The motion for a new trial was denied.

The case was then carried to the Court of Appeals and while two of the judges of a panel of three reprimanded the Government's attorney for the practices in which he indulged, i. e., multiplicity of charges, leading questions and the intemperate remarks to the jury concerning the defendants, there was a finding for the government.

The Supreme Court refused to review the case. Sober was sent to prison for a year, the two directors received nine month terms each while Ira Sober and Jack Reese were paroled on probation for three years. All received heavy fines as well. Sober served approximately half of his sentence before being paroled. Dr. Heineman and Mr. Cypher were paroled after being imprisoned for approximately a third of their sentences.

Shortly after his return from prison, Sober found a letter in his mailbox in which the writers asked for the address of the chief examiner of the Federal Deposit Insurance Corporation. The authors of a portion of the letter, who had been government witnesses, claimed they had been promised material rewards if their testimony would help to convict Sober. They stated that they had not gotten what was promised them. This letter led Sober to open an investigation of his own, and with the help of friends he received sworn statement after sworn statement, numerous letters and other documented material revealing questionable practices on the part of those who had conducted and who were aiding government agents in the investigation of The Old Freeport Bank.

Retaining an attorney in Washington to carry his case further, Sober then began to find that bureaucracies have many means of weaving webs to ensnarl, hold and halt. The term "red tape" began to have a new and vibrant meaning for him.

As soon as one phase of the investigation would be cleared, another ruling or demand would be put in its place to halt the progress toward reaching an equitable justice. In the meantime, some of the bankers who roundly condemned Sober for his practices, instituted many of the theories first espoused by him.

Thus the story stands at the present.

As stated in the beginning of the preface, this was originally intended to be a booklet or a pamphlet. However, a complete study of the newspaper accounts, transcripts of the testimony, the appeal to higher courts, the sworn statements, letters, and tape recordings of interviews with people involved, turned the pamphlet into a somewhat more lengthy story.

At first it was the intent of the author to show Sober's side of the story. This motive has not been forsaken, but there is a deeper purpose to this writing. It is hoped that it will show how small independents — whether engaged in banking or in the grocery business — are at the mercy of the faceless "bigs," who using political connections can throttle and destroy the "littles" who have the audacity to step on the toes of the "bigs."

In spite of the tribulations which have plagued Sober, he has staunchly maintained that he is not against all controls. He has repeated time and time again the need for bank examiners, the Federal Agencies that have to do with banking, the Bureau of Investigation, the Department of Justice and other agencies required for the proper conduct of business in any field. He does maintain just as staunchly, however, there should be no politics, no "conflict of interest," no personal interest in or among the personnel of these agencies. He has felt that laws should be spelled out and clarified and not used as a whip to shackle the individual initiative which in the past has contributed to the growth of this nation.

Unless corrective steps are taken, a greater threat is presented — not only to business men — but to the people. If someone with power can and does use that power for the harassment of the individual through a government bureau, then that bureau, fed through money collected from these same little people, may eventually use the power to usurp and destroy these same little people.

The danger is clearly shown. May the words which follow awaken a liberty-loving people to the danger.

About the Author

Ralph k. atchison, jr., was born in Iowa in an area which had as its prime distinction "that Jesse James and his men once rode through here." Moving with his family at an early age, his boyhood differed little from that of other youth of the period, brought up in the verdant hills and vales of Western Pennsylvania.

His interest in writing was nurtured early in life since his father and mother, of Scotch-Irish background, made available some of the world's best literature and writings. This bent was further promoted when his brother purchased an interest in a weekly newspaper, and would detail his younger brother to gather "personals" for each weekly edition. Thus, the interest in writing was coupled with an interest in people.

Formal education was furthered after high school with four years and a degree from Geneva College in Beaver Falls, Pennsylvania. The stark realities of the depression were encountered upon his graduation from college in 1934. Jobs were few and far between. However, wanderings of the author included a tour of the midwest by means of hitch-hiking, approximately a year as an employee of the Hookless Fastener Co., in Meadville, Pennsylvania, and various tasks on small daily and weekly papers in New York, Pennsylvania, West Virginia and Ohio.

With the advent of World War II the author worked for approximately a year and a half with the Martins Ferry Division of the Blawnox Company until called to the service. Of the twenty-six months as a member of the United States Naval Reserve, sixteen months of this period were spent on the island of Los Negros in the Admiralty group in the southwest Pacific. Returning with neither battle scars nor battle stars, he purchased a small weekly in Freeport, Pennsylvania, in 1946. While the job of running and editing this weekly proved rewarding as far as the study of human nature went, he found after thirteen years that he couldn't live and support his family on such rewards as above mentioned. Unfortunately it is a materialistic world.

Prior to suspending operation of the newspaper to help provide for everyday necessities, he took a position as a teacher in the Freeport Area High School. No man can serve two masters, so a year later the publication was suspended and teaching became his full time forte.

It was during his tenure as editor and publisher of the Freeport Journal that he met Charles L. Sober. While at first the the acquaintanceship was based on business relations, it developed into a strong friendship which has remained through the years.

The greatest portion of the documentary material in the story *The Web of Lawful Injustice* was furnished by the collaborator Charles L. Sober. A review of his life will be found in the story as it is told.

THE OLD FREEPORT BANK
FREEPORT, PA.

CHARLES L. SOBER

Chapter I

THE MID-MORNING sun heated the pavement of the main thoroughfare of the little western Pennsylvania town. A truck drew to a halt in front of a building of frame construction. Two stories high, it seemingly leaned as if from the weight of the many coats of paint. One of the two large windows, which were intersected by a recessed doorway, sloped at an angle to conform to the sagging window frame. As if unable to carry the weight, the sheathing above the window and doors, which had been placed perpendicularly, shed strips of the latest coating of gray paint to reveal myriad hues of the previous coatings of the past eighty years.

A bread truck braked to a stop in front of the building. The dust arose in a small cloud and settled anew, as the driver reached in the racks to the rear of the drivers' seat and pulled out ten small doughnut boxes. Jumping to the curb, he bounded up the four steps two at a time, entered the recessed doorway, pulled open the screen and strode quickly into the dull, drab interior. The spring on the screen brought the door closed with a quick stop. The front of the building trembled from the impact.

"Hey, Ma," yelled one of the group seated at a round table in the rear of the building, "that fella's here you been looking for."

A voice came from beyond a doorway to the left and rear of the table, "Leaf a couple off boxes. Der moneys in der cash register. Help yourself." The thick German accent was undimmed by years and years on American soil.

[1]

One of the five men seated at the table rose and went behind the counter. He lifted the lid of the top box recently deposited by the truck driver, pulled out a doughnut, placed it on a small plate and then licked his fingers.

"Bring me a couple of those," demanded one of the remaining four at the table.

"How many more want a doughnut?" asked the self-appointed counter-man, as he arranged small plates before the box and again dipped his tongue-cleaned fingers into the box. Two more requests were heeded and he carried the plates back to the table and seated himself before a cup, half-full of coffee.

It was part of a morning ritual in Freeport, a town of some 2600 located some thirty miles from Pittsburgh on the west side of the Allegheny River. The building was known as Kamers, and daily, business men, steel workers, railroaders and others convened in the little restaurant to drink coffee, eat doughnuts, make small talk, argue, settle world affairs, exchange information, complain, exchange confidences, which would soon be on every tongue in town providing the secrets had enough of the malicious and filth to be worthy of repeating.

This August morning in 1950 proved no different from the others. The group at the table had been arguing about inflation. There was a lull in the conversation.

One of the men, to show that he knew something the others didn't, placed his elbows on the table, held his cup in both hands, sipped slowly, and lowering his cup said, "Ya know, the Old Freeport Bank is going to change hands. Now, I got it straight . . ."

He got no further. One of the men wearing a cap which identified him as a railroader, interrupted, "Bill, where've you been? I heard that a couple of weeks ago. The fellows from the First National are buying up the stock, and they're going to consolidate the two banks, and they're going to move everything over to the Old Freeport Bank building, cause it's the better building . . ."

The second speaker didn't get much further than the first. This one had heard something, that one had heard this and another had heard that. Out of the garbled conversation, generously seasoned with opinion, rather than fact, came the news that someone was buying up Old Freeport Bank Stock. The assembly at the table agreed on that, but from that point on the news, enlarged, strained and magnified by the speakers to outdo the others, was as varied as Joseph's coat of many colors.

Before the group had departed to their businesses, their homes or their jobs, the following items had been set forth, not as opinions but as facts: the bank stock in question was being purchased by the First National Bank, the stock was being bought by a bank in Pittsburgh and the Old Freeport Bank would eventually become a branch of one of the larger banks, the stock was being bought by a Ford City Bank, by a Kittanning Bank, and by a group of individuals who intended to liquidate the assets and in some way make a financial killing.

Truth was showing through the darkness. In all stories told that morning in the restaurant, this much was true — someone was buying the stock of the Old Freeport Bank.

It wasn't long after this conference in Kamer's Restaurant that the citizenry in the little community began to receive letters from a brokerage firm in Butler, Pennsylvania, soliciting the stocks of a half dozen local and nearby banks. Included in this list of stocks was that of the Old Freeport Bank. Still in the background remained the party or parties responsible for this action. This much was known — someone was buying up Old Freeport Bank stock — this was fact.

The citizenry of the small community were not wont to let the story lie idle. What was not known was enlarged with each telling, and the tale-bearer embellished such facts as were garnered with his own interpretation. This in turn, would soon be repeated as a truth.

When the group gathered each morning for coffee, the latest, pertaining to the stock purchasing would be rehashed. Out of the maze of half-truths, came this factual statement — a man by the name of Sober was buying the stock. Again the theories ran rampant. He was buying the stock for a Ford City bank, controlled by people with the name of Dunmire. When the transaction was completed, so the story went, the stock would be turned over to the Dunmires, who in turn would make the Old Freeport Bank a "paper bank."

Some of the stories were not so mild. A young man walked down the street one day and he was hailed by a maiden lady, who having nothing better to occupy her time, delighted in keeping up with the latest stories in the community, whether they pertained to the latest "shotgun" marriage or some erring husband unfaithful to his wife or the banking business.

As the young man drew near, she rasped, "Haven't seen you for a spell. Come in and sit. Can't stand out here and talk, hard on my asthma." She brushed a wisp of yellow-white hair from her forehead, to cover a spot on her head where hair had ceased to grow.

"Well," stammered the young man, as he made an effort to go on, "I'm busy and . . ."

"Don't have any time for me, humph! Come in here," she commanded.

In deference to long training to respect the old, the young man stepped into the doorway.

"Now, you wait here. I'll get a paper and put it on this chair, seeing as your clothes are dirty. Did you wipe your feet good?" she questioned, as she scurried to another room, brought out an old newspaper to serve as a buffer from the dirt and grime of work to her overstuffed chair. She hesitated not a moment, "What do you know about this fellow that's buying the Old Freeport

Bank stock?" Her tone was not that of a request. It was imperious and commanding.

"Why, I don't know very much," he replied. "I heard that someone was trying to buy Old Freeport Bank stock."

The maiden lady beamed. She pulled a paper over a rip in her dress. "Well, I know." Her words came with a snort. "He's in with gangsters. He's tied up with that—and he's a gangster. I know, I was told by a party right in the bank." In self righteousness, she smiled. She knew a wrong and had revealed a wrong.

"I didn't know anything about that," replied the young man. "I knew someone was buying stock, but I hadn't heard who it was."

She was loath to leave her visitor go. After plying him with questions, she gave all of the details of the bank transactions, plus other stories of the type which are only whispered in small communities, she consented that he go to his work. As a parting admonition, she yelled, "If you tell what I told you, I'll say that you lied." With that she slammed the door and rushed to clutch the papers that had protected her furniture, and hurry them to the incinerator, so no germs would contaminate the house. Her biggest flaw in the story which she had repeated was that the man she had named as a gangster, later turned out to be a highly respected dentist from a nearby community.

While some continued to rehash these tales, they gradually began to diminish as truth raised its head. Myron Rowley, the Pennsylvania Railroad station agent in Freeport, paused one day on his way home from work to greet some of the townsmen. The conversation concerned the man Sober. Rowley listened to some of the exaggerated stories for a moment, and then added his voice to the conversation, "Why, you're worse than a bunch of old women gossipers. There ain't a word of truth in that. I know Sobers. Used to work for the Pennsy. He's from Vandergrift, and has been running the credit bureau there for years."

Within the period of a few weeks after the stories had originated, many of the citizens had met Sober. He had been soliciting stock in the Old Freeport Bank. These people in turn told their stories and they began to counteract the original stories.

As the group gathered in Kamer's for coffee one September morning in 1950, the topic of conversation again turned to the man who was buying the bank stock. A man sat quietly at another table for a while. The others had ventured many stories. The man turned to the group and said, "Have you met this man you're talking about?" Not one, who had been so ready to give information replied in the affirmative.

"Well," he continued, "I have. He offered to buy my stock. Don't know where he found out I had some, but he offered to buy it."

"Probably trying to steal it from you!" was the offering made by one of the group, who had been loud in his detraction of a man he had never met, never known, and never seen.

"Nope!" the retort was firm. "I got this stock when Dad died. He left it to me, so I went to the bank and inquired as to its worth. One of the fellows in the bank told me it was worth about three dollars a share. This fellow Sober offered me ten dollars a share, and I don't think I'll pass that up."

The group at the table in the restaurant turned quiet. Their so-called knowledge which many had been willing to repeat as fact, was beginning to be shown up for half-truths.

"What's he buying it for? Must be worth something to someone, if he's willing to pay ten dollars a share for it?" one in the group queried.

The stockholder volunteered the information, "I'll tell you just what he told me. He said that he wasn't buying the bank for anyone or any other bank. He has a son and he figured it would be a good investment for his son and him, and he could also see where a bank could be a lot of help to a lot of people."

"Don't see how," was the response from another. "What could

[6]

he do in a bank, that isn't already being done?"

"All I know is what he told me," answered the stockholder.

* * * * *

Similar stories were to come into the open as C. L. Sober continued his drive for stock. He made visits. He pounded on doors. From one person he would gain some information as to the possible owners of stock. From another, he would learn of a disgruntled stockholder dissatisfied with the present management of the bank. The price of the stock gradually rose.

Across the street from the Old Freeport Bank stands the First National Bank of Freeport. Even prior to the advent of Sober on the scene, some feeling, not altogether a good feeling, existed between the two banks. However, there were those connected with the First National Bank who had been buying Old Freeport Bank stock.

Now that a man by the name of Sober came on the scene, the drive for stock on the part of those connected with the First National Bank began to step up. However, those who were buying stock and who were connected with the competition bank, were loath to meet the par value price. They had been buying the stock on the basis of loyalty to the community, that a stranger was trying to get control, and that it was the duty of the Old Freeport Bank stockholders to sell to a friend and neighbor. This appeal was good for some. There were others who frowned on this buying technique, and held that the stock would go to the party or parties who offered the most money for it.

This attitude resulted in some ill feelings—feelings which continued for a long time. A railroader walked into the First National Bank. He was approached by one of the officers. "Hear you're selling your stock to that man Sober," he stated.

"That's right," was the rejoinder from the railroader.

"Don't think you ought to do that. Wouldn't be right to sell to

[7]

him. He's not a man of very good moral character. You wouldn't want that kind of a man in this town, would you?"

The railroader set his mouth in a straight line. He answered with a question, "I suppose you know all the moral standings of the men in the companies you own stock in. Are you getting rid of it just because they're not the type of men you think they ought to be?"

"You are being unreasonable now— I'll give you ten dollars a share for your stock," replied the bank officer.

"You're away off base. Sober offered me more than that, and what's more, what's moral about trying to get something for nothing, when it's worth more than what you are offering?" With that statement, the railroader gave a snort and strode out of the bank.

The autumnal hues turned dark and drab. The dead leaves rustled as the winds heralded the approach of winter. As the leaves were ripped from the trees, the battle for stock went on and on. The late A. M. Johnston who was at that time president of the Old Freeport Bank, was approached one day by the owner of the small weekly serving Freeport.

"Is there any truth to the report that this man Sober has enough stock to control the bank?" the editor asked the president.

The old gentleman was non-committal. "Don't know, don't know."

The editor questioned further, "He has been getting some stock in the bank, hasn't he?"

The interview came to an end as the old banker walked away with a shake of his head, "I guess so," was the reply.

There were times when Sober was not successful in purchasing stock. Some of the reasons were personal, some were odd, and some were the result of a pure dislike because of the stories making the rounds that had never been allowed to die.

He had heard of a lady living near Pittsburgh who owned a block of Old Freeport Bank stock. He journeyed to the area and found her residence, and made his wants known. He stated a price he would pay.

"No," the lady replied, "I'll not sell my stock to you."

"Am I not offering enough for it?" asked Sober.

"Yes," she answered, "but if I sell to anyone it will be Hugh Ralston. He's the cashier, you know."

"I know him; I've met him, but why are you holding the stock for him?" Sober asked.

"He was one of my Daddy's pallbearers," she replied and with that the conversation was closed.

Regardless of the favors done in the past, there were slights and hurts that had not healed through the years. Perhaps it was this attitude on the part of many which helped Sober in obtaining stock.

One lady, who had worked in an office for years in Freeport, was in charge of settling an estate. Included in the estate were several shares of Old Freeport Bank stock. She went to one of the officers of the bank, revealed her plight that the estate was in need of money. The offer made her was seventy-five cents a share. This she took as an insult and a couple of years later when contacted by Sober, sold the stock to him. She gloried, not quietly, but loudly, that she had enough sense to wait and boasted that she had gotten more than par, which was $10 per share.

Sober was gradually getting stock. How much he had, no one knew for sure—but he was buying stock.

As he became known around town, one of the citizens ventured to query him, "Say, Sobers (it was common practice for many to put the 's' on his last name) why are you making such a big blow about buying the stock? Why didn't you pick up a little at a time and on the q. t. You coulda had it for a lot less. Lot o' people never expected to get more than two, three dollars a share."

Sober replied, "I don't want to drive them away. I'll want them for customers. They won't be customers if they feel they have been cheated."

[9]

The battle was gradually growing to a climax. It was nearing the Christmas season and early in January, the annual stockholders' meeting of the Old Freeport Bank would be held. Once again the rumor mills started. The stories were varied and wild, yet sometimes they were factual. The morning coffee gatherings had Sober with enough stock to gain control, with not enough stock to do anything, and a half-hundred other tales both in support of his drive and with a note of distinct disfavor.

A flurry of activity preceded the meeting that cold January morning of the second Tuesday in 1951. Sober was represented by an attorney. The "old guard" of the bank had an attorney and as the voting progressed during the meeting which was just as cold as the January day, tempers were being brought to a white heat. Every proxy was challenged. In the end, C. L. Sober was a member of the board of directors. The "old guard" chose the late Dr. C. M. McLaughlin as the "scapegoat". He was removed from the board.

This was just another step in the war. One battle had been won, but victory is only counted by the final accounting. Sober demanded and received a list of the stock holders. He began in earnest to buy stock.

One thing was certain in the small community. More interest was being shown in the Old Freeport Bank than had been shown in a long, long time. Sober did not intend to let the interest lag. He was out among the farmers and the tradespeople, the millmen and the railroaders, children and the aged—he was boosting the Old Freeport Bank and picking up stock or proxies whenever he could.

As the year 1951 rolled to a close, interest in the fight for the control of the bank was renewed. Rumors and stories again gained ground as the groups gathered in their favorite loafing places. However, on these occasions one or two supporters of Sober could be found.

With a list of the stockholders, Sober continued to contact them far and near. He went to a farmer who lived within a few miles of the town. He was a man known for his frugality and his keen ability to discern a good investment. As Sober told his story to the farmer, which included his plans for making the bank grow, the old gentleman, well up in years, rubbed his chin, cast his eyes to the ceiling and then gave his answer. He would sell one half of his stock, give the newcomer his proxies for the other half—for if it was going to be as good as promised—he wanted to remain a stockholder.

Then there was the incident of the Sunday School stock. A class in a small church near Freeport held a few shares of stock. The stock had been obtained after the bank had reorganized following the crash of the early thirties. Upon reorganization, a percentage of the deposits held by individuals and organizations was released to them as stock. This was the reason that there was so much stock, scattered far and wide throughout the area. Anyway, Sober contacted the officers of the class concerning the purchase of the stock. The class agreed and the transaction was to be consummated at the home of one of the officers. The money was paid in cash, and the stock was turned over to Sober. Upon returning to his home that evening, he found that he was twenty dollars short. He chalked it up to experience and promptly forgot about it for the time being. However, there are in this world those who cannot keep their good fortune to themselves. The Sunday School officer had to tell friends how careless that man "Sober" was, and how she was twenty dollars to the good. She forgot to tell her benefactor about this carelessness—and hasn't to this day.

The trumpets were sounded, the call to arms came that second Tuesday of January in 1952. It was the annual meeting of the stockholders of the Old Freeport Bank. The forces arrayed against the "old guard" were many and strong. In spite of strong speeches, of the bickerings of the attorneys, when the proxies were counted

C. L. Sober was in control of the Old Freeport Bank with a definite majority on the board.

A new era in banking was about to begin—not only in Freeport —but in western Pennsylvania.

Chapter II

LOLLYPOPS

The annual meeting which saw Sober gain control hadn't any more than been adjourned, when the new executive vice president began to work. The meeting of the directors, held within a week of the stockholders session, resulted in Franklin V. Bush being named president. The late A. M. Johnston, who had served as president since 1932 when the bank was reorganized following the closing resulting from the bank holiday, was elevated to the position of Chairman of the Board. Ira L. Sober, son of the executive vice president, was named vice president, and Jack C. Reese, a young man raised in Freeport, was named as one of the assistant cashiers.

As the new board assumed its duties, Sober continued to work. In spite of the resentment shown in the immediate local banking circles, there were those in banking who were friendly with the new executive vice president.

Here was a small-town bank. The resources were little over a million dollars. Where was the progress to come from? What was the next move to be made? Sober's advisors, even while making the recommendations, shook their heads in unison — as much as to say — that is what needs to be done, but it can't be done. The bank must grow, and where in a community the size of Freeport could this growth come from?

These were not the only problems confronting the new officers and members of the staff. In concentrated and self-centered small towns — and Freeport is the epitome of them all — the resentments against the newcomers, the would-be and successful interlopers are strong. The deposed directors in some instances withdrew their accounts, and urged their friends to do likewise. There were some who made withdrawals.

One doesn't live in a small town without becoming associated with every facet of its life, one does not make everyone a friend. Whether in the course of business, in politics, in religion, in social affairs or in just being alive, resentments, dislikes and even hates are fomented along with the friendships. It may be that small-town people get to know each other too well, or it may be just a trait in human nature to want to do the opposite of what someone else is doing. As the word was passed in devious ways that the "good" citizens were withdrawing their money, there were those who made it a point to deposit funds. So the drive to discredit the new banker bogged down as January became history and February merged into March in 1952.

While Ira Sober and Jack Reese were making an effort to learn the workings of the bank by asking questions, the elder Sober was sticking his head and his arms into every cranny in the bank. One day he saw a "pigeon hole" to the right of the tellers drawer. As he walked back to the counter, he noticed a similar cranny at every tellers cash drawer.

"What are these places for?" he asked Mrs. Hilgert, a long-time employee of the bank.

Before she could answer, Hugh Ralston came onto the scene. "That's where we keep our revolvers."

Johnston, the board chairman, noticed the three with their heads together and soon joined the party. He added his information to that of the others, "They're for protection, in case we are ever held up." With that he reached into one of the openings and drew forth a revolver. He held it up to his mouth. A small cloud ascended into the bank as he blew on the weapon.

"That thing loaded?" asked Sober.

"Certainly," Johnston replied.

"When was the last time it was cleaned?" Sober continued his questioning.

Johnston slid the revolver back into its place, pulled out his hand and then wiped the dust from it on his handkerchief. "Hum, let me see. Oh, I'd say maybe five years ago we had them all cleaned. I don't remember exactly."

Hugh Ralston had returned to his window, and Mrs. Hilgert turned her attention to a customer at the window.

"Huh," Sober snorted, "they'd probably blow up in your face, if you ever did get them out in time to point at a robber.

With that the subject was seemingly dropped. The bank's employees, having by that time become acquainted with some of the traits of their new supervisor, noticed that he paced back and forth in the bank's interior, casting a glance every now and then in the direction of the crummy holes to the right of the tellers' cash drawers.

"Something's up. I can tell by his actions," Mrs. Hilgert confided to the young lady who occupied the window adjacent to her.

The next morning Sober strode into the bank long before the opening hour. Under his arms he carried several boxes. He deposited them at the tellers' windows and awaited the employees to show up.

After the regular morning tasks of getting cash for the drawers, getting other working supplies out was done, Sober walked behind each teller's window. He reached into the pigeon-holes and brought out the revolvers. These he deposited in a box. As each cranny was emptied, he ordered the vacated places thoroughly cleaned. The tellers' eyes bugged as he opened the boxes which he had earlier deposited at the windows—before them were lollypops—hundreds and hundreds of lollypops.

"Now, you take these suckers," he indicated to the tellers as he issued the orders, "and put them in there where those guns were. Everytime a kid comes in here with his dad or mother make sure he gets a sucker."

"Any age limit?" asked one of the employees.

"Naw, I don't care whether you give them to any kid from nine weeks to ninety. Just give them a sucker." With these words, he turned to return to his office. He found Johnston blocking his path.

"I don't like this at all, not at all," proclaimed the old gentleman as he shook his head negatively. "In the first place, you're leaving the tellers without any protection at all in case we are held up. Furthermore—"

Johnston got no more words out in his protest.

"Nuts. Those guns are so dirty, they probably wouldn't even fire. And if any guy would try to stick up this place, they'd be here and gone before anyone would get their hands on the gun. I don't believe in taking chances anyway. If some bird comes in here and demands money at the point of a gun—we'll give it to them. The money's insured anyway." Sober paused for a breath.

Johnston was ready by this time. His words were precise and clipped, "We should do everything in our power to protect our funds. You just might be able to get a shot at a bandit. I used to be a fair shot with a revolver myself."

"When was that? Thirty years ago. Ha! Betcha you couldn't hit the side of a barn door, now," Sober retorted.

Johnston was through. His ability, his judgment and in a sense his authority, which he had held so long, had been challenged. He continued, "And another thing, what is this about giving children candy. This is a bank. This is a dignified business. This is a business dealing with a person's most precious possession—money. We'll become the laughing stock of the banking circles." His eyes snapped as he made valiant but vain efforts to uphold

[16]

his philosophy—the philosophy of a century. There was no place for warmth, or for that matter, personal feeling. The banker was a stalwart figure in the community. The banker had dignity and he maintained that dignity. A banker never lowered himself to the "gimmicks" used in other businesses. As for a child, the paternalizing pat on the head was sufficient. As for lollypops, the idea was ridiculous.

"Give lollypops," ordered Sober, and he turned and walked away.

At first there was some hesitancy on the part of the tellers. If a child accompanied by an adult happened to walk away from a teller's cage without a lollypop clutched in his fist, Sober was out of his office presenting the child with candy. If there were indications of more children at home, enough suckers were presented to the parent, so that none of the wee bairns remaining at home would be forgotten.

It was not long until the little boys and girls, when accompanying their parents, would tug at skirts, hands, sleeves to urge their parents into that place where they could get a lollypop. Even the late A. M. Johnston, who at first opposed the move, soon found delight in handing out the goodies to the children.

However, all was not sweetness and light. Among the members of the defeated and opponents of the new Freeport banker, it was customary to hear such phrases as, "Oh, you mean the lollypop banker," or "Humph, trying to buy business with suckers."

The people in the area hardly had time to digest the appeal to the children, when the papers serving the area came out with huge ads, with captions: "Now—Open Saturday Nights." The signature at the bottom of the ad was The Old Freeport Bank. This was unheard of, and the other bankers in the area grumbled. Banking hours had been set for a long time. As if by collusion, banks had set hours from 9 to 3 Mondays through Fridays, and from 9 to 12 Saturday mornings. Yet, here was this upstart

[17]

banker, who had the audacity to open a bank Saturday nights. And this was not all, while other banks took advantage of every holiday marked on the calendar, the ad also announced that the Old Freeport Bank would be open for business every day except Sundays, Memorial Day, Fourth of July, Labor Day, Thanksgiving, Christmas and New Year's. The announcement further stated that the bank would be open on Good Friday from 9 until 12, at which time the other businesses closed.

The move which brought about the new hours, was not one that came with ease. While the new board had voted in favor of the hours, there was reluctance on the part of some of the members. It is often difficult to step from established practice, regardless of how necessary such moves are. There were some who felt that the move might antagonize competition, and they also felt that competitors, already angered, should not be given any more grounds to whet the hate which had been started. Johnston, the chairman of the board, opposed the move and stated that he would not be on hand to serve, even though the clerks and tellers were being paid extra for the additional hours of work.

The first Saturday night under the new plan came inexorably. Time will not be stopped. The date and the hour had been set. The tellers and clerks had indicated a willingness to serve. At six o'clock, the late Charles Cassel, who was then the custodian of the building, unlocked the doors. For a few moments Sober paced in the lobby of the bank. When decisions had been made, there are always the little doubts which creep into the mind. Had those people really meant what they said when he had been soliciting proxies? Did they want longer and more convenient banking hours? Would they take advantage of these additional services, or would they, too, feel that such a move was off the beaten path of accepted banking practices? As these thoughts tumbled one after another through his mind, he heard the door open. Sober quickly raised his head to greet the first customer—it was A. M. Johnston, who had opposed Saturday night openings.

As he started for his desk, he nonchalantly removed his hat as he said, "Thought you might need some help." His words proved to be prophetic.

The customers wandered in by one and twos. At times, that first Saturday night there were ten and twelve customers in the bank at one time.

As word spread around the area, more and more people began to take advantage of the Saturday night opening. Even some of those who at first opposed any change, found that the Old Freeport Bank offered a convenience. With the trend to the suburban areas on the part of the people, with only one car to serve the family, with the bread-winner at work during daytime hours, many had found it difficult to bank during the regular hours. Now, here was a bank that catered to their needs.

Prior to the decision to open the bank on Saturday evenings, Ira Sober, son of C. L. Sober, and Jack Reese had been brought into the bank. Both of these young men had had some experience in accounting. After completing a stint in the armed services, the young Sober with the Army Air Corps and Reese in the U. S. Air Force, both had continued schooling. Sober had gone to the Robert Morris School of Accounting, and Reese to the New Kensington Business College. The young men had come into the bank with hopes, aspirations and feelings of pride. Little did they realize the jealousies and resentments their presence would create, not only among the members of the "old guard," but also among the group who actively opposed the elder Sober's control of the bank from the very beginning.

As the young men assumed their duties, they sought the help of those who had been in the banking business for years. This help and instruction were not forthcoming rapidly. The younger people, who had been in the bank previous to the change in management, were somewhat hesitant in opening wide the secrets of the bank. At the same time the elder members of the staff would dismiss questions with, "I'll take care of that."

However, Ira sought to learn as did Jack. When the clerks were posting the ledgers, they would literally look over their shoulders.

One day while examining the file which contained the postings of the checking accounts, Ira noticed penciled notations at the top of various accounts. Upon looking closer he found the words in pencil, written in a plain, but very small hand, "No charge." His curiosity aroused, Ira turned to one of the bookkeepers standing near him. "What does this mean?" he asked. The bookkeeper turned, and with a shrug of the shoulders walked away. Ira was still bothered. He pulled out one of the cards and examined it. He noticed that at no time was there a charge made for checks. He pulled out another card, bearing a similar notation. Again there was no charge being made on the basis of the number of checks written, only the balance carried in this account was practically non-existent.

Ira knew that immediate inquiries, based on his previous experiences, would net him little, so he searched until he found a list of the rules governing a checking account. In black and white the rules were set forth. A minimum balance must be carried at all times, to elude a charge for writing checks. This minimum balance would give the holder of the account a certain number of entries (deposits or written checks) without a service charge. The greater the balance in the account the less the charge would be, or the more checks one was permitted to write without charge. However, Ira could find no rhyme or reason for the accounts marked "no charge." Some carried substantial balances, while others, most of the time, had balances of zeroes with no supporting figures before them.

He took the discovery to his father, the elder Sober. That evening, after the bank had closed to public business, there was a conference. Why, Sober wanted to know, were some people charged for checking accounts, and why were some people never charged?

Out of this meeting grew the revelation that the people who were not charged, regardless of the balance carried, were friends of the bank. Further examination revealed that some of these "friends" were the severest critics of the bank, and one of them had been actively engaged in promoting a merger of the Old Freeport and the First National Bank of Freeport prior to its acquisition by Sober and others.

The matter of charges for checking accounts was resolved at the next meeting of the board. Sober presented the findings and urged that the board adopt a policy of "no charge for checks, no minimum balance required." However, before the motion was carried, there was some debate. Question after question arose. Wouldn't there be a financial loss? After all checking accounts brought some funds into the bank. Wouldn't such a move be deviating from the course pursued by the other banks in the area? What other bank in western Pennsylvania had such a policy? They all charged for checks. Finally, the board acceded to the request of the executive vice-president.

Within a few days huge ads in the area papers carried the announcement — "No charge for checking accounts! No minimum balance required! Free checks furnished! Checks cashed free!" While the announcement was greeted happily by some, with skepticism by others, there were those who raged openly that this upstart, this newcomer had the audacity to kick over all traces of established practices on the part of other bankers.

Even before the air had cooled, other innovations were introduced — yet they proved to be almost as ancient as the Old Freeport Bank itself.

As the word spread that the Old Freeport Bank had "free" checking accounts, activity in the bank proper increased. More and more customers crowded the lobby and the Saturday evening hours became particularly popular. Still the new officers were busy delving into the dusty, musty files that contained the records of half a century. They noted the books and ledgers penned in a fine Spencerian hand. The figures were neat and orderly, and the occasional flourish gave them the appearance of the copybooks used in schools more than a half hundred years ago. It was while Ira and Jack were going over some of these old records that they came across a packet of forms which bore the printed heading "Certificates of Deposit."

They carried a couple of the forms to the elder Sober. The paper on which they were printed was in good condition, and in spite of its antiquity, did not crumble and fall to pieces when handled. The elder Sober looked over the form.

"Hey, Johnston," he yelled, "what are these things?" The white-haired old gentleman, known throughout the banking circles in Pennsylvania and even further, walked to Sober's side and took the proffered paper from his hand. His hand shook slightly as he read the print on the slip of paper.

"Certainly, I know what these are. They are Certificates of Deposit!" he answered.

"What's Certificates of Deposit? I can read that, but what are they for? How do you use them?" Sober put to Johnston in a series of questions.

Johnston was in the height of his glory. His dimmed eyes grew brighter as he told of banking practices long forgotten by many of the modern day financiers, and completely unknown to the novices in the Old Freeport Bank. "Why, these," he exclaimed, "are forms used when a person desires to leave money in the bank for a specified period of time. Usually they were written up for a period of a year. For example a person would come in with a thousand dollars. If this person knew that he wouldn't need this money for a year, he would put it in the bank on a Certificate of Deposit. Since the bank would be assured that this money was available for a specified period of time — that it wouldn't be withdrawn — a little more interest would be paid on this than on a regular savings account."

Sober evinced still more interest. "Are these things legal?" he asked.

"Certainly," was Johnston's rejoinder.

"Why don't banks use 'em now?" Sober continued to query.

The old gentleman smiled knowingly. This man must certainly be naive, he thought. The answer was easy. "Why," he replied with a question, "would a bank give additional interest when most people already put money in savings accounts at one per cent and ask no questions?"

The new executive vice president mulled this over in his mind for a time, and then put a final question to Johnston, "Well, now, let's say that someone puts money in the bank on a Certificate of Deposit, and they need the money before the time on the contract has run out. What then?"

"Usually," his instructor stated, "if a statement is made showing dire necessity on the part of the holder of the certificate, payment is made and interest is paid to the date of withdrawal." With that the old gentleman dropped the subject and returned to his desk and picked up The Wall Street Journal.

Sober continued to look at the paper for a long time. He turned it over in his hands. He studied the print, read and reread the words not once, but many times.

It was not long after this that again the papers brought out big ads proclaiming: "Earn more on your Savings! Buy a Certificate of Deposit. Get up to (2½) two and one half percent interest." The ad went on to detail the plan.

The plan caught fire and the business at the bank continued to grow.

There were anxious times, however. Hearsay had not been quieted. Wagging tongues, fed with the bits of fuel of half-truths, flamed anew with scandal of truth, as the new management put into practice each new innovation. Again the source was traced to the defeated in the battle for control and disgruntled employees, who had left the bank.

The time had arrived for the examiners. It was their first visit since the new management had taken over. Some of them, too, had been apprised of the vicious tittle-tattle that had been flowing from tongue to tongue.

Upon completion of the examinations, it was found that the assets of the bank had increased almost two hundred thousand dollars. The report on June 30th, 1952, showed a total of $1,250,055.05. The examiners had some criticisms, too. The law did not permit the paying of three percent interest, and Sober was ordered to correct this offer being made by the bank at once. Further, the examiners learned of some of the stories being spread by word of mouth, being spread by people who should have known better. The examiners called on these people and informed them of the law—that it was a serious offense to start, tell, repeat or spread stories that might be harmful to a bank, if these stories could not be substantiated. The stories soon died down. The lie, the half-truth and the innuendo had not been successful in halting the activities of Freeport's new bankers.

The first hurdle was over. Six months of business had resulted in a substantial growth considering the problems involved. There was more work. Employees, who had formerly devoted hours to personal affairs, Boy Scout work, church activities and sundry other projects, now found that they did not have an opportunity for such work. Their duties at the bank required their full time. Some were disconcerted over this state of affairs, while others accepted it as a part of life and joined in promoting the growth of the institution.

There was no resting now. The growth during the first six months under the new regime was only the start. If other bankers had shaken their heads over the problems, Sober did not take time to question. To be of service and successful, the bank must grow.

As the summer months of 1952 turned into fall, when the leaves began to lose their luster and dress the valley wherein Freeport is located with their reds and yellows, a new ad bearing the signature of the Old Freeport Bank appeared urging savings accounts for youngsters. The "Hopalong Cassidy Savings Accounts" were designed especially for the young element of society. Besides being a stimulant to savings, each young depositor was enrolled in the "Hopalong Cassidy Club." As the savings grew and as various stages in the individual accounts were reached, the child would receive a button signifying the duties of a cowboy, such as a ranch hand, wrangler, foreman, etc. Added interest in these accounts continued to grow, clomping down the main thoroughfare of Freeport on Saturday came a man dressed in chaps, wearing a ten gallon hat and riding a white pony. He was advertising a Hopalong Cassidy movie to be shown in the local cinema. The showing was sponsored by the Old Freeport Bank and the admission was free.

Even children learn from their elders. As the young fry gathered in groups on the street awaiting the theatre to open there were many arguments as to whether the man on the pony was Hopalong Cassidy or not. The youngsters were clamorous in their debates, with one claiming to be just as much an authority as the other. When the doors of the theatre swung open they rushed for the seats, and were soon turning their attention to the hero on the screen who outran, outrode, outfought the dastardly villain to clutch the heroine to his manly chest.

At the intermission, Ira Sober and Jack Reese marched to the front of the throng. The Old Freeport Bank had door prizes for the children.

That night hundreds of children relived the drama of the silver screen, while their parents talked about the Old Freeport Bank. The Hopalong Cassidy Accounts continued to grow and grow.

With the advent of the holiday season, while men with their

mouths proclaimed "Peace on earth, good will towards men" the animosity toward the new bankers was not left to die. The Old Freeport Bank paying interest on savings accounts from December 1st, had not advanced the interest rate on savings accounts. The closest competitor, The First National Bank of Freeport, paying interest from January 1st to July 1st, had shown no indication of raising the interest rate on savings deposits. It was in the early part of 1953, the competitor bank came out with a huge announcement that it would pay two percent on savings accounts.

This move, in a sense, caught the Old Freeport Bank unawares. There had always been an unwritten agreement that any such major change in policy on the part of one bank or the other would be discussed between the officials of the two banks before being put into effect. The clash had grown into open conflict. There was no collusion; there were no secret meetings; there were no open meetings.

The officers of the competitive institution claimed that cooperation on the part of the Old Freeport Bank was lacking; that no effort had been made to work out plans regarding the certificates of deposit or on the free checking accounts. So, agreements, verbal or otherwise, did not hold. Now, in respect, it was each institute for itself.

The move on the part of the competitor did not put it in an advantageous position for a very long period. The announcement on the part of the First National Bank had only been out for a few days when the Old Freeport Bank came out with an announcement that it, too, would pay two percent on savings accounts.

While the play and by-play regarding the savings accounts was taking place, other moves were being made to entice customers and build good will.

One day prior to the Christmas season, a man walked into the lobby of the bank accompanied by his four wee progeny. As he completed his transaction, the teller handed lollypops to each of them. Just at this moment the elder Sober walked out of his office into the lobby. He greeted the customer and smiled at the children, who were busily engaged in getting the wax-wrappers off the suckers in preparation to jamming them into their mouths.

"Say, Sober," the man questioned, "where is the sucker for the dad?"

Without a word, Sober reached into his pocket and pulled out a couple of cigars and handed them to the questioner.

"Aw," went on the customer, "I was only a kiddin'. You know that." He made a feeble and half-hearted attempt to hand the smokes back to the bank official.

"No, you keep 'em," Sober replied.

The group left the bank in high spirits, as Sober returned to his office and immediately began to root through his desk. He looked for a folder he had received only a few days previously. He found the folder and immediately began going through the items listed thereon. Of course, it had been the custom for years not only for the Old Freeport Bank, but other financial institutions and stores to give calendars near the end and at the beginning of each year. Figuratively speaking, wouldn't the grown-ups like "lollypops" as well as the children. Sober busied himself with the folder and finally satisfied with his actions, sealed an order in an envelope and sent it on its way.

Within a few days a number of parcels arrived at the bank. There was no need to clean out any musty, dusty cubbyholes. Sober removed the items from the boxes and placed several of them at each of the tellers' windows.

"Now, when a customer comes in," ordered Sober, "you give them one of these or a couple of them."

"Even if they just come in to cash a check?" asked one of the clerks.

"Yeah, if they only cash a check. Just hand them out."

It was not long until the Old Freeport Bank's customers were being given, not only calendars, but book matches, ball point pens and pencils, all carrying the bank's name.

Before many years had passed the gifts to the customers included not only the above mentioned items but address booklets, plastic rain hats, hot panholders, yardsticks, and other sundry items used for advertising purposes. Coupled with the free checking accounts, free check books and many other services offered, the Old Freeport Bank soon became the talk of the district.

As the year rolled on, the time came for the report of condition required by the Pennsylvania Banking Department and the Federal Deposit Insurance Corporation. At the close of business on June 30, 1953, the assets stood at $1,832,864.69. At the same time the report showed that the surplus and undivided profits had increased almost ten thousand dollars. Better still the dividends to the stockholders were increased from five to seven and one half percent based on the par value of the stock.

But in spite of the growth and advances, all was not well. An elderly merchant banker left his place of business on Saturday evening, and while he rested in his chair would question those who passed as to their destination and advised them not to go to the Old Freeport Bank.

Chapter III

JUST BANKING

THE ACTIVE OFFICIALS of the Old Freeport Bank were too busy to pay any attention to the slights and innuendoes that all was not well. The horde of people using the bank's service increased daily and the Saturday night throngs helped not only that institution but the merchants as well. Here was one bank open, when every other bank with one exception, Merchants Nat. Kittanning, Pa. in western Pennsylvania had closed its doors, serving the people at a time the people desired to be served — not at the banker's convenience.

As the word spread of the bank's new approach to customers and banking problems, some people who had distrusted such institutions since the bank holidays of the thirties, were once again bold enough to try this new bank. Still behind the willingness, were the memories of what had happened in the past.

It happened in the late summer of 1953. An old, grizzled farmer walked into the bank. He hesitated once he was within the doors and looked over the tops of his glasses, noting the plaques above the tellers windows. Finally, he saw one which said "Loans." He ventured to the window. "Say, there, young feller," the man of husbandry stated, "this where I make a loan?"

The young man back of the window greeted the man pleasantly and automatically reached for a series of loan application forms which might be used. He then invited the farmer into the office adjacent to his window.

The usual questioning began. "What did he want the loan for? How much did he propose to borrow? Did he own property? As this line of interrogation continued the set of the customer's mouth became more and more rigid. The relaxed jaws became tight and small knots of muscle appeared along the neck.

"Jist a minute, now," and his words came with such force and clarity that they could be heard throughout the bank, "I came in here for a little money. I wanted to borrow a little money, but dad blame it, I ain't a gonna begin ta give ya my life's history for it. First thing you'll be asking me if I kissed or kicked my wife this morning."

The sound of his own voice gave him added confidence, and looking over the railing that separated the small office from the lobby and seeing that he had an attentive audience, he continued, "Yep, that's what gets me about you bank fellers. You want to know everything. What about this bank, here? Betcha if I was to bring in some money, you wouldn't ask me a lot a silly questions. You'd think I was crazy, if I'd start pumping you about the time of day and a lot of other questions."

The potential customer was about to continue his tirade, when the elder Sober, hearing the voice, stepped from his office into the adjacent cubicle where the conference was taking place. He extended his hand, and the man of the soil took it rather reluctantly. Sober introduced himself and invited the farmer into his office.

"Couldn't help hear you," exclaimed the elder Sober. "Seems as if you don't think much of bankers."

The man who had been invited into the office had been diverted for the moment. Sober took advantage of the lull, and offered him a cigar. "That young fellow was only doing his job. After all, this money we lend out belongs to our depositors. We have to have a little idea where it's going, and we have to know if it will be returned." Sober eyed the man thoughtfully for a moment. His long experience in the credit business, revealed many things about the person. He could tell from his calloused hands and the wrinkles about his eyes, that he had looked into the sun. The reddish brown complexion resulted from wind-burn as the result of hours in the fields. "You are a farmer, aren't you? He asked.

The startled man of the soil looked at Sober in amazement. "Yep, but how'd you know that? Didn't think we hicks showed it so much any more?"

"I can tell a man that works," answered Sober.

"Ain't changed my mind much about bankers, though. Just because you guessed what I do. No, sirree, I still think the same about bankers."

Sober didn't realize that his next question would unloosen a torrent of feeling held within the heart and mind of the man, when he asked, "Well, what's wrong with bankers?"

"What's wrong with bankers?" The prospective borrower's voice rose in a crescendo. "Why, I'll tell you. You act like a customer is a worm crawling to the corpse to feed on a pittance of dried blood — now, I ain't meaning you alone — but bankers, bankers in general act like funereal, craven so-called humans. And look — jist look at your banks — marble and steel, cold, unfeeling and heartless. Why, they look like overgrown mausoleums, 'stead of warm, friendly business places. And another thing, you bankers sit in your soft chairs, work a couple of hours a day and call that a hard day's work." He took a deep breath and was about to continue, when Sober interrupted.

"You talk about hard work. Why you farmers don't know what

[31]

hard work is anymore. You've got machinery to do everything. The hay is bailed in the field. The manure is spread by machinery. A tractor pulls the plow, and instead of plowing one furrow, you plough several furrows at a time. You milk by machine, you feed your cattle by machine — what do you mean 'hard work'?"

The farmer's mouth, which had held to the straight line, except when talking, fell open in amazement, "What do you know about farming?"

"My dad," Sober went on, "ran a country store and a farm over at Weinel's. When I was a boy I had to work on that farm. Talk about spreading manure, I helped do that too and it was by back-breaking labor. We'd load the wagon, drive to the fields, and then fork it off. And making hay wasn't what it is either. Remember the hummocks and how you'd go out with the hay rack? Then you had to fork it onto the wagon, drive back to the barn, stick the mow fork into that load, pull it up to the mow, trip the fork and a third of a rack of hay would come tumbling down in the mow. Then it had to be spread. The timothy seeds would get down your neck; you'd be sweating up under those barn eaves, but you couldn't stop — the hay had to be gotten in. Now then, talk about plowing. My dad wouldn't stand for any of this cut and cover business, and walking behind a plow and horse, keeping your furrows straight . . ."

Sober got no further. His visitor's mouth relaxed, "Well, Sobers," he said as he extended his hand. "I guess you do know what hard work is." He got up to go, "Guess there ain't any use of expecting any loan here after what I said about bankers. I still mean it though. Need a little money to build a silo, but this is the third bank I been too—the others acted just like I told you—just as if they was doing me a favor by even talking—got a little tired of it. Good-by, Sobers, and thanks for the cigar." The man grabbed his battered felt, jammed it on his head, shoved his toilworn hands in his jacket pockets and started out of the office with his head high. The heritage that was his, the heritage of being an American, independent, bowing to no one, catering to neither the rich nor the poor showed in his demeanor.

"Wait a minute," Sober yelled.

The farmer turned and looked at Sober.

"I didn't say we wouldn't loan you the money. Come in and sit down." It was partly order and partly request.

After a moment of hesitation, the husbandman returned to Sober's office. Soon there were roars of laughter as the two men met on equal ground. The conversation continued for twenty minutes, and as the two men parted Sober said, "Yep, we'll be out to see you real soon. I'm sure we can help you."

The thoughts were many and varied that ran through Sober's mind after his return to the office. The complaints voiced so succinctly and plainly concerning bankers, he had heard before. He had to admit that banks were not the most pleasant places in which to do business. The very architectural designs, while perhaps promoting the feeling of strength, also had a tendency to exclude any feeling of warmth and friendliness.

It was only a short time after the farmer's visit that Sober and Johnston made a journey to the farm. Here they found acres and acres of well-kept land; the fences were in good order; thousands of dollars worth of machinery was housed in the barn and adjacent sheds; the living quarters, not pretentious, were good and adding to their value was their setting in well kept lawns. Added to all this was a herd of cattle that would bring several thousand dollars on any stock market.

Sober and Mr. Johnston returned to the bank to complete the work on an appraisal. What Sober found bothered him. Here was a farm, well equipped and well stocked. Subsequent investigation revealed that the farmer had a good reputation and would be considered a good credit risk. Yet this man had been turned down twice before coming to the Old Freeport Bank. The words he had spoken—the words of truth revealed with feeling—pointed out a salient fact concerning banks. There were times when they were too cold and unfeeling, when they apparently did ask too many questions, especially when the prospective borrower was often worth more than the capital stock issued by the bank. These were items for correction, and this farmer and hundreds like him must be given an opportunity to secure needed capital when they required it.

This particular problem had not any more than been solved for the moment, when a lady who first saw light of day in sunny Italy, walked into the bank. She approached the teller and demanded to see "Dis a man Sobers."

She was soon ushered into his office and in halting English told her story. She wanted to borrow twenty dollars. She revealed that she and her husband, long residents and citizens of this country, had a small savings in the bank. However, she did not want to bother this nest egg. She would rather borrow a few dollars to have money to pay certain of the utilities which were due before her husband's pension check came.

Sober looked at the lady. What was one to do? A small amount such as the one she asked involved a certain amount of paper work. The interest on the loan would hardly pay for the work involved. So, the new banker reached into his pocket, pulled out a twenty and handed it to the lady. Her thanks were profuse and loud.

On the date proposed for repayment she walked into the bank. Imperiously she walked to the window of the teller. "I justa wanta see dis man Sobers!" When he was free of another customer, she walked proudly into his office and pulled out twenty dollars and laid it on his desk. "You onea gooda man, Meester Sobers. I tella alla my friends about you. You coma to my house sometime. I givea you drink of wine." With this offer of hospitality, she marched out of the bank.

[34]

Sober was not to see the last of her. Whenever pressing bills amounted to more than the small monthly pension which she and her husband existed on, she would march to the bank to "seea my friend, Sobers," get a small amount of money and repay just as promptly.

It was not not long after this incident, that several accounts were opened in the bank. Many of these were carried under names that proclaimed the depositer was either a native, or had forebears from this country of romance. His newly found friend had been urging and advising all of her friends and relatives to go to The Old Freeport Bank.

The new customers in the bank were many and varied. While the Old Freeport Bank was becoming known throughout an area that continued to grow wider and wider, other things were happening at the bank than taking in and handing out money.

With the words of the farmer still ringing in his ears concerning the "mausoleums of stone and marble, cold and heartless," the management resolved to do something about this accusation. The first move was to fix a window with slab boards. For the convenience of the younger customers, too small to reach the window, a small set of steps were erected. Above the window hung a crudely lettered sign, "Hi, pard! Hopalong Cassidy Corral."

Not only were the comforts of the youngsters catered to, but two drinking fountains were placed in the lobby, and rest rooms were provided for the customers. Each added convenience seemingly brought more and more customers, while the opponents became more bitter in their denunciations, with such remarks as "Humph! That bank's beginning to look like a side-show tent at a circus."

The new management couldn't win all of the time. Efforts to please the customers occasionally backfired and the "favor" hurt more than helped. One day a prominent citizen of his respective community walked into the bank. He approached Sober and declared, "Sober, you've got to help me out. My son is coming here for a loan. I don't want you to give him the money."

"Why not?" queried Sober. "I know you have some money. Why don't you loan it to him?"

The man hung his head. It is rather difficult for a boy's father to admit that his son isn't just about perfect. It was rather hard for a man to admit that he had told his son he didn't have any ready cash, rather than say "no;" he had told him that he could have the car he wanted, if he could get the money from the bank.

It wasn't very long following this conversation that the young man came into the bank. He didn't ask, but demanded audience with Sober. Within the confines of the office, he poured out his story. He wanted a car. He needed a car. He didn't have any particular use for the car except to run around and that all of the other fellows had one.

Sober listened to the story for a time. He looked the boy in the eye steadily for a time. The young man, bloated from over indulgence and lack of physical exercise, his face cluttered with pimples, could stand the stare no longer. He dropped his eyes.

"How you going to pay this money back?" asked Sober.

"Oh, I'll pay it back, all right. I can pay it back. My old man's worth a lot. If I don't, he will. You won't lose nothin'. All I got to do is raise a stink around the house about what a tight-wad he is—you'll get your money."

"Yep, I'll get my money, all right, just because you are a stinker. You've told me you've been out of school for quite a time. No job—no nothing—. You go on living off someone else. It's about time you wakened up. You're not going to have your dad forever, and if you keep up the way you're going you'll ruin yourself and your dad. The thing for you to do, young man, is to stop being a sponger. Get out and get a job, and prove your value to yourself and others. When you do that we'll begin to talk about a loan—"

Sober had not finished his lecture when he noticed two huge tears rolling down the cheeks of the young man. Without a word the youth pulled himself out of the chair and walked out of the office. He had been humiliated; he had been frustrated, but worst of all his demands, which had always been so successful with his father, had failed to gain him his desires. The hard lesson of life, never even acquired before because of overindulgent parents, was brought to him fully. There were people—at least one person—he couldn't fool.

Thoughts of the encounter were put aside for only a few minutes when a shadow fell across Sober's desk. As he looked up he saw the young man's father standing before him. Half in anger and half in pleading, he said, "Sober, why in the world were you so rough on the boy? After all he's only a boy, and he needs help and understanding . . ."

"Understanding!" yelled Sober. "He understands you too well. He knows that when he turns on the waterworks, you'll . . ."

The doting parent interrupted, "You get a note ready and I'll sign it." Then rationalizing, he added, "Perhaps he'll find a job if he has a car. Anyway he promised to pay it back. He will; I know he will; I'm sure he will." The words tumbled out rapidly as the man tried to assure himself that his son would do all that he in his heart hoped he would do.

There were other incidents, literally thousands of them, that added to the bank's growth and assets. Yet when the clouds of adversity opened to pour troubled water upon the institution's officers, those who stood fast were not the so-called "big people," but the "little people" who would not forget the help offered in times of need.

A young man walked into the bank one day and requested a loan to buy a car. He was rather hesitant. His previous experiences in trying to borrow money had not met with success. He told the teller that he wanted to borrow money to buy a car and was directed to Ira Sober. The information was taken and the young man was informed that the money would be available.

The transaction was but one of many similar transactions taking place daily. It was forgotten for the moment, and nothing transpired to bring it to the attention of the officers at any later time, because the customer was prompt and sometimes ahead with his payments.

One Saturday evening, as the bank lobby filled with people, doing sundry tasks which necessitate the bank's services, the elder Sober was summoned to his office. When he went in a man and woman, husband and wife, and a young man were standing in front of his desk. They were greeted and before time was dilapidated in small talk, the woman in the party drew a check out of her handbag and laid it on Sober's desk.

"I want you to deposit this for me," she commanded calmly. The check was for $19,000.

"I will call one of the girls," answered Sober, as he turned the check over in his hands. "How do you want it? Checking account? Savings account? Certificate of Deposit?"

"Well, you fix it any way you want to. Don't make it too easy for me to get, 'cause every once in a while I get a hankering to spend money," was the woman's reply.

Again the question was repeated by Sober, and again the answer was the same, "You fix it any way you want to."

The teller who had been called into the office was given instructions to put a part in a checking, a part in savings and the remainder in Certificates of Deposit.

When the employe had departed to complete the records, the lady, who was the spokeswoman for the group, put the question to Sober, "I suppose that you are wondering why we're putting this money in your bank?"

Sober had been curious ever since the people had come to the office instead of going directly to the teller's window. He made a half-hearted attempt to fain disinterest by commenting that it was all a part of a bank's business, but within his mind he wondered why these people, whom to the best of his recollection, he had never seen before, were making this deposit.

Again the lady spoke, "Know this young man here?" She pointed to the youth. "He's my son."

Before she could continue, the banker being politic, said, "Oh, yes, now I remember him. You did some banking here, didn't you?"

The younger of the two men nodded in the affirmative.

"Some time ago," the lady continued, "you loaned him some money. He'd been to several banks before he came here. The others wouldn't do anything for him. You loaned him the money he needed. He said at the time, 'Mom, if you ever get any money, I hope you put it in The Old Freeport Bank. They were nice to me.' Well, Mr. Sober, I was in an accident some time ago. Fact is, I was laid up, when my boy here, needed some money. This money is from a suit for damages, and when people are good to my boy . . . "

The youth could hold back no longer, "Yes sir, Mr. Sober, I said to Mom if she should ever get any money to put it in your bank."

By the time the story had been told, the teller had returned to the office with the account books, checks and certificates. The usual parting pleasantries ended; at the close of business the Old Freeport Bank showed a substantial increase in assets.

The new bankers learned, somewhat through trial and error, that it didn't pay to say "no" too quickly, or to be too prompt to say "yes." Often the man or woman who appeared at the bank looking as if they had stepped out of a page of a style book, owed for the very clothes they had on their backs. On the other hand the man in the ill-fitting suit, wearing a shirt that was frayed at the collar and cuffs, and decorated with a necktie that showed signs of a thousand knots, soiled with the drippings of sundry

[39]

foods during a decade, might be an excellent credit risk or a potential customer of inestimable worth.

A man walked into the bank one day. While his clothes showed signs of being good, they were worn and of a cut and style that had been in vogue some few years prior to the date of his visit. He approached the teller and inquired for Mr. Sober. Upon being ushered into his office he stated his business promptly. He said that he wanted to buy some Government Notes (U. S. Government 90 day bonds), and inquired whether it were possible for an individual to make such a purchase. The elder Sober declared that he didn't know, and in turn summoned his son Ira and put the question to him. Ira turned to the books and pamphlets on Banking Laws and stated that he could find nothing in these books regulating the sale of such "paper" to individuals. The visitor then asked if he could purchase such bonds through the Old Freeport Bank. The answer was yes! He was told that such government "paper" was allotted to the various small banks from the larger banks and that it was available upon occasions. The price agreed upon was the market price at the time of delivery, plus a small broker's fee.

It was but a short time later that the Old Freeport Bank had some Government 90 day bonds. The person soliciting these securities came to the bank and completed the transaction, writing a check for approximately $100,000 on another bank.

"You know, Mr. Sober," he said, as he turned over the check and received the bonds, "I was told that I couldn't buy government notes at two other banks. Thank you, Mr. Sober. Good day, and you will see me again."

It was not very long until the individual kept his word. A substantial checking account was opened in the Old Freeport Bank, and until the time of the man's death his transactions brought close to $400,000 in business to this little Western Pennsylvania, small town bank. It was business taken from the bank's competitors, large and small, because they would not accommodate him in his just and legal desires.

The growth through the years, from 1953 until 1958, did not come from large accounts which had been transferred from competitor banks. The growth in all departments was from just plain "little people." The people who borrowed small amounts, and the people who deposited small amounts. The growth came from the inherent justness in people, who being favored, in turn like to favor.

A salesman walked into the bank one day and sought an order for various banking supplies and forms. The items were needed, and after the order had been placed Sober approached the visitor regarding the opening of an account. The visitor replied that it would not be feasible for him to open an account in Freeport. "After all," he declared, "I live in Brookline, and I only call on your bank once every three months. Just would not be convenient for me to have an account here. Furthermore, the bank where I do business, is also a good customer."

"How about a Hopalong account?" Sober asked.

"Oh, sure, I could open a little account for the son. I thought you meant something larger."

"We'd be glad to have a small account," was Sober's reply.

Thus the account was opened — the original deposit was five dollars. Later the salesman was to admit that this small account had grown into a savings of approximately $1,400. So the bank grew and grew and grew.

In the late fall of 1953, the new management of the Old Freeport Bank—those upstarts as they were called by competitors—brought about a new innovation for the times. Not since the twenties, the period before the crash, had any bank paid interest on Christmas Savings Clubs. Upon the mailing of the Christmas checks for 1953, a folder announced that one percent interest would be paid on Christmas Clubs paid in advance or kept up to date. At the same time huge ads in all of the area papers proclaimed the same thing.

While the opposition to Sober and his methods roundly condemned such a program, more and more people were drawn into the bank. The customers would line-up at the windows with a handful of Christmas club books—one for each member of the family.

Even at the beginning of this program, the elder Sober did not realize that one day it would spare him trouble. As the deposits went up, so did the loans.

Sober and Johnston had made an appraisal on a proposed mortgage. The prospective mortgagees were told that as soon as the money was available, the loan would be granted. As the deposits increased Sober ordered Johnston to prepare the papers for the mortgage. Sufficient funds were in the bank to grant the loan desired.

The papers were prepared in due order and the mortgage was taken. Some few months following this transaction bank examiners made one of their periodic visits to the bank. The examination hadn't any more than been completed when Sober was summoned to appear before the examiners. The examiners were blunt and to the point. The Old Freeport Bank was over extended on mortgage loans. According to the law, on a specific date a mortgage had been taken, and this particular mortgage put the total of mortgage loans over the percentage permitted to be loaned. This percentage was based on the amount in time deposits, which bore interest to the depositor.

Sober looked at the figures which were shoved toward him by the examiners. He looked at the mortgage which had been the veritable straw "to break the camel's back." It all came back to him. He had remembered telling Johnston to prepare the papers for this loan, but he had not reckoned on a large savings withdrawal which had been made that day. Yes, the figures were correct. From all appearances, he was in trouble. He had authorized a loan which had resulted in the total loans exceeding the percentage permitted by banking law.

"What law says that we can't make over a certain percentage of the savings deposits?" Sober asked.

One of the examiners leafed through a manual and finding the edict, read it to Sober.

"Read that again," ordered the banker.

It was read again.

"Why, I'm all right. I haven't broken any law," Sober yelled at the examiners.

There was a stunned silence for a moment. The very audacity of this man proclaiming that he hadn't broken any law, when it was here in black and white.

One of the examiners, his face flushed, slammed the manual on the table, 'What do you mean, you're all right? It says right here," he paused for a moment and his index finger went to the book on the table before the group, "that you can't loan over a certain percentage of your deposits on interest bearing accounts and Sober" he wagged his finger under Sober's name for emphasis, "you did just that."

"Well, now, wait a minute," Sober pleaded. He put his hands on the table and shoved himself and the chair backward to give him room to rise. "Look at this figure, here." He pointed to the examiners' records. "This shows the time deposits. Right?"

"Right," responded the spokesman for the examiners.

"Well, now," Sober continued, "look at this figure." He pointed to the column listing the Christmas Savings.

"What has that got to do with it?" was the rejoinder.

"That law you read," Sober stated, "just said that you couldn't make mortgage loans over a certain percentage of a bank's deposits on interest. Well, we didn't loan over the amount allowed.

[43]

You add our time deposits and our Christmas Club accounts . . ."

"What are you trying to pull, Sober? Add the Christmas Clubs to your savings — do you think we're crazy?"

"No, but the law doesn't say what kind of accounts as long as they're interest accounts. We're paying one percent on Christmas Clubs. On this day that you said we were over extended, we had $79,000 in Christmas Clubs."

One of the examiners grabbed the reports. He scanned the figures quickly. His only comment was "Humm! Humm!"

A short time later Sober was called into Pittsburgh to confer with the Pennsylvania State Secretary of Banking. After the usual amenities, the question of using the interest bearing Christmas Clubs was brought to the fore. But the conclusion was "All right, Sober," said the gentleman across the table, "You won this time, but don't use Christmas Clubs as backing for mortgage loans after this. I'm making a ruling." This affair was settled. But laws and the rulings by bureaucrats were to plague Sober in the years to come.

In spite of seeming reverses and set-backs, banking continued and the growth continued. Innovations, both in banking and as attractions to customers, continued to appear almost monthly.

As 1954 passed into 1955, the resources of the bank had leaped from $2,366,167.32 to $3,336,101.89 on June 30th. All departments of the bank had grown. The circle of customers came from ever widening areas. Dividends were being paid regularly, and surplus was growing along with the bank's climb.

While the officers and tellers and employees were busy caring for the needs of the customers, the bank itself was taking on a different appearance. A low wall was erected on the outside of the bank. The enclosure built of canyon stone, added to the appearance of the structure and between this wall and the bank building proper, small shrubs and flowers were planted. Changes were taking place in the interior of the building, too. The old marble columns, "cold and heartless" as one customer described them, were being removed—customer and banker were meeting on more convenient and equal grounds. At the Eastertide, lily after lily decorated the interior of the banking quarters, and at Christmas the bank was a galaxie of color with the lighted Christmas tree in one corner of the lobby, and poinsettias placed in every conceivable spot that did not hamper the business operations of the bank.

Customers came to look for the changes taking place. Children scampered to the indoor, decorative fountain and clapped their hands in glee when they beheld six fluffy ducklings placidly treading the water of the pool.

The bank became a meeting place for people who desired to transact business. A desk in one corner of the lobby was provided for those who could meet more easily at a central point. It was not long until the bank became a central exchange for hundreds of people. All of these services resulted in more business for the bank. The resources continued to grow and grow.

While all of these progressive innovations were taking place, business was being conducted. People were making deposits, people were borrowing money and transacting such affairs which required the services of a bank.

A young man walked into the bank one day and requested information regarding a G. I. loan. He had served in Korea, and having returned to his homeland, he looked forward to a full and rich life. The papers carried news story after news story about the many beneficial services which the government was offering to young men who had served their country in time of danger. But visits to other lending institutions had resulted in negative results. In spite of the stories, banks, he found, were not making G. I. loans. He walked into the Old Freeport Bank. He had married recently. He wanted to build a home under the G. I. loan plan. Yet he had been turned down by the banks which he had visited. Here as a last resort, he sought the people who had been known to help, when all other avenues had been closed. He made inquiries and was directed to the executive vice-president.

"Well, son, why did you come here?" asked Sober.

"I've tried every place else," the young man stammered, "and they say they won't make G. I. loans."

Sober leaned back in his chair, "You know," he chewed on his cigar, "there isn't much money to be made on G. I's. Takes a lot of work to prepare all of the papers. Besides we give a lot of stuff away around here, and that costs money. Why don't you get the money from the bank in your town?"

"They won't lend it on a G. I." repeated the customer.

Sober knew that the bank to which he was referring had purchased a million dollars worth of G. I. mortgages from contractors and builders through brokers, but they wouldn't be bothered with all of the paper work, reviews and appraisals which such individual loans necessitated. He continued the conversation, "Well, I just don't know. You have come here from another place. You know, son, we can lend all the money we have to lend on regular mortgages. That's why you've been turned down other places, probably." Sober got no further.

The young man's expression showed disappointment. He shuffled his feet, his head fell. The sigh that came from his lips was audible. "Well, thanks for your time." He arose slowly from the chair.

"Now, wait a minute, don't get in a hurry!" Sober commanded, "I didn't say we wouldn't do anything for you." He then explained the workings of the bank to the young man, and how depositors made money available for loans. He also told him how the stockholders must be satisfied, because they in the first place put up the capital to start a bank.

"Mr. Sober," the young man volunteered, "if you'll loan me the money, you won't be sorry. You've told me stuff that I never knew before. I never knew where you got the money to loan other people."

So the loan was put through. The process of getting approval from the Veterans Administration for a G. I. loan, the appraisals, the inspections and the paper work were completed.

Even before the veteran's house was completed, several new accounts were opened in the Old Freeport Bank. The veteran being of Polish origin, had been trained from early youth in the value of close relationships and loyalties. He had spread the word that the Old Freeport Bank had acquiesced to his desires, and it was not long until parents, brothers, cousins, aunts and uncles had opened sundry accounts in the bank which had favored a relative. These accounts were taken from other financial institutions—the very institutions which had refused to talk G. I. loans in the very beginning.

As the year of 1954 rolled into 1955 the banks assets continued to show phenomenal growth. The management decided to show its appreciation to friends and customers by staging an open house. During the week of June 13 through the 18th, people were invited to visit the bank. They were taken behind the counters and shown the interior workings of a bank. But, what was more impressive to them was the fact that they walked on carpet. The management had covered the lobby with carpeting, and following the inspection of the bank, which was adorned with basket after basket of flowers, the guests numbering into the thousands were taken to a restaurant in the basement, fed and given souvenirs. A booklet giving the history of the bank from its inception in 1868 was handed to each one as they left. The opening, marking the remodeling of the building proper did much to help dispel the fact that a bank was a "thing of marble and steel, cold and heartless."

Even with this, the officers were not content to rest on their laurels. Business continued and growth continued, and as 1955

[47]

blended into 1956 the June 30th statement showed resources of $4,528,998.27. The directors increased the dividend from 7½ to 10 percent based on the par value.

As in any business, regardless of the thought and care expended, errors were made. While The Old Freeport Bank grew, there were problems created over which the officials seemingly had no control. Ira walked into his father's office one day and declared that there was some difficulty with one of the bank's customers. He said that one of the parties who had borrowed on an F.H.A. loan was not satisfied with their house and wanted a final inspection on the part of the F.H.A.

"Well," declared the elder Sober, "let's notify the contractor or the F.H.A. or whoever you notify and get the final inspection. If the house isn't right, then it's up to the contractor. If it is right, let's get the thing completed. They been keeping up their payments?"

"Yeah, Dad, but it isn't that easy," responded Ira. "You see, this is one of those properties where the contractor went broke . . . he had a few little things to do, and these people are getting a little huffy about things."

"Humm, humm," the elder Sober mused to himself, "We'd better get the things straightened up. What do you suggest?"

"We have two attorneys on the board. Let's put it in their hands and see what the proper steps are," Ira responded. "I'll tell the people what we are doing, and that we'll fix things up as quickly as possible." So the problem regarding the F.H.A. loans was turned over to Attorneys McCue and Paz. Even efforts to correct things over which these Freeport bankers had no control, were to plague them in the months to come.

There were times, however, when the affairs of the institution were not centered on big exchanges of money. Since Freeport had installed parking meters some years before, an advertising promotion consisted of an announcement that The Old Freeport

Bank would pay for the first hour of parking. The ads read, "Just ask the teller for a nickel." Some people took advantage of this offer, while others were loath to even ask for the nickel.

The lobby of the bank had cleared for a few minutes and one of the tellers slammed her pen down on the counter, slid from her stool and marched into the vice president's office, "Mr. Sober, I'm getting tired of it, and I'm not going to do it any more. If that old buzzard thinks he's pulling something on me or on the bank he isn't. I'll tell that old goat off . . ."

"Wait a minute, wait a minute," snapped Sober, "what's this all about anyway?"

"You know Henry Blank? He lives out here in the country. Well, ever since we've been giving nickels for the parking meters, he comes in and gets his nickel, and, Mr. Sober, that parsimonious old miser isn't even parking his car by the meters. He is parking on Sixth Street where there aren't any meters . . ."

Sober laughed, "Oh, give him a nickel anyway. It won't break us, and he is a customer."

"But that isn't all," continued the teller. "As I understand it we're giving that fee to aid customers when they come into the bank to do business. He comes in for that five cents whether he has any business in the bank or not. One morning he said that he had some other business to attend to first, and he'd be back. Well, I just found he went back all right—back home, never did come in again . . ."

"Give him the nickel," laughed Sober. "He must need it more than we do."

The teller returned to her window, but as she left the office one could hear the epithets issuing from her lips, "Pinchpenny, scrounger, money-lover. . . ."

As time went on and as the bank became known as a haven for those who were in deep financial difficulty, the customers increased both in types and numbers. Due to Sober's experience in the credit business, one of the most difficult types to deal with were those who were known to have little financial responsibility. They were people who were dupes for every sales-gimmick, and who paid for everything on time. They lived from one payday to the next, and as a rule were broke three hours after the check was cashed. If some event transpired to disrupt their lives such as illness, or a lay-off then they were in deep trouble. Banks, as a rule, have little to do with this type of borrower. Bankers shunt them off to the agencies who prey upon them, by loaning a few dollars at a time at rates of interest that run anywhere from 18 to as high as 42 percent.

When they would appear at the Old Freeport Bank, they were given audience. If a loan were considered, then these people would of necessity consolidate all of their debts into one, and the bank would take a chattel mortgage on all of their possessions. While the bankers at the Old Freeport were condemned for this practice, Sober well knew that, if such steps were not taken, these same people within a short time would be again deeply in debt, owing everyone.

Sometimes this practice served as a real boon. It lifted the customer from a slough of despondency as the result of debts and bill collectors; it taught a simple lesson in economics, and their gratefulness was displayed by opening small savings accounts. In others, this practice only created resentment and dislike. Once free of the sword of many and various debts, consolidated into one, which hung constantly over their heads, they would look covetously upon every new item on the market; their neighbor's car, television, boat, or furniture, would only serve to make their own appear shabbier than it was. They wanted to go out and buy, but were often thwarted when the seller would find things tied up on a chattel mortgage. Then they would turn their resentment toward their original benefactor, the Old Freeport Bank.

As the years rolled on and 1957 wandered to the end of the lane, the Old Freeport Bank was once again a galaxie of color.

There was the usual Christmas tree in the corner of the lobby, while poinsettias graced the interior. In a prominent place was a huge candle and the customers were given an opportunity to guess the length of time required for it to burn out. Prizes in the form of Certificates of Deposit would be awarded those who guessed the number of hours and minutes it would burn.

As the holiday approached, the activity in the bank grew from a flurry to a rush. Children scampered around the Santa who presented them with candy and gum. Even the older customers were favored with small gifts bearing the bank's insignia. Finally, the bank closed its doors. The employees wended their way homeward, laden with gifts after having tucked safely in their pockets a check representing a Christmas bonus. Sober leaned back in his office chair. He put his hands behind his head and chewed on a half-smoked cigar. Santa Claus, a local citizen who had agreed to play the part for the bank, stuck his head in the office, "Sober, you want me any more tonight?"

"Have anything to do?" Sober questioned.

"Nope, nothing special. Why?"

"How about going along to the hospital. We've got some candy left and things. We'll take them to the kids. Must be pretty lonely in a hospital on a night like tonight."

So Santa Claus and Sober climbed in the car. They were laden with gifts. It was not long until they entered the Allegheny Valley Hospital. Sober approached the nurse on duty at the desk. He inquired concerning the children, and discovered that there were very few in the place of healing. It was a practice to send as many patients home as possible, except those whose condition was such that it was imperative that they stay.

"However," the nurse stated, "you can go up to the children's ward, if you care to."

Sober and Santa made their way to the ward. They looked down on a few small forms. The eyes were dull. Sober managed to stammer out a few inept phrases and pushed a box into this child's hand and then the next. "What do you say to a child," thought Sober, "How do you cheer them up on a night — especially on Christmas Eve."

One little golden-haired girl upon receiving her gift, mumbled "Thanks," and then turned her head away, but not before Sober caught sight of a single tear which rolled down a pallid cheek.

He walked out of the ward, followed by Santa. "Hump," he turned to his companion, "Christmas isn't going to mean much to some kids, is it?"

He couldn't describe his feelings as he started down the hall. There were some things he couldn't do, and at this time he wanted to do them in the worst sort of way. He wanted to drive the pain, the hurt and the anxiety from the eyes he had seen. He was a banker . . . cold and heartless . . . that was the way bankers were described. What business did he have in a hospital. He coughed and then brought the back of his hand to his cheek, to draw it across his right eye.

"What's the matter?" Santa asked.

"Nothin', nothin' at all," Sober replied. "Just something I got in my eye."

He hadn't any more than gotten the words out, when he heard a voice, "Hey, Sober, what are you doing down here?"

Sober turned on his heel, and peered into the room from whence the voice was issuing, "Jim? By golly, they got you penned up for the holidays," was the greeting as he recognized the man who had summoned him from the hall. "You look like a million."

"Won't let me out yet. Sent the family home early, you know, it's Christmas Eve, and Mary has a lot of things to do for the kids. Come in and set for a spell."

Sober went into the room and took a chair. He introduced

Santa and visited for a time with the patient. He learned that Joe and Mike and Jerry and others were hospitalized for the holidays. He plied the man in the bed with gifts and then made the rounds. It was near the midnight hour when he left the hospital. The rules had been relaxed. Visitors had been permitted to stay for a time, but he felt good. He knew in his heart that Christmas meant as much to these adult patients as it did to the children. He hoped that he had lessened the hours in length for those whom he visited.

Sober didn't relate these experiences. He couldn't turn them into promotion for the bank. There was something about them that he held closely, as if to reveal them would break the spell in which he was held. He then went to Citizen's General Hospital, New Kensington, Pa. for a similar tour, and finished around 2 a.m.

Gradually, as the year '57 gave way to '58, banking business required most of his time. Occasionally, he would relax and think of the visits to the hospital. "Funny," he thought, "got about as much pleasure out of them as out of banking."

Chapter IV

STORM CLOUDS

THE PROGRESS and growth of the Old Freeport Bank had been unusual and outstanding. The critics maintained that something had to be wrong for a small bank, such as this one, to show such phenomenal growth. The statement issued on June 30, 1957 showed resources of $6,322,784.93. The capital stock outstanding amounted to $143,330 and the surplus and undivided profits had climbed to almost $243,000. In the grand plan for the bank, none had been forgotten. While the customers were being given added services, the employees were paid for overtime, taken under a pension plan, and dividends to the stockholders, based on the par value of the stock, were being paid at the rate of twelve and one half percent.

All of the business did not come from Freeport and immediate vicinity. The circle of customers was ever widening, and a review of the accounts revealed that there were many from the Lower Burrell township area, now the City of Lower Burrell. Watching this growth and noting the progressiveness of the area, Sober confronted the directors with a proposition that a branch of the Old Freeport Bank be opened in this latter area. The usual debate followed, with the matter being weighed both pro and con. In a final analysis, the directors voted to take steps which would eventually, they hoped, permit the bank a branch in Lower Burrell.

Sober little realized the wrath this proposal would stir up among competitors. The fact that the Old Freeport Bank was already dealing with thousands from the area in which the branch was proposed, made little difference. However, this time the opposition did not confine its actions to tales alone. Where there are human beings, it was found that human beings could be touched, and some of these were touched to aid in the destruction of not only an institution, but humans as well.

Sober realized that his plans would result in gnashing of teeth, but he little realized the extent to which some people will go to smash that which stands in their way.

The signs of the storm clouds were there, but like the man intent on his work, the storm unleashes its fury before shelter can be found. The grayness of the skies, as the clouds seemingly pull together for the onslaught, the turning of the underside of leaves skyward, the gusts that pick up dust particles to send them skittering through the atmosphere, and the first splattering drops of rain, were all present in the case of the Old Freeport Bank. These storm warnings preceded the furious, rolling, black, ugly clouds that opened to pour forth hate, envy and vengence, which resulted in arrests, convictions and eventual prison sentences.

One of the first signs came after a visit of the bank examiners. As usual the examiners called the principal officer of the bank for a review of the examination. This was routine. Criticisms are made, suggestions are put forth, and sometimes orders are given to cease certain practices or definitely correct items that do not meet with the approval of the examiners. Sober was called to confer with the examiners. The routine matters were taken care of, and then one of them approached the subject of give-aways. Definitely condemning the use of book matches, yardsticks, sewing packets, pens, pencils, address booklets, rain caps and

[55]

sundry other items which the bank had been using. Sober was told that these resulted in too great an expense to the bank. The executive vice president was wont to argue the matter, "But look, fellows, these have been good advertising . . . the bank hasn't lost anything. Fact is, the profits are the highest they've ever been."

"Too much for advertising. No other bank of this size spends as much," was the reply received.

"You fellows told me once that this bank was too small. You said that it had to grow, and how are you going to make it grow unless you advertise?" Sober reiterated.

"You should just grow naturally, just take the customers as they come . . . anyway, we want to see the advertising budget cut."

Sober knew that this was an order. Even though he did not adhere to a belief in the philosophy expounded by the examiners, theirs was the last word.

It was during this same visit of the examiners, and after the conference, that Sober was approached in his office by one of them as they prepared to leave. "Say, Sober, how about a couple of those good pens you've been giving away. I've never seen any ball points as nice as those," the examiner requested.

"Sure," answered Sober. He reached into a file case near his desk and brought out a box of the pens bearing the imprint of the bank.

The examiner reached into the box and took a fistful. Sober opened his eyes in astonishment. His visitor then undid the clasp on his brief case and dropped the loot into the interior. "And say, how about a couple of those heavy yardsticks? I saw some around here, and they're so much better than the ones we get around Harrisburg."

Sober got up from his chair slowly and walked into the bank lobby. He went to a steel cabinet and brought forth a half dozen of the three-foot pieces of wood bearing the Old Freeport Bank's name and slogans.

As he walked into the office, he laid the yardsticks on his desk.

The examiner reached down and picked up one of them. "No, sir, you don't see yardsticks like this back home. My kids are pretty rough on them. I'll just take a couple while I'm here. You might not have any on my next trip. Oh, yes, Aunt Minnie would like one. I know she would. If you don't mind, Sober, I'll just take all of these. Certainly make nice things to hand out to my friends. Thanks a lot, Sober," uttered the visitor as he picked up his brief case, tucked the yardsticks under his arm and started for the door.

Sober was speechless. He had just muttered a "So long," when the examiner turned on his heel and stuck his head in the office. "Now Sober, let me give you a little tip. Don't take offense, but you know I'm in a position to hear talk. You'd get along better if you'd act a little more like a preacher. Thanks again." The examiner finally departed from the bank.

A few weeks later, while exploring the avenues to be followed in the application for a charter for a branch bank, there was an occasion for several of the Old Freeport Bank officials to meet with officials of the Pennsylvania State Banking Department. The methods, growth, and earnings were reviewed. All of the state officials showed their approval verbally, with the exception of one.

"Well, I don't know," the words came out in half a whine. "Every department of a bank should pay its own way, and Sober, as I study the figures from the Old Freeport Bank, your checking department certainly isn't a paying proposition. You should go by the national averages." The examiners used this statement many times in 5 or 6 years.

"Now, Mr. Poe," Sober began his defense of the bank, "these free checking accounts have been a big boost to the bank. We're a small bank, so we don't expect every department to pay. We must give some services. The business these checking accounts bring in more than pays for what little cost is involved in them."

The former employee of the Mellon National Bank and Trust Company, still loyal to his original employer, continued, "We didn't do it that way at Mellon's."

"Anything illegal about free checking accounts?" questioned Sober.

"Oh, no, only I still think that every department in a bank should make money for the bank."

His criticism, which went unheeded by the Old Freeport Bank, was just the wind of the gathering storm, collecting the dirt to be thrown into the atmosphere to becloud, besmirch and hurt.

Even those who had been favored by the Old Freeport Bank could not refrain from seeding the gathering storm clouds.

Small banks do not keep huge amounts of cash on hand. They have correspondent banks, usually large city banks. The Old Freeport Bank had at various times close to a million dollars in the Mellon National Bank and Trust Company in Pittsburgh. While these correspondent banks may and often do use the funds of correspondent banks in making loans to their customers, they pay no interest to the smaller banks. At one time the "bigs" paid small interest for this money until laws rescinded this—even the Christmas Clubs, which the Freeport Bank was forbidden to put on mortgage loans—was being loaned by the "bigs" to all types of customers.

For more than fifty years the Old Freeport Bank had been a correspondent bank of Mellons. However, even the big human gets rough as the annoying little fly buzzes around its head. As the Old Freeport Bank began offering more and more services, they drew customers from some of the larger institutions. The clouds became rolling and black.

Irate customers began stamping into the bank with more and

more frequency, stating that checks written on the Old Freeport Bank were not being honored by the Arnold National Bank and the Mellon National Bank and Trust Company in New Kensington. There was nothing that could be done. It was the legal prerogative of a bank to refuse to cash a personal check when presented. However, the story took a different turn when one of these banks was presented with a draft drawn on the parent bank.

A potential customer approached the cashier of the Old Freeport Bank one day and inquired concerning the possibility of a loan to consolidate debts, which included a loan on a car. The party's credit rating was checked and found to be in good order. The transaction was completed and Johnston gave the customer a draft drawn on the Mellon National Bank and Trust Company in Pittsburgh.

The feeling and anger of officers and employees of other banks had apparently risen to a white and unreasoning heat. When the man who had approached the Old Freeport Bank for the loan presented his draft, drawn on the Mellon Bank, to the Mellon Bank in New Kensington, a teller in the latter refused to cash or honor the draft drawn on the parent institution in Pittsburgh.

The customer wasted no time in getting back to Freeport. He stormed into the bank lobby and demanded, "What in the hell goes on here?" His voice, loud and angry, aroused the interest of all who were near. Sober rushed from his office, Ira came to the man as did Jack Reese and Mr. Johnston. The story poured forth. "What's the matter, ain't your bank any good?"

Sober could feel his head throbbing. There had been incidents lately, but the incidents had been coming with increasing regularity. "Just a minute, you wait right here!" he ordered the customer and headed for the office.

His hand shook as he picked up the phone. It was just a few minutes until he had a Mr. Frazier, a vice president of the Mellon Bank in Pittsburgh, on the other end of the wire. If Sober had ever made any attempt to "act like a preacher," such attempts were forgotten at the time. He poured out the story in no uncertain terms. His language wasn't found in dictionaries nor in the best drawing rooms. "Wait a minute, wait a minute," cried the man on the other end of the line, "I'm sure it's just a little error. Now, don't get excited, Sober, you know we consider your bank an honored and valuable customer. No . . . no . . . Sober, we don't approve of things like that . . . I'll call you back . . . yes, in a few minutes. Now, Sober, you know better than that . . . we think a great deal of you and the job you're doing there in Freeport . . . yes, I'll call you in ten minutes."

Sober slammed up the phone. He pounded into the office where the group had gathered, "I don't understand this, I don't understand this," he repeated to himself more than to the others.

It was but a few minutes that the phone rang. Mr. Frazier was on the other end of the line. He informed Sober that it was all an error, and that someone would be at the Old Freeport Bank within a short time bearing the title, note and other pertinent data relative to the transaction. Mellon's, he informed his party, would accept the draft.

While such incidents came with increasing regularity, it still did not dawn on the officers of the Old Freeport Bank that a concerted effort was being made to discredit the institution. It was but a short time after the incident when a teller at the Mellon Bank in New Kensington refused to honor a draft, that rumors of a much more serious nature began to filter back to the Old Freeport's officials.

Various customers had intimated to Sober, his son, Ira, or Jack Reese that all was not well with the money institution. Efforts to reach the source of these stories came to naught. Yes, this person or that person had heard such a tale, but they couldn't or wouldn't tell who had ventured the information. The invisible, destructive "they" was used time and time again when the detractors would repeat as a truth, "they say that the Old Freeport Bank is going broke."

A resident of Butler County, who resides approximately half way between Butler and Freeport, walked briskly into the bank one morning. He had been and was a good customer. He knew most of the bank's personnel, and after greeting those at the windows, he inquired for the elder Sober. The greeting had not been any more than ended when he said, "Say, Sober, I'm going to ask you a question, and I want a straight answer. None of this double talk, mind you, but I want to know."

"Well, what's the trouble?" Sober asked, little expecting the kind of a question he was going to get.

Again came that old, indefinite, questionable "They say." "They say," the visitor proclaimed, "that the bank here is going broke."

Sober's face became red; he rose from his desk and started to pace the small area in his office, "Who says so?" roared Sober.

The visitor repeated his question, "Well is it so?"

"Have I ever lied to you?"

"No."

"Well now," the banker offered, "I'm not going to begin now. The bank is in good shape. We're growing, and we have good backing for all of our loans. "You know, Fred," he faced the man in the office, "we've been hearing these stories from time to time, but we can't get to the source of them. Fred, do you know where they're coming from and who is making such statements?"

"Sure, I know where they're coming from. Fact is, I had a fellow tell me, and I know the fellow."

"Will you stand back of the statement, you've just made?" Sober continued to interrogate.

"Yep! You've been square with me, and if someone is trying to hurt you, I'll do what I can to stop it."

The visit continued and it was revealed that an employee of the Saxonburg Branch of the Mellon Bank had been soliciting accounts in that area and had been liberal in his denunciation of the Old Freeport Bank, and had been planting the seeds of distrust during his conversation.

The informer had no more than left the bank, until Sober was out of the door and into his car. He, never a rapid driver, increased his speed slightly on the journey down the valley. He wasted no time in formalities upon being ushered into a Mr. Sullivan's office. This vice president of the Mellon National Bank and Trust Company with offices in Pittsburgh, extended his hand. Sober at first hesitated and then relunctantly put his hand out to meet that of Sullivan's. The latter sensed that something was amiss.

Sober was blunt and to the point. He informed the officer that he was going to move the Old Freeport Bank account, and wasted few words in telling him why.

Mr. Sullivan, in polished and precise speech, requested, "Give me 24 hours to clear this matter up, before you do anything."

Sober returned to Freeport. The next morning an abject and apolegetic young man appeared at the Old Freeport Bank. He introduced himself as a Mr. Kelly from the Mellon Branch in Saxonburg. As he was ushered into Sober's office, he lurched into his story. He was deeply troubled, and he hadn't realized that he had done anything wrong. He declared that he thought his actions were all a part of business. Anyway, he couldn't keep the Old Freeport Bank from taking his customers, because of services offered, which were not offered by the bank he represented. He also revealed that he had been warned by a Mr. Copeland, of Butler, his superior, that if he didn't stop the flow of customers from the Saxonburg branch to the Old Freeport Bank, and if he couldn't get back those customers who had already left the bank, he would be fired.

A twinge of pity was experienced for the young man as his story poured forth. The Freeport banker thought as he looked at the youth, here is another doing the bidding of his superiors, and yet they do not share the blame when trouble is involved.

The young man left disheartened and worried. He wondered who was responsible for ethical practices, when orders had been given on threat of dismissal.

The incident was dismissed in Freeport. It had been chalked up as an experience, and not as a part of a concerted drive to create trouble.

There was little sunlight to dissipate the roiling clouds of trouble and adversity. While the bank continued to grow, the first few drops of the deluge were splattering down upon the bank and its officials.

Sober suggested to Jack Reese one day in the late spring of 1958 that they attend a district bankers' meeting which was being held at the Sewickley Heights Country Club. The two reached the club grounds and found bankers from throughout the district. As Sober and Reese sat at a table which overlooked the rolling greens and fairways, an official of the Pennsylvania State Department of Banking weaved among the tables and eventually wound up at Sober's side. His tongue was thick and his words were slurred. He had been at the meeting long enough to make frequent visits to the 19th hole. "Shay, Shober, why weren't you at sha hearing for your branch bank in Washington, D. C.?" As he asked the question he slid into a chair at the table.

"What hearing?" inquired Sober.

The guest at the table launched into the story. A second hearing into the matter of the Old Freeport Bank opening a branch in Lower Burrell had been scheduled. None of the officials of the Old Freeport Bank had been notified. However, the guest informed Sober, members of competitor banks had been told, as was their right, and had appeared at the hearing voicing opposition to the proposed branch. Volunteered also was the information that among these who had been there, were Frank Irvine, president of the First National Bank of Tarentum, and Samuel Kauffman, president of the First National Bank of Freeport.

Sober disclaimed any knowledge of this second hearing scheduled by the Federal Deposit Insurance Corporation in Washington, D. C. "Funny," he muttered half aloud, "that we weren't told."

Yet, the story was not completed. The state official called for another drink. He hunched his shoulders, and looked about him. Confident that no one was paying attention to his table, he lowered his voice, "You know Shober, I'm drunk. If I weren't sho drunk, I wouldn't tell you thish. You shouldn't have made that loan and shtuck on that two thous extra. You know the loan."

Sober shook his head negatively.

"You be shure and watch that loan. I'm tellin' ya, Shober. I'm tellin' ya. An' if you shay anything about thish, I'll shay you're a damn liar Shober, I'll say your nothin' but a damn liar." With these words the state official put his finger to his lips, went "sh" and weaved through the tables to the place from whence he had come.

His return to his duties in the bank left Sober little time to ponder these various happenings. The business continued to be brisk and demands on his time were many and varied.

As the spring of 1958 evolved into summer, the bank became a mecca for people from a wide area, especially on Saturday nights. If the executive vice president was not occupied at his desk, he would saunter through the lobby, greet this one and that, hand out a pen, pencil or yardstick. On this particular Saturday evening, as he was making his rounds through the lobby, he was greeted by a customer. The man, a Mr. Montgomery from the Sarver area, beckoned to Sober. "Someplace where we can talk alone?" The two went into the office. Sober thought little of the request at the moment. It was often the practice for customers to impart what they believed choice bits of information regarding the affairs of the area.

"Charley, if I were you, I'd be careful," began the interview. The exact words have been lost in the pages of time, but the farmer in a blunt and straight speech, informed him that a director from the competitor bank, The First National, located across the street, had told him that he (Sober) was going to be arrested. He wasn't sure of the charges, but it had something to do with the banking business. His friend was concerned, "Charley," he continued, "them skunks won't stop at nothing. You be careful."

Since there was a lapse of time between the various incidents, the warnings were usually relegated to the recesses of mind. Literally the Old Freeport bankers were unaware of the impending storm, in spite of gathering clouds, the winds and the huge drops that preceded the downfall.

On another occasion, a Mr. William Rhodes walked into the bank and said that he desired to pay off his loan. He informed the bankers that the First National Bank of Tarentum would give him the money he needed in his steel business, at a lower rate of interest than he was getting the money for at the Old Freeport. "Charley, you won't be mad if I move my loan?" he asked as he completed the transaction.

"Not a bit of it. We can use the money, and I don't blame anybody for getting money at a cheaper rate. You've got to protect yourself," Sober replied.

"Boy, they sure have it in for you down that other place, but I can't very well turn down the offer they made me."

Little more than a week had passed when Rhodes rushed into the bank. His usual custom was to greet Ira and Jack and any others who might be at the windows. He dispensed with any formalities. He moved in half a run to Sober's office, and finding the door ajar with no others present, he went into the cubicle. He didn't wait for an invitation. He caught his breath. "Charley," he stammered without giving Sober time to speak. "Something's going on, and I don't like it. Frank Irvine has been down at my plant and brought a fellow with him by the name of Canaday, who he says is a head man with some government bank agency. He says that any help I can give them to help convict you will be appreciated. And Charley, since then young Irvine, you know— Frank, Jr.,—has been at my plant with this fellow, and I'm getting a call from Canaday about every night from Pittsburgh. What in the hell is going on?"

The examiners were in the bank. The splattering drops had turned into an incessant drumming. The storm was coming.

Chapter V

THE DELUGE

THE STRIDES MADE by the bank seemingly created new and difficult problems. The officers of the institution looked upon these as the result of quick and rapid growth. At no time was there an abundance of trained employees. It was a period of hitherto unknown prosperity. Wages were high and jobs were plentiful. The young man or young lady, taking a position in the bank, would often use it as a training period to gain a similar and better paying position with a larger institution. About the time a novice would learn the workings of the place, either marriage or a more munificent paying job would lure them from the Old Freeport Bank.

In early August, the inspectors from the Federal Deposit Insurance Corporation, accompanied by the inspectors from the Pennsylvania State Department of Banking, descended on the Old Freeport Bank. Like a swarm of locusts they delved into every facet of the bank's business. Yet, in all innocence, the officers and employees little realized what this was leading up to. They deemed it just a thorough examination of the bank.

The examination hadn't any more than been started, when Alonzo Canaday, examiner at large for the Federal Deposit Insurance Corporation, walked into Sober's office. He carried a ledger sheet with him and fistful of other papers. "What's the meaning of this, Sober?" He pointed to a name on one of the papers which showed the distribution of the moneys relative to the loan.

"What do you mean, 'What's the meaning of this?'" asked Sober.

"You heard me the first time!" Canaday shouted.

"Tell me what you're driving at, and I'll tell you what I can, but I don't know what you're referring to," the banker stated as he reached for the paper which Canaday still held in his hand.

"You're a fast worker, you bastard. You know damn well what I'm referring to, and you'll find out more." Canaday strode from the office and returned to the rear of the bank, giving no heed to Sober's call.

"What in the world is he up to now. A plague on these examiners," thought Sober. "They can pick up some little thing and turn it into a mountain."

It was but a day or two later that Sober happened to glance at a statement of condition, which he had had printed after the close of business June 30, 1958. "Well" he mused, "the examiners can't find much fault with that." The report showed assets of $8,103,798.19. Unearned interest was up to $176,000; the capital stock was $200,000 and the surplus and undivided profits amounted to $343,000. The bank had an exceptional record on loans, with losses in this category running approximately five hundred to a thousand a year based on outlays of five and a half million. "Probably some little thing that can be straightened out," went through Sober's mind, as he reflected on the conversation of the Chief Examiner a day or two previously.

Mrs. Hilgert put her head in Sober's office. "There's a party out here to see about a loan. Can you see him now?"

"Can't he talk to my son or Jack?" he asked.

"They're busy with the examiners," the teller answered.

"O. K., send him in."

The doldrums of the year had descended. The hot noon sun of that day early in August of 1958 beat mercilessly down upon the town and the stone bank on the corner. Within those walls the air-conditioner labored to force some comfort into an atmosphere laden with the heat of tensions. An occasional fly buzzed noisily against the window in the office, which was to the left of the main entrance. Sober wondered why the examiners were giving the books such a thorough going over, but he had business to attend to at this time. Anyway a private firm of auditors had recently examined the books and had found the bank to be in good condition.

The customer introduced by Mrs. Hilgert entered the office and made application for a loan. The work was routine and following the usual adieus, the man left the office.

Another customer stepped into the doorway of the office, the moment the man cleared the entrance. He had no more than filled the doorway with his frame, when two neatly dressed men bruskly pushed the customer aside and walked into the office. Sober was about to make a remark when one of the men unceremoniously pushed him back in his chair as he began to rise.

Sober was stunned for a moment. Words didn't come. Several thoughts flashed through his mind. Was this a joke? No, that couldn't be. There was something about the demeanor of the men which forbade anything of humor. Was it robbery? Sober glanced around the men to the lobby of the bank. No unusual activity seemed to be taking place there. If it were robbery, then it was a smooth operation. One of the men stepped to Sober's side and deftly ran his hands over his body. The strangers identified themselves as members of the Federal Bureau of Investigation, and one pulled a warrant from his pocket which he read. It charged Sober with several violations of the United States Banking Code. Efforts to question the members of the FBI met with little success. They ordered Sober to get his hat. They told him to walk to the waiting car in front of the bank. Sober was placed in the rear seat and the officers rounded the machine and crawled into the front seat.

By the time this action took place, a group of curious onlookers gathered in front of the bank. In the small town, which had seemed only deserted before, little knots of people were at various spots on the main thoroughfare with their heads inclined toward one another. If someone whom they did not know would approach, the conversation would cease only to be resumed more earnestly the moment the stranger had passed.

By the time Sober arrived at the Federal Building in Pittsburgh, the news was already being blatted over the air-waves. Before he was given a chance of a formal hearing, the jury of public opinion — whetted and driven by newscasters and the press — had already begun to try the case. "Freeport Banker Arrested," "Banker Charged With Loan Sharking," and similar other banners and titles blithely gave the one side before the defense ever had an opportunity to fight.

The daily paper serving the local area sent extra copies to Freeport that afternoon. The details of the entire affair, even down to the specific charges, and on whom they were purportedly against had been placed in cold, heartless type, and the ink seared not only one man, but the reputation of a community. The stories were designed to burn a man's reputation but in many instances they branded those who had been helped, when no other help was to be found.

Sober was formally charged and released on bail to secure the services of an attorney or attorneys. The charge also included the information that he was not to return to the bank. There were personal belongings, such as anyone will gather in a place of business in time, there were changes of clothes to be secured. What would be the best thing to do?

Always a man of action, Sober lost little time in setting a course for himself. He took a room in one of Pittsburgh's hostelries, and began preparations for the fight which he little realized was not to end four years from that time.

Thoughts turned to legal counsel. Sober had employed many lawyers in his time, but these were men adept in civil matters. Who would be the very best in a situation such as the one he was in? His question was partially answered within a few days when he received a call from a lifelong friend, Andrew Uncapher of Vandergrift.

Uncapher informed Sober that he was coming to see him, and that he thought that he would be able to help him. An appointment was made and after a brief conference the two men journeyed to Harrisburg.

Upon their arrival in the capital city of Pennsylvania Uncapher was profoundly pleased that he was able to introduce Sober to George Bloom, chairman of the Republican Party in the commonwealth. Bloom listened to Sober's story intently. At the close of the story, he pointed a finger at the teller and asked, "Did you get any money?"

"Not a cent," replied Sober.

"There is one man that I can recommend to defend you. I think he'll take your case. He's a former judge, and has seen the courtroom from both sides of the bench. He's the man who can get you out of your trouble." With these words the party chairman dismissed his visitors.

"Can I say that you recommended him?" asked Sober, as he moved toward the doorway.

"Sure, sure," affirmed Bloom.

Sober and Uncapher went directly to a phone and called Judge Cooper in Pittsburgh. The Judge had some slight knowledge of the affair as the result of the searing publicity, and granted the two men an interview in his home that same evening at seven o'clock. The two hurried back to western Pennsylvania. The trip was made with lighter hearts. At least the appointment with an outstanding attorney was like a ray of sunshine piercing the dark clouds of trouble and adversity.

At approximately seven o'clock the two men were ushered into the Pittsburgh home of the attorney. In the Judge's library, he began, after completing the usual banalites, to question Sober regarding the case. Sober again related the events which lead to his arrest. The judge leaned back in his chair, placed the tips of his fingers together to form a steeple, and looked towards the ceiling. Slightly on the portly side with a round, ruddy face topped with white hair, he looked like a benign Solomon sitting in judgment.

"Hum, hum," was heard coming from his throat. Finally, he brought himself erect in his chair. "How much money did you get out of this?" he demanded of his visitor.

"I didn't get a red cent," Sober replied.

"Not anything?" Cooper repeated in another manner.

"No, not a thing," reiterated Sober.

The visitors were ushered to the door of the Judge's home with the knowledge that an appointment had been made for a later date.

It was during this latter visit with the Judge that Sober was ushered into his private office. Again Cooper repeated the question, "What did you get out of this?"

And again Sober echoed, "Not a cent, not a cent."

As the conversation droned on, the attorney put the question in another way, "What payment did you receive for the services you gave?"

Somewhat irritably the visitor repeated, "Not a cent!"

"Now, Sober," the attorney began for the fourth time, "between me and you and God, no one else, how much did you get?"

It was with anger that Sober replied, "I've told you once, and told you again and again that I didn't get a cent. What do I have to say to make you believe me?"

"All right, all right. I believe you — I just wanted to make sure. I'll take the case and I'll win it for you," the Judge answered. His earnestness, forcefulness and the way he hammered his fist on the desk seemingly vouched for his sincerity. But Sober was to hear again and again, even from his own attorney, the question, "How much did you get?"

It was but a few days after the news of his arrest had been broken, that he met one of the officials of the Pennsylvania State Department of Banking. The greeting was sincere and warm. It was not too many words later that the official commiserated with Sober over his problems. As the charges were discussed the official put his hand on Sober's shoulder. "You know, Charlie, I was awfully sorry to hear of what's happened to you. You know the law — a banker isn't to take or accept any fee, gift or any-think of value for procuring a loan — you didn't, did you?"

"As certain as God is my maker and witness, I never got a cent from these deals," Sober replied with some weariness.

"Even indirectly?" his visitor questioned.

"No, not even indirectly. Not in any way."

"Well, I'm sorry and I mean it. I wish I could do something for you, but this is a Federal charge and Charlie, between you and me, it's pretty hard for a state man to buck the Federal boys. I knew there were some kicks about you getting a branch bank, but I never realized that it would be carried this far. I'm sorry, Charlie," the speaker reiterated. "Our examiners found nothing in your bank but a few minor errors. The things you are charged with is going on in all other banks."

"Well, I'm going to fight it. I knew I could depend on you for some good advice. I tried to call you right after I was arrested, but I couldn't find you in. Your secretary said you were on vacation . . ."

"Oh, yes I took my family to Ligonier. We were the guests of the Mellons. You know they have cottages, horseback riding, swimming pools . . . oh, just about anything and everything a person would want. Certainly had a grand time. Didn't cost much either. The Mellons offer these accommodations to banking personnel and officials every year . . ."

"Thought you said something about bankers not receiving a fee, gift or anything of value for any service rendered . . ."

"Why'er, ah, well, Charlie, you understand. It's not the same in my case," the official stammered.

"What would you do if you had to make a decision against the Mellon organization?" Sober queried.

Sober turned on his heel and began a retreat. The visitor stammered a few inept phrases; "But this wasn't the same. Now, Charlie, you understand . . ." He then hung his head in thought. "I would like to testify for you but that will depend on my boss, Secretary Myers."

There were many things to be done. One which was required was that of resigning as an officer and director of the Old Freeport Bank. There was the search for evidence which could be substantiated by witnesses, but at the same time Sober was advised not to talk to any of the government's witnesses.

He returned to Freeport on frequent occasions. He could not enter the bank. So his chances of meeting many whom he had known decreased as he would drive to the main street of the little western Pennsylvania community. There were those who would deliberately avoid him. Walking down the street, they would glance up to see the man who had once befriended them, then lower their eyes and cut diagonally across the thoroughfare. The pretense was only in their hearts that they hadn't seen this "criminal" as he was labeled. Their eyes and minds told them differently.

Then there were others, who in their self-importance, wisdom and knowledge, would seek Sober out to offer advice. The advice of one often would run counter to the suggestions of another and soon Sober's ears were dinned with "do this," "plead guilty," "sell out," "don't do this or that," "now I know a fellow who knows someone who knows someone high up in government," and a thousand and one other proposals by self advisors.

Sober sat in his car on the main street of Freeport early one afternoon. He was trying to think of the next move to make. He had an attorney. He had people who said that they would testify in his defense. What else was there to be done? He looked out of his car window. He saw a woman going into the town's variety store; he saw a man entering the bank; a mother dashed into the street after a toddler, who had broken from her hold, to grasp him by the wrist. Sober could even hear her reprimand and the shriller wails of the child as he was forcibly yanked back to the walk.

The world rotates on its axis in its orbit. Some place a banker was making a loan; some place a mother yelled at her child; the loafers in a thousand little communities like Freeport talked about the weather, the coming elections, work, employment, unemployment, taxes and a thousand and one other subjects in which they think they were well versed. Sober knew this. He began to wonder if he counted for anything at all, if all the protestations of friendship meant anything. He wondered if any single individual, caught in the maelstrom of legal maneuvering coupled with the desires of aggrandizement, and the forces of envy and hate, really meant anything to anyone.

There were a few bright spots in the picture. Sober was accosted one evening by a man to whom he had, as an official of the bank, loaned money. "Hey, Sober, wait a minute, I want to see you. I've been looking for you." The speaker was Richard J. DeSalvo, who had taken over what had been known as the Stam farm near the Freeport Brick Company plant. He had laid a portion of the farm out in lots, and was making efforts to develop the sub-division.

He didn't wait long to go into his story. The two men leaned against the First National Bank, and DeSalvo poured forth his tale. "There were a couple of men to see me yesterday, Sober. They said they were from the FBI and they came to ask me questions about my dealings with the Old Freeport Bank and what connection I had with you. And Sober, I answered everything they asked me and then they started to get mean. I asked them to act as gentlemen and I would do the same."

"What happened then?" Sober queried.

"Well," DeSalvo continued, "they twisted their questions around several times. They said that did I know I could go to jail if I didn't cooperate with them in their investigation. So they started all over again. I gave them the same answers. They said I was lying and told me what could happen if I didn't tell the truth . . ." DeSalvo paused for a breath.

"What happened then?" asked Sober, seeking the entire story.

"You know me, Sober. No one calls me a liar. I don't care whether he's a government official or not. At the same time, my wife and daughter got scared and were crying. Sober, it ain't right that people can come into your home and upset things like that. I don't know much, but seeing my wife and daughter like they were, I invited them outside to settle the matter. Maybe I called them a couple of names, too. They still said I wasn't telling everything, so I told them to leave," the speaker concluded his story.

Sober was speechless for a moment. He had heard that these were the tactics being used to elicit information from people with whom he had dealt, but he didn't know how far it had gone.

Before parting, DeSalvo put a question to Sober, "Haven't people got any rights, any more? Can government men come into your house and call you a liar and threaten you with jail? Isn't there a law, someone to protect me and people like me?"

All Sober could do was to shake his head. "I don't know, I don't know."

While Sober's affairs were caught in the whirl of conferences and decisions, activity on the part of the examiners and Federal Bureau of Investigation officers had not ceased.

A short time after Sober's arrest, Dr. Richard Heineman, who was also a bank director, was arrested, while in the process of performing an operation, in the Allegheny Valley Hospital where he was on the staff. He was charged with receiving a fee for securing a loan.

A few days following Heineman's arrest the FBI picked up John E. Cypher who was also a director of the bank, on similar charges in connection with another loan. Both Heineman and Cypher had to undergo the tortures and glaring publicity which had accompanied Sober's arrest. The papers again had a field day as they reprinted all of the charges. The trial by public opinion, giving only one side of the case, continued.

But the officers, seemingly intent not only in destroying individuals, but a banking institution as well, were not through. Charges of false entry and embezzlement were filed against Ira L. Sober. He, too, was removed from the bank.

Jack Reese's turn came later. One day in September of 1958 a government representative approached Reese. "Reese," he said, "Teitelbaum, the U. S. Attorney, would like to talk to you in his office. You better go and see him."

"Is that an order?" Reese asked.

"No, just a request," was the reply.

A day passed and Reese mulled the request over in his mind. After all, he had done nothing. There was no need for him to see the attorney. This coupled to the lurking fear, induced by viewing proceedings with lawyers on the television, told Reese to remain away.

Again the government man approached Reese. "Did you see Teitelbaum" he questioned.

"No, I didn't," replied Reese.

"Well, if you don't go to see him, you'd better write him a letter telling what you know about the affairs here in the bank." With this thinly veiled threat, the man walked away from Reese.

Reese lost no time in seeking Attorney Frank Paz, who was also a member of the bank's board of directors. He told Paz the whole story, "You know, Frank, you being an attorney, know how they can twist your words around. They can even make written words sound different from the way you mean them. Would you advise me to see Teitelbaum or write him?"

Paz didn't hesitate, "You're exactly right, Jack. I wouldn't go unless you are ordered, nor would I write a letter. You haven't done anything anyway."

Reese took some comfort from the advice. He continued to work in the bank, trying to care for the burden of work as a result of the upset, and at the same time trying to answer the myriad questions put forth by the examiners. It was but a short time later when the FBI representatives made another trip to Freeport. This time Jack Reese joined the four others, and once again the brutal glare of trial by public opinion, induced by repetitious newspaper accounts, seared into the heart and soul of a young man who had never harmed anyone.

Left to operate the bank were the late A. M. Johnston and a staff of clerks and tellers. The self-righteous waited in anticipation for the bank to close its doors, while the examiners sought more and more evidence. A teller was at the window. A customer came in to make a deposit. The teller had no more than marked the amount in the pass book, when a hand reached in front of her and grabbed the book as she was returning it to the customer. The lady looked at the examiner in amazement and then with a certain fear, when he slapped the book down in front of the customer without so much as a "pardon me." The lady who had received the book retreated from the bank hurriedly.

The teller could withhold the tears no longer. She laid her head on the counter and sobbed, "Why are you doing this to us, why, why, why?"

Gaining some control, she blew her nose, and wiped her tear-stained face. "What in the world are you trying to find? Do you go over every bank's records like you've been going over this one?"

The examiner was somewhat taken back by the display of emotion. He could stand being cursed and threatened, but a woman's tears were another matter. The hardness of heart he had developed as a member of a government bureau had inured him to many things, but not a woman's tears.

"Now, now, perhaps I was a little hasty, but we have to check everything."

The teller grew bolder. "Wouldn't you find things wrong in other banks if you conducted such an examination?"

"Yes, we probably would, but this is the bank we're examining, not others." With these words he walked away from the teller.

During this same period of examination Sober received a call. The caller would not identify himself. "Say, you want out of the mess you're in?"

"Who is this?" Sober shouted.

"Never mind who this is," the voice responded, "if you want out of your trouble, it can be fixed."

"Well now, what do you mean by being fixed? Anyway, I'm not talking to someone I can't see," Sober informed his caller.

[79]

"I'm sincere," the voice went on, "if you'll agree to certain things, I can have the indictment quashed, after certain obligations are fulfilled."

"What are these things?" came the next question, as Sober's curiosity was aroused.

"If you'll agree to sell your stock and get out of the banking business altogether . . ."

Sober slammed up the phone as he yelled, "Never!"

Chapter VI

GENESIS
OF A JUSTICE

THE U. S. FEDERAL ATTORNEY lost no time in taking action. A True Bill was found by the Grand Jury on August the 15th of 1958. Both Sober and Dr. Heineman pleaded "not guilty" in open court on August 25. Subsequent charges were filed and another True Bill was found by the Grand Jury on January 12, 1959. The findings of the Grand Jury involved not only Sober and Dr. Heineman a second time, but included the charges against John E. Cypher, Jack Reese and Ira L. Sober. The charges were many and varied and were repetitious. As in all law, when one runs afoul of an interpretation, it usually results in a multiplicity of charges. The law under which Sober and Dr. Heineman were first indicted reads as follows:

"Whoever, being an officer, director, employee, agent or attorney of any bank, the deposits of which are insured by the Federal Deposit Insurance Corporation, of a Federal Intermediate credit bank, or of a National Agricultural Credit Corporation, except as provided by law, stipulates for, or receives or consents, or agrees to receive any fee, commission, gift, or thing of value, from any person, firm or corporation, or for any other person, firm or corporation, from any such bank or corporation, any loan or extension or renewal of, or discount or acceptance of any paper, note, draft, check or bill of exchange by any such bank or corporation, shall be fined not more than $5,000 or imprisoned not more than one year or both."

Not only were Sober and Heineman charged with the violation of this law, but additional charges or counts were incurred which were termed "conspiracy" and "aiding and abetting." While the charges of receiving a fee were not directly attributed to Sober, he was involved in all the counts of the case, as a conspirator, or for aiding and abetting.

The days between the arrests, the finding of a True Bill on the part of the Grand Jury, and the subsequent opening of the trial in the Federal Court in Pittsburgh, April the 14, 1959, were busy ones. There was much legal maneuvering, and the U. S. District Attorney Hubert I. Teitelbaum kept the matter before the public by frequent releases to the press and newscasters. The terms "loansharking" and "kickbacks" were printed frequently and freely during the intervening months.

It was with something akin to confidence and belief that justice would prevail — faith if you want to call it that — that the defendants entered the court room on that April day. There had been no perjury, no lies, no attempts to circumvent the processes set up so that all men might be tried fairly and impartially. That is, no such attempt had been made on the part of the defendants.

The jury had been selected. They were people from all walks of life, and little did the defendants realize that these twelve, good and true, would soon be lost in a maze of legal and technical banking jargon that at times even troubled the attorneys.

If the confidence of the bankers were shaken in the least, it happened during the address of Teitelbaum to the court and jury during which he outlined the charges and then and there decided on the guilt of the defendants by painting them as cruel hoaxers of the humans who had placed their trust in them; the cold-hearted, dishonest bankers who were taking the last mite from the widows and orphans. The district attorney played his hand well. In the opening address to the jury he played more upon the emotions, than to the pure process of reasoning. The bankers, sitting in that court, slightly below the jury box, were the blackest of black fiends and most certainly henchmen of a demon. Yet, at no time during his address did he mention that these same people, whom the government had subpoenaed as star witnesses, had utilized every possible avenue before they came to the Old Freeport Bank. Thus, reasoning in a court is devoid of reason, because all of the reasons behind actions are seldom brought forth. Only those reasons which serve their purpose are brought forth and used.

Leo Gallagher operates a road house or inn on Route 28, approximately two miles southwest of Freeport. Gallagher, according to his testimony, wanted to buy out his partner. But that wasn't all he wanted. He had some other obligations which he hoped to consolidate into one loan at the time he approached the Old Freeport Bank.

Gallagher was sworn and appeared on the stand. Under the rehearsed questions of Teitelbaum, the story of the events leading up to the transaction which had placed the bankers in jeopardy was brought out.

Sober did not recall everything about that first meeting, but as the course of the conversation delved into Gallagher's problems, he was informed that representatives of the bank would make an appraisal of his property in view of possibly granting a loan.

Later, accompanied to the Sunlight Inn by Franklin Bush, who at that time was the president of the Old Freeport Bank, Sober went to make an appraisal. There are certain things that are taken into consideration when making an appraisal. These items were carefully checked at the time. But the big holdup, as far as granting Gallagher the full amount he wanted to borrow, was the fact that the bank did not loan on a liquor license, and the water situation at the inn was not all it could have been.

Gallagher was informed of the results of the appraisal and was told that the bank would loan him $9000. A great deal was made of this figure later in court. Teitelbaum continued to play up this figure as being a "come-on" for Gallagher to approach and get security from other people. Coached by the attorneys for the government, Gallagher replied to their questions from the stand in this manner:

"Then he (Sober) says, 'Well that is all the bank will do.' Then I asked, 'Do you think, do you know anybody who would want to lend out some money?' He said, 'I don't know, I will see what I can do.' So a couple of days went by, I went around, he said, 'I think I've got the fellow who will lend you the money.' He says, 'I'm not sure, I will have to see him again.' So a couple days went by, I went down, he said, 'Yes, I think I can get it for you.' I asked him who it was."

"Did he tell you who it was?" asked Teitelbaum.

"Yes, he did," replied Gallagher.

"Who?" was the single worded question.

"Dr. Heineman," was Gallagher's reply.

The district attorney continued with his interrogation and established for the court and the jury who Dr. Heineman was, by having Gallagher point him out. He then had Gallagher describe his visit to Dr. Heineman's office.

"What did you talk to Dr. Heineman about?" was the question put forth by Teitelbaum.

"I told Doc I came down to see about getting that money for taking the Inn off."

"Did he know anything about it when you first talked about it?"

"Yes, he knowed about it. He knowed I was coming down."

"He knew you were coming down, he didn't ask you whether you were sick, what was wrong with you physically?"

"No, sir," Gallagher replied.

"He knew about the loan?" asked the attorney.

With an affirmative answer, Gallagher implied that Heineman had already been informed of any conversations that might have taken place in the bank. He told the assembly, "I told him about needing this here money. I said, 'Mr. Sober told me to come down and see you.' He said, 'I got it, I can lend it to you.'"

The lawyer continued to draw Gallagher out regarding the amount he would need, "Had anybody said to you well, the bank will loan you nine, Heineman six, or the bank ten and Heineman five?"

Gallagher answered in the negative.

"Where did these figures come from?" Teitelbaum asked as he pressed the point regarding the transaction.

Gallagher hesitated for a moment. "Well," he stammered, "Mr. Sober said the bank would only go so far."

"He said ten?" came the next question.

This time Gallagher's answer was in the affirmative.

"I want to know," Teitelbaum let his voice boom over the courtroom, "where did the figure six come from; why was Dr. Heineman offering six instead of five?"

"Well, it was $6000 and then," Gallagher looked toward the ceiling as he seemingly tried to recall the event, "he said it would be $2000 extra."

"Who said it would be $2000 extra?"

"Dr. Heineman," answered Gallagher.

Then came one of the first of a series of leading questions

which marked the entire trial, "Had Sober said anything to you about extra payment?"

Gallagher looked blandly at the government attorney, "He said it would be extra payment for it."

"Did he (Sober) say how much?"

"He said it would be around $2000. I said, 'I don't want to pay that much.'"

"Charlie Sober told you that in the bank before you ever went to see Heineman?"

"Yes, sir."

"That it would be about $2000 extra?"

Again Gallagher nodded in the affirmative.

"What made you change your mind?"

Gallagher drew a deep breath, "I waited about two weeks, studied it over, I figured I will have the place in my own name, I will just have to work for three months for nothing to make that up, I will have the place in my own name."

The direct examination continued. Teitelbaum continued to not only draw out this witness for the government, but to weave a story which implicated not only Heineman, but Sober as well.

As one example of this questioning, he asked Gallagher, "Did Dr. Heineman give you any money that night?"

"No, sir," was the reply.

"What did he do?"

"He said he'd take care of Sobers at the bank."

So the inference was drawn that Sober "would be taken care of" and since the conversation was about money — there was only one conclusion which could be drawn. This was what the district attorney was striving for at the time.

As the questioning continued, Teitelbaum continued to bring out the details of the transaction whereby Gallagher received the money.

* See Gallagher's sworn statement on Documentation page 17.

The government's attorney walked over to the table to the left of the bench, picked up a piece of paper, "I show you what's been marked Government Exhibit No. 30 and direct your attention to the backend of that, ask you if you recognize the signature on that check?"

"Yes, sir." Gallagher nodded affirmatively as he answered.

"Now whose signature is on there?"

"There is my signature on there and my wife's signature."

Teitelbaum smiled as he directed the next question to the witness, "Look at the front of the check; now look at the front of it; did you ever see that check marked Government Exhibit 30 before?"

"Well," replied Gallagher, "I saw it the night he brought it, Mr. Sober brought it down to the tavern for me and my wife to sign it."

"How soon," the attorney seemingly relished the question, "How soon did Mr. Sober come down to the tavern after you signed the note for $17,000?"

"I would say about three or four nights."

"He brought with him that check?"

"Yes, sir."

"What did he tell you?"

"He says, 'I want you and your wife to sign this check.'"

"Did you know what the check was for?"

"Yes, sir."

"What was it for?"

"The $2,000."

"The $2,000 for what?"

"All I can figure out was kickback."

"The kickback you were supposed to give Heineman for getting the loan?"

Gallagher answered again in the affirmative.

It was then that Sober could begin to see the web being woven to entangle the defendants. The testimony was damaging. The terms "kickbacks" were being placed before the jurors and the court through leading questions to the witness. He knew that a great deal of the testimony given was a mixture of both truth and lies, but how far it could go toward being refuted, he had no idea.

Before the government's attorney was through with his witnesses, he brought out the interest on the loan and then made an effort to point out that this witness had a year later secured a loan for $17,000 to pay off the Old Freeport Bank, and that he needed no security for it.

To this line of questioning, the banker's attorney, Judge Cooper, objected vigorously. "I am objecting to a question which I do not believe—

Judge Miller leaned over the bench, "What is your reason?"

"Because," said Cooper, in answer to the court's question, "what this witness did in his refinancing a year later certainly is not material to what happened in this case, has nothing to do with the charge that is brought against this defendant."

"I think that's right," confirmed the court.

However, Teitelbaum in his persistent way, continued, "I think we are going to show he refinanced a loan of $16,000. I think that is quite relevant, at another bank. I think that is very relevant. In other words, he paid off this loan."

The court came into the word battle, "Well, he paid it off all right, but where he got the money, what difference does that make?"

"May we come to a side bar? I don't want to say anything I shouldn't in front of the Jury," the government's attorney requested.

"You said more than you should already," snapped Cooper.

Again the play of legal manipulations was brought to the fore. The jury was not to hear this conversation at the bench, as was to be the case so many times. Teitelbaum continued to plead for the right to bring out in open court that Gallagher had gotten a loan later to pay off the mortgage held by the Old Freeport Bank, and that he hadn't needed any additional collateral than his building.

Looking back, Sober wished that his attorney had let this matter come to open court. Gallagher had made improvements to his premises; he had drilled a well for additional water supply, and he had enlarged it. It may have been that the Inn was worth a great deal more than when it was first appraised by the Freeport men.

Gallagher was turned over to Judge Cooper for cross-examination.

As the attorney made efforts to bring out the various points in the defendants' favor, he said to Gallagher, "Never went to any?"

"No," was Gallagher's firm reply.

"So that when you needed money—"

"Yes, I did;" Gallagher on second thought changed his story, "I went to the Natrona Bank and asked them if they would give me more on the loan and they said they didn't want to loan any more on the tavern."

"And then you saw Sober?" continued Cooper.

"Yes, sir."

"You didn't know him at all?"

"No, sir."

"And he said he'd have to see the property?"

"Yes, sir."

"And he came up with Mr. Bush?"

"Yes, sir."

"After he saw it, he told you that he'd have to submit it to the Board?"

"And the Board turned you down?"

"They turned me down for $15,000."

At this point in the cross-examination Teitelbaum injected himself into the matter.

Cooper began another question, "They said—"

He was not to go on, for Teitelbaum had interrupted and before he could be stopped said, "Of course if he knows that of his own knowledge. Mr. Sober told him that, as I understand."

Judge Miller offered his judicial advice, "That is what he testified, Mr. Sober came to his home and said he could only lend him ten."

Cooper reiterated, "Yes, that is what we are talking about. I don't know, are you objecting to something?"

Teitelbaum countered with, "I don't want you to ask him what the Board of Directors did."

"Will you let me," said Cooper with some irritation, "conduct my cross examination. If I do something wrong, you object and let the court tell me."

"I suggest you both address your objections to the court," the court admonished, "quit bickering among yourselves."

Later Sober was to learn that this was to be a continual practice. It seemed to him that such confusion and "bickering" as it was described by Judge Miller always came at a time when the defense would be on the threshhold of making a point, and as the cross examination would continue the point would lose its effectiveness.

Anyway, Cooper continued to impale Gallagher with his own words: "You went to see Sober, didn't you?"

"Yes, sir."

"Well, he didn't run after you, did he?" Cooper asked.

"Naturally, he wouldn't come up and try to lend me money; I'd have to go to see him," Gallagher replied.

"When he told you the bank would lend you a certain amount of money, he stopped, and he didn't come and ask you to do anything else; he was through, that is all the bank could do, isn't that right?"

"That is all the bank done," was the answer.

"You kept on going after him for him to try to get you somebody to make the loan?"

"I only went once," Gallagher answered.

According to Gallagher's direct testimony, brought out by Teitelbaum, he admitted coming to the bank not once, but at least four times prior to making arrangements for the loan. Yet, this matter was not brought forward by the defendants' attorney at all.

The cross examination continued with Cooper going into the actual transaction as it occurred that night in the bank, when the actual distribution of the funds took place.

"Mr. Gallagher, I show you a paper which has been identified as Government Exhibit 28. Look at the back of this exhibit, and I ask you whether or not these items do not appear: Proceeds of Mortgage—"

Again it was time for the government's attorney to step into the picture. Apparently, he knew that the questions would not show his witness in a favorable light. "Your honor," pleaded Teitelbaum, "shouldn't that be admitted before it is read from?"

"We will admit it technically before or after."

"All right," stated the Court, "What is the Exhibit number?"

Mr. Cooper answered, "Exhibit 28."

This exhibit was admitted by the Court, and the brief intervention into the questioning came to a close, as Cooper continued with the witness.

"Now then, on the back of this there appears the following items: "Proceeds of Mortgage less cashier's check to Dr. Heineman, $2000. Is that right?"

"Yes sir," came the answer from Gallagher.

"Check to the First Natrona Mortgage, $4920.23." "Check to attorney fees and taxes, $396.95." "Check for attorney for other taxes, $285.81." "Check to Gallagher balance, $9226.91." And then there is an appraisal fee for $170, making a total of $17,000. You knew about these figures, did you not?"

"I knowed these here checks had to be paid off, yes."

Cooper put the next question, "Weren't they given to you at the bank when this deal was closed?"

"Yes," came the answer, "after we paid the bank off, yes, we got all of the stuff back."

"When they gave you all of these checks, the check for $2000 made out to you and Mrs. Gallagher was right among those checks, wasn't it?"

Gallagher thought he wasn't going to be trapped. He had said previously that Sober had delivered the check to the Inn a few nights after the deal was closed, so he answered the question put forth by Cooper, "No, I never got that."

Cooper was warming to his task, "You just take a look at it, Mr. Gallagher. Take a look at all these checks. Didn't you get all of these checks the night the deal was closed at the bank when Mr. Johnston was there? You know you got them there that night?"

Teitelbaum came to the defense of his witness, "Your Honor, I am confused as well as this witness. I don't understand what we are getting at."

"I do," replied the court.

Teitelbaum continued to inject himself into the verbal fray.

He made an effort to befuddle the issue, by saying, "All right. I didn't understand that. He talks about checks plural."

Judge Cooper, Sober's attorney, again turned to the witness and again pointed out that the entire distribution of the loan was made up at the bank and turned over to the parties involved at the bank. Even Judge Miller, from the bench, tried to aid the witness when he said "He means by that Mr. Gallagher, including the check for $2000."

But Gallagher was adamant in his statement, "No, that check for $2000 wasn't given to me at the bank."

In repetitious questioning, Gallagher continued to claim that Sober had brought the check for $2000 to the inn some two or three days after the closing of the loan at the bank. At one point he even said that it might have been five days later.

Cooper proceeded to introduce the checks, showing the numbers, the perforations which show when the checks had been cancelled. "Now then, I show you this Exhibit No. 30, this check for $2000, dated September 11, 1953, No. 24570, and looking at this, you will find that it cleared through the bank and was paid on September 13, 1953 two days, the same date as your check, as the check for $9200."

The witness only nodded his head.

"Now then," continued Cooper, "certainly this check could not have been brought to you three or four days later, could it, Mr. Gallagher?"

"I said," answered Gallagher, somewhat falteringly, "I just can't recall the exact date he brought the thing in there."

"Mr. Gallagher, it seems to me that you showed an amazing memory when you told the story of this closing. You remembered what Sober said, you remembered what Heineman said, and you remembered that Mr. Sober said, "It will cost you $2,000," and that Dr. Heineman said, $2,000. Don't you remember that this was given to you the same night?"

Even the government's attorney could see the trend of the questioning, and once again, to free his witness from the position he was in, he jumped to his feet and strode across the front of the courtroom. The eyes turned from the witness to the attorney, "Your Honor, I object to the addresses to the jury being made out of order. The check stands for itself. Whatever is on there is on there. This kind of questioning is entirely improper."

The Court blandly replied, "Objection overruled."

"Don't you know as a matter of fact that you got this check for $2,000 and your whole story about Sober bringing you the check is a fabrication, and it never did happen?"

Gallagher fell upon a question as a defense. It gave him a little time to collect his badly battered thoughts. "What didn't happen?"

"That Sober ever brought a check for you to sign?"

The witness had been drilled in how to answer—even though he had been tripped before, he continued, "He did so fetch a check down for me to sign for $2,000, to take down to Dr. Heineman."

The Judge injected his voice at this time and asked if Sober's attorney was going to have any further cross examination. When he was informed that there would be, he stated that he thought it had better be deferred until the next morning. He then added, "I am going to have a little talk with the members of the Jury. This is off the record."

We do not know what he told the Jury. There is not any court record.

But the record does state that at four p.m., the trial of this case was adjourned until Thursday, April 16, 1959 at ten o'clock a.m.

The time of adjournment and the time set for the resumption of the trial is told here for a specific purpose. It serves to illustrate one of those points, which has continued to plague and bother the defendant ever since the trial was concluded.

The most of the morning session on April 16, 1959, was taken up with a repeat of the questions of the previous day. Gallagher was shown the various exhibits and was asked to identify them. There were the checks which were included in the loan made to Gallagher. Gallagher again claimed that he endorsed all of the checks the night the loan was consummated, except the check to Dr. Heineman. He continued to claim that Sober had brought that check down to him, and that it was a kickback.

When Cooper questioned him regarding the definition of a kickback, he said that it was hand money.

Where did Gallagher get the term "kickback"? Was it of his own making, or had he been well drilled to present a word which would place in bad light the defendants in the case?

Cooper continued his questioning. Even though the day was not hot, and the pleasant April sun cast heartening rays through the high windows of the courtroom, Gallagher was becoming more and more uncomfortable. At one point he pulled a handkerchief from his pocket and wiped his forehead.

"I show you a paper," Sober's attorney directed it toward the witness, "which has been identified as Defendant's Exhibit D-1, and ask you to look at it and tell us what it is?"

Gallagher stammered, "This is a copy of what Mr. Canaday took."

"What is the date on it?"

"Fourth month, 16-59," said Gallagher, now more sure of himself since he was reading from a paper.

"59," Cooper raised his eyebrows, "Is it signed by you at the end of the last page?"

"Yes, sir."

"That is your signature?"

"Yes, sir."

Cooper then began to question the witness as to what efforts he had made to secure a loan, other than the Old Freeport Bank. He elicited the information that Gallagher had gone to only one bank and that was the First National Bank of Natrona. He also drew out that the Natrona bank would not increase his mortgage.

Then Cooper returned to the statements again. "Mr. Gallagher, I now show you a paper which has been identified as Defendant's Exhibit D-2 and ask you to look at it and tell us what that is?"

"This was a paper made out by Mr. Canaday, and was taken to Tarentum and sworn to."

"And you signed it?" interrogated Cooper.

"Yes, sir."

"Your name appears on the second page?"

"Yes, sir."

"Now then," inquired the attorney, "on the first page this is what it says: "I went to the bank at Ford City, Pa., to borrow sufficient funds on a note to pay Mr. Gross. The Ford City Bank did not care to loan the money in this area." "Did you go to the Ford City Bank?"

Gallagher hesitated a little. He remembered that he had said previously that he hadn't gone to any other bank, but the Old Freeport Bank, so he made it right with this answer, "That is when I went the second time to get the money to pay the Freeport Bank off, not the first time."

Cooper played with his witness much as a cat plays with a battered mouse. He would let him go so far, and then pounce before he got away. "So that this information that you gave to Mr. Canaday did not have anything to do with what you did before you got the loan, is that what you are willing to tell us?"

"Yes, sir."

"You did not go to the Ford City Bank to ask for a loan in '53 before you got your money from the Freeport Bank?"

"No, sir."

As Cooper continued to wind his web he said to the witness, "I wish you would start reading right here, or start, read the whole thing, start from the beginning."

Teitelbaum spoke from his chair at the table for the government's attorneys, "I have no objection to counsel reading it. I think that is easier."

Cooper turned his head toward Teitlebaum, "Let him read it. He is pretty good."

"If your Honor please, the Exhibit speaks for itself. I think it could be introduced, counsel can read it. I don't think this man should have to sit here and read this thing."

Cooper ignored his opponent's request. "Would you," turning to Gallagher, "start reading here, and read the first three sentences."

Gallagher started to read, "I first went to the bank in Ford City, Pa., to borrow sufficient funds on a note to pay Mr. Gross."

"Stop right there," commanded Cooper.

Teitelbaum was on his feet. His words were polite. He had a favor to ask, "May we go to a sidebar a minute?"

Cooper said, "Sure."

So again away from the ears of the jury, Teitelbaum made efforts to open the web which Judge Cooper was drawing about the government witness. "This transaction that we are talking about occurred in 1953, this statement refers to something that happened in 1955.

Attorney Schwartz, assistant to Cooper, pointed to a discrepancy in the statement, "If you will notice, on the original copy he scratched '55 out, put '53 in and initialed it."

Cooper added, "Just a minute, please. On the other copy, '55 is scratched out and '53 is written in. In the second place the contents of these two sentences show that he went to Ford City for the purpose of borrowing money to pay off his partner, which happened in September when he borrowed money from the Freeport Bank."

Teitelbaum continued to try to evade the issue at hand, "If Judge Cooper reads it himself, and starts from here, instead of doing what he is doing."

[97]

"He's asked him to read three sentences, so we will permit him to read it," the Court replied. The matter was returned to open court.

"Please look back at Exhibit D-1, Mr. Gallagher, and I want you to notice at the bottom of the first page and see if the word— in this sentence, "About the first of September 1955", "55" is crossed out and " '53" is written on top, and your initials appear right there, is that right?"

"Yes, sir."

"All right now. Does this Exhibit—and does the same thing occur on Page 2, where the words "55" are crossed out and " '53" is written on top, and your initials appear right there, is that right?"

"Yes."

"Now, you watch this as I read this. "In early part of September 1953, I went to the Peoples National Bank, Ford City, Armstrong County, to borrow sufficient funds to buy Mr. Gross' interest in your business." "Is that what you say here."

Gallagher only nodded his head.

"Look at it and read it and see if I read it correctly?"

"Yes," was the answer, which came slowly.

"So you did go to Ford City to try to borrow this money, didn't you, Mr. Gallagher?"

Like a small boy caught on the shelf with his hand in the cookie jar, Gallagher hung his head, "Yes, I did."

Chapter VII

COURTROOM DRAMATICS

AFTER GALLAGHER had been caught in his statement to the effect that he had gone only to the Old Freeport Bank, and Teitelbaum's efforts to extricate him from the ordeal were of no avail, the next witness for the prosecution was called. She was Mrs. Sylvia Burkett of Natrona Heights. Mrs. Burkett came into the courtroom that day in high spirits, and gloried in the attention being shown her. What financial troubles had plagued her and her husband in the past, seemed to vanish. She was the center of attention.

With the eyes of many focused upon her, and the solicitous attention of the prosecuting attorney and his staff, Mrs. Burkett at long last had an opportunity to display the histrionics which seem to be thwarted in all humans. Of course she had been coached.

Mrs. Burkett was called to the witness chair, sworn, and then the questioning began by John R. Gavin, First Assistant United States Attorney. The questioning opened with establishing the identity of the witness.

Gavin then asked, "Now Mrs. Burkett, in October of 1954, did you go with your husband to the Freeport Bank, the Old Freeport Bank at Freeport, Pa.?"

* See Sylvia and John Burkett sworn statements in Documentation pages 14, 15, 16.

[99]

"Yes, we did," she replied.

"Why did you go there?" Mr. Gavin continued questioning.

"To get a loan," Mrs. Burkett replied with haste.

"Who did you talk to when you went to the bank?"

"Mr. Sober, Sr."

"Charles L. Sober?"

"The father," she answered to this query.

The next question was for her to point him out. This she did answering at the time, "Yes." Of course, the counsel for the government developed the question by saying, "Seated right behind his counsel, Mr. Cooper. Did you talk with Mr. Sober at that time?"

"Yes, we did," Mrs. Burkett answered. "We had a long talk. I told him my troubles, and I guess he felt sorry for us and he told us to go see Dr. Heineman. It came out in the conversation that Dr. Heineman was our family doctor."

Again the questioning delved into the business transaction, "Did you discuss making a loan with Mr. Sober?"

Mrs. Burkett hesitated a moment, as if seeking to recall the event, and her answer came forth, "Well, yes, we asked for a loan. He told us to go see Dr. Heineman."

Attorney Gavin continued with this phase of the examination, "Did Mr. Sober say at that time whether or not the bank would make you a loan, or did he just refer you to Dr. Heineman?"

"Well, he talked real nice to us," said Mrs. Burkett, "and the way it sounded to me, if we seen Heineman we would get the loan."

"Do you know Dr. Heineman?" was the next question put to Mrs. Burkett.

Mrs. Burkett informed the court that he was the family physician and then pointed him out to the assembly.

Again the question, "Did you go to see Dr. Heineman as you were instructed to do by Mr. Sober?"

Mrs. Burkett knew her role well, and replied quickly, "Yes, we went directly to Dr. Heineman's office on Brackenridge Avenue in Brackenridge."

"At the time you went to see Dr. Heineman," Attorney Gavin asked, "did you owe him any money?"

"A few office calls or house calls," was Mrs. Burkett's reply.

As the attorney delved deeper into the problem, he brought out the information that the Burketts had gotten to see Dr. Heineman during this visit and had talked of the loan.

She brought forth the information that Sober had told them to go and see him about the loan and then she added, "He told us it would cost some money."

The attorney led her on and on. When the questioning took place regarding the actual signing of the papers for the loan, Attorney Gavin continued to paint a black picture of the transaction as he questioned, "You signed some papers at that time, didn't you?"

Mrs. Burkett dabbed her eyes with her handkerchief, "I signed my life away, I think."

"Did you sign a note?"

"I signed a chattel mortgage, a note, my husband's life insurance, he signed over."

"Signed a chattel mortgage; what was that for, your furniture and personal possessions, appliances, and you signed an assignment of your husband's proceeds in his insurance policy; you also signed at that time, did you not, a note for —"

Attorney Cooper jumped to his feet, "Just minute please."

But before Cooper could get any further, his opponent, Teitelbaum solicitiously asked Mrs. Burkett, "Would you like some water?"

"I object to that form of questioning," Attorney Cooper pleaded.

"It is leading," Judge Miller stated from the bench.

However, it was not long until Attorney Gavin again led the witness into making statements such as signing a bond for double the amount of the mortgage, which is standard practice for all mortgage loans. Again Sober's attorney objected.

Mrs. Burkett's testimony continued on the vein of payments to creditors. There was a check to the First National Bank of Tarentum, one to the Personal Finance Company of New Kensington, to the Freeport Finance Company for a car, to a clothing store and others. Finally the government's attorney brought out as an exhibit a check in the amount of $800. There was a typewritten endorsement on the back reading "Pay to the order of Dr. Richard W. Heineman."

"What was the purpose of this check, Mrs. Burkett?" asked Attorney Gavin.

"A commission, fee, for us to get the loan to consolidate all of our bills."

"A commission fee to Dr. Heineman?"

"Yes."

"For obtaining a loan for you?"

"Yes."

"You said," continued the attorney, "at the time you saw Dr. Heineman in his office about securing a loan, you owed him some money for professional services?"

"Yes."

"I believe you also stated you didn't recall the amount?"

"No."

"Was it more than $10.00 that you owed Dr. Heineman?"

Even though she was a government witness, Mrs. Burkett became somewhat befuddled, "It could have been, it couldn't have been any more."

This double answer was not even questioned by the defendants' attorney.

Mrs. Burkett went on to say, "Well, I knew we had to pay a commission before, because when we went to see him he told us it would cost some money. I never dreamed $800; I thought maybe $50 or $100, but never $800." Then, for emphasis, she added "God."

"You didn't owe Dr. Heineman $800 for medical services?"

"No, my husband had Blue Cross. Thank God, I didn't have sickness in the house."

Yet it had only been that same morning that Mrs. Burkett testified to this same government attorney that she owed the doctor for a few house or a few office calls. Later on she testified that she could have owed the doctor ten dollars, it couldn't have been any more. Still, during the same period of quizzing by the government's attorney, she testified that she hadn't had any sickness in her home, but still admitted going to the doctor for a few office calls. In the cross examination, no reference or questioning of this obvious discrepancy was challenged.

After bringing to the attention of the jurors that the Burkett house was going to be put up at Sheriff's Sale in 1955, the witness was turned over to Attorney Cooper. Cooper gradually developed the trend of thought by bringing up the statements which were signed by both Mr. and Mrs. Burkett.

"Did you give them a statement?" Cooper asked.

"Not that day, no. My husband wasn't home," was the reply.

Teitelbaum brought forth a practice which he was to use throughout the entire trial with little or no admonition from the bench. "We are getting off of what she was doing in my office."

Cooper turned to his opponent, "I am coming back. I am cross-examining her, I am coming right back to your office in a little while."

[103]

Later on in the cross-examination, the attorney for the defendants, asked, "In the course of your visits to Dr. Heineman, you had many conversations with him?"

"Oh well, sure."

"You were friendly with Dr. Heineman?"

"Yes."

"He was your family physician?"

"Yes."

"If you had any troubles you would tell Dr. Heineman about it, wouldn't you?"

Mrs. Burkett replied with a question, "What kind of troubles?"

"All kinds of troubles. Wouldn't you talk—"

"I don't know. Sickness maybe, but I don't know of any other troubles," replied Mrs. Burkett now feeling sure of herself. She had been warned of what to say and what not to say when being cross-examined. This fellow, Cooper, she thought is a nice old fellow. She could answer his questions.

Cooper, however, was warming to his task. He was looking for the opening, regardless of how small, which would break down the confidence of the woman on the stand. It was not long in coming.

"Didn't you have," Cooper asked quietly, "in October of 1954, you had a lot of trouble didn't you, Mrs. Burkett?"

"Oh yes, we had a first mortgage, a second mortgage, and all the bill collectors wanting their money."

"And you weren't paying on your first mortgage, you were behind on that?"

"Yes, we were behind," admitted Mrs. Burkett.

'You were behind on your second mortgage?" was the next question.

"Second mortgage," with the nod of her head made it affirmative.

"And you had loans from two finance companies?"

"Yes."

"You couldn't make any payments?"

"No. My husband was sick and he was laid off. I had all kinds of trouble ever since I have been married."

"Didn't you say that your husband was working?"

"Yes, he was working then."

"All right. If he was working he was well. Now let's get this straight—"

However Cooper was interrupted in his quest for more concerning the conditions at the time the Burketts sought financial help. Teitelbaum interjected his voice into the words of Cooper, "Your Honor, all that is, is a statement which may or may not be right. I object to that kind of a statement by counsel, and ask him to ask questions."

The court concurred with the attorney for the government. "Yes, counsel should ask questions. I can agree on that." Teitelbaum was just beginning a practice which was to mark the entire course of the trial. He would inject a statement, a request, or apparently make a ruling when the questioning of a government witness came too close to the whirlpool of confusion in answers.

Cooper continued his questioning. He stressed the point that the Burketts owed many institutions and people. The witness on the stand readily admitted this.

The strands of questioning were drawn ever tighter. And as the attorney cross-examined his witness, the acting continued with the witness dabbing her eyes occasionally and she made an effort to impress the jury with cruelness of the bankers.

"Isn't it a fact that you talked to Dr. Heineman and told Dr. Heineman all your troubles and he said that he would, might help you, if you go down to the bank?" Cooper asked.

But the answer was not direct. Mrs. Burkett had been well coached. "We talked to Sober about our troubles."

"Before you talked to Dr. Heineman?"

"Yes."

"How did you happen to get to Mr. Sober?"

"How did we?" Mrs. Burkett replied with a question.

"Yes."

"We were taking a ride through Freeport and I told him, I says 'Honey, let's stop here and just see what they say. Maybe they'll help us out.'"

"Was it in the daytime?"

"Yes, it was in the afternoon."

"During banking hours?"

"Yes."

"In the middle of the week?"

Mrs. Burkett became irritated. She raised her voice as she answered, "Oh, I don't remember that. I don't know what day it was, but I know it was in the afternoon, because the children were in school."

"You and your husband were taking a ride, your husband wasn't working that day?" Cooper questioned.

"Yes, he was off I guess."

The attorney for the defendants took another line of questioning, "Is there a bank across the street from the Freeport Bank?"

"Yes, there is a bank there."

"Did you try the bank across the street?"

"No."

"Why did you pick the Freeport Bank?"

"I don't know."

"When you walked into the bank, did you ask for anybody in particular?"

"No, we—"

"To tell the truth," Mrs. Burkett drew a deep breath, "I didn't talk to anybody. What I can remember, we just went right in his office."

Cooper arched his eyebrows, "You just walked in his office and told him who you were?"

"Yes."

"The moment you told him who you were, he said, 'I will send you to Dr. Heineman, he can get you some money.'"

Mrs. Burkett hesitated a moment, as if trying to recollect the event, "We talked to him, who we owed; our first mortgage was back, our second mortgage was back, that they were pressing us, and we needed money."

Cooper countered this with a statement, "He said, 'Go to Dr. Heineman.'"

"He told us—it came out in the conversation that Dr. Heineman was our physician."

"How would you tell Mr. Sober that Dr. Heineman was your physician, Mrs. Burkett?"

"How would I tell?" The wording of the question had apparently confused Mrs. Burkett and she countered with another.

"Yes?"

"Well, he was a director up there or something, wasn't he?"

"You knew Dr. Heineman was a director when you went down to the bank, is that right?"

"He was, wasn't he? No, I didn't know for sure, but he was."

Cooper began to show a little irritation with the witness's answers. "Oh, sure he was. You knew that he was, didn't you, Mrs. Burkett?"

Mrs. Burkett sighed her answer, "I guess I did."

"Because you knew he was a director, you talked to him and asked him to give you some help at the bank, didn't you?"

"No. Oh, no. I never dreamt of Dr. Heineman being the way he is."

"Did you tell Mr. Sober who your lawyer was?"

Mrs. Burkett was somewhat puzzled by the question, but she answered, "We didn't have a lawyer at that time."

"Did you tell Mr. Sober where you were dealing and what grocery store you were dealing with?" Cooper's questioning was plaintive, coaxing.

"No."

"Then why," Cooper permitted his voice to rise, "did you tell him who your doctor was?"

"I didn't tell him who my doctor was."

The trap was sprung. It was too late to retract the words. Cooper worked on this theme, "Well now, Mrs. Burkett, didn't you just tell me a little while ago in the conversation between you and Mr. Sober it came out that Dr. Heineman was your doctor?"

"Yes, he's our doctor. He was our doctor. As far as him being a doctor, he is a wonderful doctor but—"

"Did you tell people you were coming down here to testify because you were promised that you would get your property back?"

"No, definitely not. I come on my own."

"Before you went to the bank you were threatened with fore-closure by the people who held your first mortgage and your second mortgage?"

"Yes."

"So that if you did not get a loan from somebody, you were going to lose your house, is that right?"

"Yes."

"When you made a loan, you made it with the idea of saving your home?"

"Yes."

"And this loan was made to you on October 12, 1954 or '55?"

"'54."

"Fifty-four. Your husband was working at that time?"

"Yes, he was at that time."

"What were your monthly payments on the mortgage to the Freeport Bank?"

"They were $85."

"Did you make any payments after you got the mortgage?"

"I believe we did," Mrs. Burkett replied.

"How many?"

"A couple."

Cooper repeated her statement as a question, "A couple?"

"One or two."

"After that, what happened to the payments?"

"Well, to begin with, my husband really didn't want to sign those papers."

"Wait a minute." Cooper pleaded, "All right did somebody force you to sign them?"

"No, I told him he'd better sign them."

"And if he didn't sign, what would happen? Why did you tell him he'd better sign?"

"Because we were back on our second mortgage."

"In other words, they were going to foreclose on you and take your house away, is that right?"

"Yes."

"So you got this money and you paid off the first mortgage, is that right?"

"Yes."

"Paid off the second mortgage, is that right?"

"That's right. I didn't pay it, the bank paid it."

"That's right, out of this loan paid off everybody you owed and consolidated so you'd have to pay only $85 a month or something, is that right?"

"Yes, that's right."

"And then after you got your loan, you made about one or two payments and that was all?"

"My husband got laid off," Mrs. Burkett replied.

Thus the questioning went on and on. Finally, Cooper brought out an Exhibit, which was identified as No. 49 (the court's method of keeping exhibits used during the trial clear with a minimum of confusion). The attorney made an effort to have Mrs. Burkett read the notation on the back of the exhibit to the Jury, but after a discussion, read it to the jury himself at the court's direction.

"For value received I do hereby assign, transfer and set over unto The Old Freeport Bank of Freeport, Pa., the within certificate of deposit and all monies represented thereby, to be held by the said bank as additional collateral security for the prompt payment of the whole principal and interest on a certain mortgage dated .... and given to said bank by John R. Burkett and his wife, Sylvia J. Burkett, for the sum of $5900. This assignment is to be held by said bank as security aforesaid and at its option during the full period which the said mortgage has to run, and if beyond the maturity date of this certificate, then renewal certificate shall be issued under the same terms and agreement as above. Witness my hand and seal this 12th day of October 1954."

The assignment was signed by Richard W. Heineman and the certificate bore the signature of C. L. Sober as a witness.

A little later Cooper relinquished the witness. Teitelbaum called for a re-direct examination. As the questions were forwarded to Mrs. Burkett, he asked, "That day that you first went to see Mr. Sober about a loan, and during the discussion about whether or not you were going to get a loan, was there any discussion with you as to how much it was going to cost to get that loan?"

"No."

"Were you not told that it was going to cost you something?"

"Not in Sober's office."

"Where was that?"

"In Dr. Heineman's office."

"Who told you that?"

"Dr. Heineman."

After a few more questions, Mrs. Burkett's part in the drama was brought to a close. Her answers revealed that they (she and her husband) were in deep financial difficulties prior to going to the bank, and as additional security Dr. Heineman had to put in the bank three thousand dollars which he eventually lost because the efforts to help these people were of no avail. They had not, even after having a multitude of payments consolidated into one — much lower than the many — done their part.

Now those who had come to their aid were being held up before the public as Shylocks who had demanded the "pound of flesh."

The testimony of John Burkett, the husband of Mrs. Sylvia Burkett, was called for next. His statements, under the gentle prodding of the government attorney, were much like those given by his wife. However, Burkett continued to build on the theme that there was collusion between Sober and Heineman.

"Well, I talked about getting an application for a loan, told him about the first mortgage and the second mortgage, all the other bills I had. I told him I wanted to consolidate them all into one so I have one place to pay, so in the course of conversation, he asked me where I lived, where my home was located at. I told him it was in Brackenridge. It came out in the conversation about he asked me if I knew Dr. Heineman. I says yes."

Thus did Burkett create the impression that Sober had brought up the name of Dr. Heineman.

His further testimony detailed the transaction which took place in the bank the evening of October 12, 1954. During the direct examination by John R. Gavin, First Assistant United States Attorney, Burkett replied to a question concerning the $800 cashiers check made out to Dr. Heineman, "I didn't want to sign it. My wife says, after we discussed it over before about taking the loan, I figured I might as well go ahead and sign it. I handed it over to Sober and him and Heineman went out from his office in the other part of the bank."

Gavin continued to question, "Did Mr. Sober, as soon as you signed it, take the check from you after you signed the check?"

"I signed the check," Burkett answered, "I laid it back down across the desk. He picked it up and him and Heineman walked out from his office out to the other side of the bank."

"What was the purpose of that $800 check?"

"That must have been for getting the loan, $800, that was their fee. I think they were sort of mad because it was only $800."

Thus did Burkett add to the stories already started concerning Sober's part in the transaction. Yet there was no objection from Attorney Cooper. The die was cast, and penetrating the minds of the jurors by innuendoes and "thoughts" of what others "felt", the web was begun to ensnare the banker and his associates. It made no difference that the Burketts were in deep financial trouble and could not get help from other sources; it made no difference that they had not fulfilled their obligations. These were the bad bankers.

When it became Burkett's turn to be cross examined by Cooper a great deal of the testimony already covered by the government's witness was reiterated. The attorney agreed with Burkett, "You had plenty of troubles."

"That is for sure," Burkett confirmed.

The statement was repeated in the form of a question, and Burkett replied in the affirmative.

"You were looking for some place," continued Cooper, "where you could get rid of all your troubles and put them behind you, and then you would have payments, just one place to make payments?"

"Yes."

"That's right."

"That's right," parrotted Burkett.

"And that is why you wanted a loan?"

"That's right, that is why I wanted a loan."

"That is why you went to the Old Freeport Bank?"

Burkett's mind raced to keep up with this series of repetitious questions. He answered, in confusion, "That is not why I went to the Freeport Bank. Yes, I in a way, that is the way, reason I went to the Freeport Bank. I was going to try the Freeport Bank, I was going to try anywhere I could to try to get a loan."

"You did get a loan, didn't you?" counsel for the defendant asked.

"Yes."

"Now Dr. Heineman, out of the payments that were made in distribution, Dr. Heineman got a check for $800?"

"That's right, I think. Yes, that's right."

"Did you know before that night that you came down to make the settlement what the charge was going to be?"

"No, definitely no."

"You never knew?" Cooper pressed the question further.

"That's right," responded Burkett.

"And the first time you saw $800 was on that check?"

"That's right."

"That was the first check?"

[113]

"That was the first check I signed, that's right."

"Mr. Sober didn't bring that check to your house, did he?"

"No, he didn't. I signed it right there in the bank."

"When you signed all of the other checks?"

"That's right. That was the first check I signed."

"I believe you told us, Mr. Burkett, that you were told the night of the closing that your monthly payments would be about $85, is that right?"

"That's right."

"That you complained you thought it was too much?"

"That's right."

"Was $85 more than you had been paying?"

"No, no, no!" Burkett shouted from the stand.

Further testimony on the part of Burkett told of his being accompanied by Attorney John McCue, making a trip to various places in the valley to pay off the Burkett's creditors. So at one place in Burkett's life he had been freed of the pressing demands of the many and the threatened suits. He admitted the payment to the Old Freeport Bank at $85 per month was less than he had been paying out before, yet it was too much.

While in the courtroom dramas—which have become plays with attorneys seemingly intent on winning cases—the movements are directed to keeping certain facts under cover, while others seek to bring facts out. The truth, even though it is only a partial truth, is sometimes more damaging than a falsehood.

The trial moved into another day. Burkett resumed the stand and Cooper shot another question at him, "I believe you said yesterday, Mr. Burkett, that you knew what a certificate of deposit was?"

"Well, I have a general idea what it is."

"Tell us again what it is?"

"Well, it's security for a loan somebody puts up in the bank."

"That's right; you knew that you couldn't get this loan unless Dr. Heineman put up security at the bank?"

"There was never nothing said about any security he was going to put up for me," Burkett insisted.

"You thought you got this loan on your own credit?"

"Yes, I thought he felt sorry for me."

Even this answer brought an objection from Teitelbaum, "What he thought I object to, Your Honor. That calls for the same conclusion."

The Court answered, "That's right, it does."

Cooper was not to get away from this line of questioning. He repeated, "But you say you thought he felt sorry for you, is that right?"

"Yes, that's right."

"And helped you get the loan?"

"That's right."

"Even if he had to put up security?"

"I didn't know nothing about security, never heard of it until it was brought out here."

You mean to tell me, Mr. Burkett, that when Mr. Canaday was out there, when the agents of the F.B.I. were out there and you talked this whole case over, that there was no discussion about this certificate of deposit that Dr. Heineman put up?"

"That's right."

"It was never mentioned—"

"No."

"By any of the agents?"

"That's right, never no mention about it."

"You never knew about a certificate of deposit Dr. Heineman put up until you heard it in this courtroom today or yesterday?"

Again came that repetitious answer, "That's right."

Thus was Burkett given the impression that nothing had been placed in the bank as security. He had been sold on the story that he had paid dearly for a loan, even though his benefactor lost three thousand dollars because as Burkett stated, "I thought he felt sorry for me."

It was a costly sorrow for Dr. Heineman.

Chapter VIII

SUPERIORITY
OF NUMBERS

F OR SOME REASON the case of Sober et al and
the government was becoming a "cause celebre" in western Pennsylvania. The newspapers each day were carrying accounts of the
witnesses testimony in detail. The picture darkened for the
bankers as first one and then another was called to the stand.
Appearing after John Burkett as a witness for the government
was John (Jack) Devereaux.

Jack, as he was familiarly known throughout the Freeport area,
had made arrangements with Dr. Heineman to purchase a garage
and agency for $5,200. As the transaction was consummated
Devereaux signed a demand note for the money, which was to
be covered by a chattel mortgage as the equipment was inven-
toried. However, Devereaux paid Dr. Heineman $2,600 and re-
tained, with the permission of the doctor $2,600 as working capi-
tal to operate the business. The government was attempting to
show that the $2,600 paid to the doctor was a kickback.

Devereaux was being questioned by Attorney John R. Gavin,
First Assistant United States Attorney, concerning the transaction
and the questions were so worded and the answers given to in-

* See sworn statement by Jack Devereaux in Documentation pages 37, 38, 39.

dicate that somewhere along the line $2,600 was given to someone.

Gavin asked his witness, "Who was there; was that the second meeting you had?"

"Yes," Devereaux replied, "There at the time was all the employees of the bank, because this was in the morning."

"That was the morning that you went back to the bank, was it, to arrange for a loan?"

"That's right."

"And what was the purpose of this check? You told the jury that you were making a loan for $5,200, there was to be a credit to your checking account of 25 or $2,600. You didn't remember the specific amount. What was this check for $2,600; what was the purpose of that check?"

"Well," Devereaux answered quickly, "that was to be returned to Dr. Heineman."

"Was to be returned to Dr. Heineman;" Gavin's eyebrows were arched, "Why?"

The answer was not direct. Devereaux countered with "Well, I signed a check for $5,200."

He was corrected by the government attorney, "You signed a note."

"A note, I agreed to take only $2,600 out of the 52."

"In other words, you signed a note for $5,200, you were only to get one-half of that?"

"That's right."

"Dr. Heineman was to get the other half?" came the question from Gavin in the form of a statement.

Again Devereaux answered as he had been coached, "That's right."

"That is what the check was for?" Gavin again countered with a statement for a question, with no effort being made to ascertain that the check was for something more than than just a gift for the doctor.

Later during the questioning, Gavin asked, "And to whom was the note payable?"

"Payable to the Old Freeport Bank, Freeport, Pa."

"So that you signed a note for $5,200 to the Old Freeport Bank."

"That's right," replied Devereaux.

"And you got $2,600 from the Old Freeport Bank?"

"That's right," was Devereaux's stock answer.

However the repetition of the questions, the same questions over and over was not lost to Cooper, Sober's attorney. Without moving from his seat at the defendants' table, Cooper injected his rather soft voice into the courtroom, "If your Honor please, I object to this method of questioning a witness, where after he has been asked twice and given answers to the questions, all of the testimony of the witness is then embodied into another question by counsel in which he is asked to repeat the same thing all over."

The Court concurred with Cooper, "I think that is right."

As the questioning continued, tempers became more heated. The legal wrangling broke into the open more frequently. At one point, prior to the dismissal of Devereaux from the stand, Teitelbaum turned to counsel for the defendants, "I wonder if we may ask whether defense counsel has a statement taken by one of their investigators from this witness. Did you take a statement from this witness?"

"I don't believe you are entitled to ask," snapped Melvin Schwartz one of the defendants' attorneys.

Teitelbaum turned quickly on Schwartz, "Why not? We turned all of ours over, why shouldn't you furnish us with yours, if you have them?"

[119]

Again came the voice of the gentleman of the "old school." Practically every opening statement addressed to the bench was "If your Honor please." Cooper, drilled in the formalities of court etiquette began, "If your Honor please, I think that Mr. Teitelbaum knows he furnished us statements because under the law he is compelled to furnish us these statements."

"That is true," the Court affirmed.

"There is no law that is different for one side from the other, as I know." Teitelbaum countered.

Judge Miller looked over the bench, directly at Teitelbaum, "Does the Act of Congress provide for that, Mr. Teitelbaum?"

"The Act of Congress," Teitelbaum answered, "only provides that under certain conditions prior to putting a witness on the stand and questioning him, you can't ask for statements of the government. It doesn't say anything about defense statements. I submit in all fairness—"

"I understand what you are getting at," the Court replied. "I know nothing in the law that requires the defendant to give you statements they have taken."

"I am going back to the old *Jencks* case that said if you put a witness on the stand, you ask him questions, you ought to produce the statements that you have."

"All right, now—"

But the younger element in the court that day forgot the niceties of the former generations. Attorney Schwartz interrupted the judge, "Let me say — "

"Does that apply to the defendants?" Judge Miller continued his sentence.

"I don't see why not, in fairness," Teitelbaum injected.

Judge Miller turned to his clerk, "Get me the *Jencks* case, Mr. Moses."

"If your Honor, please, before the court starts reading the *Jencks* case — "

"Just a moment," the Judge interrupted.

"Your Honor, if there's some reason — " Teitelbaum pleaded.

The Judge was visibly showing signs of annoyance at the interruptions. He raised his voice, "Just a minute, please."

"I was going to withdraw my demand," Teiltelbaum countered.

Cooper looked at his opponent with some surprise, "Oh no."

"If you have a reason you don't want to give us the statements, I will withdraw it," Teitelbaum spoke ingratiatingly as he nodded his head toward Cooper.

Cooper turned toward the bench, "I object to the remarks by counsel for the government. They are prejudicial to the defendants. It is done for the purpose of prejudicing the jurors against our case. That is the only purpose these remarks are being made."

"Just a minute. Just a minute," Judge Miller ordered.

Cooper forgot his early training for the moment, and without so much as a "If your Honor, please," he turned to the government's attorney, "You know it."

"I don't know it," snapped Teitelbaum. "I am going to withdraw my demand.

"I think you should," commented the Court.

"Since the defendants—" Schwartz was on his feet and talking as he walked to the front of the bench.

Judge Miller showed exasperation, "Just a moment. It has been withdrawn, that is it."

The defendants stared in amazement at the government's attorney. Never having had occasion, prior to this time, to see the workings of law and justice, they realized that somehow this legal by-play had worked against them.

Sober glanced at the jury. The members were looking at Teitelbaum, and the words of the witness on the stand were forgotten. There was something wrong when the defendants' attorney would not willingly submit a witness' statement to the prosecution. No word from the judge ordered the jury to discount the statement made by Teitelbaum.

The government was not through. After Devereaux had been dismissed, more and more were to be called to add brick after brick to the theory that something was wrong and had been wrong with the bankers' dealings with people. It made no difference that charges were to be dismissed later, the words of these coached people would weigh heavily when the verdict was handed down.

Called to the stand next, and sworn, was Rudy Kelosky.

The story as revealed by Kelosky's testimony showed him to be a dreamer. He had dreams of a trailer park first, and then because of his location in Butler County, along a beautiful winding stream, his desire was for cabins, so the place would eventually become a resort. Kelosky, like many others had no capital with which to work. He, too, had turned to the Old Freeport Bank and eventually to Sober.

It was not long until the lawyers for the government and for the defendants were into a legal battle over what the indictment covered.

As Teitelbaum questioned his witness, he asked, "What was the gist of the conversation; what were you talking about; why did you go and see him?"

"Well," Kelosky answered, "I had a pretty rough spot, I wanted to talk to Mr. Sober, C. L. Sober, and I explained to him that I had got behind in my payments and things were pretty rough, I couldn't make the payments."

"That was under the G. I. mortgage?"

"Yes, sir, I believe so."

"What was the result of that conversation; did you and Mr. Sober reach any agreement?"

"I don't remember," Kelosky stated as he shook his head, "to be honest."

So the government attorney repeated the statement made previously by Kelosky in an effort to draw him out, "Well, you went in and told him you were having a pretty rough time making the payments, you were in a rough spot. What did you want him to do for you, what did you talk about?"

As Kelosky continued to testify, it was revealed that he did not have enough equity in his property to borrow more money from a bank. He had appealed to Sober for funds so that he could construct facilities for a trailer park, and thus the land would become more valuable in a commercial sense.

Sober had acquiesced to his request and had loaned him money personally.

Grasping for any testimony which might reflect on the defendants, Teitelbaum continued the questioning of Kelosky, concerning the investment in the trailer park.

Kelosky replied, "I wouldn't actually say it was an investment. The money I borrowed from Mr. Sober, that is the reason I signed a note for $5,000 more or less as security."

"Did you get $5,000 is my question?" prodded the attorney.

"In time, yes."

"When you borrowed the $14,000, what happened to the proceeds of the $14,000?"

"After I borrowed the $14,000, when the mortgage came up to the $14,000, all these other items were paid," the witness responded.

"Paid back?"

"Paid back, yes, such as, oh, for instance, the excavating and the material used on it."

Again Teitelbaum brought the principal defendant's name into play, "Did Mr. Sober give you back the note for $5,000 at that time?"

"No sir, he didn't, not at that time."

[123]

"Now so that, if we understand each other correctly, ultimately you needed $14,000 and you borrowed and gave a mortgage for the $14,000 with which all debts and loan were paid back, is that right?"

"That's right."

"And Mr. Sober still had the $5,000 note, is that right?"

"Yes, at that time, yes."

"Now after you borrowed the $14,000 did you have to, subsequently, have to borrow more money from the bank?"

"Yes."

Cooper rose from the defendant's table, "Wait. Wait a minute. I object to that, if the court please. Anything that happened subsequent to what is charged in this count is certainly not material or relevant to the issue in this case."

"Let's go to sidebar. I'm willing to discuss it here if counsel wants me to."

So, the legal technicality was settled by the court out of hearing of the jury. It was to become a long and arduous ceremony to be indulged in with increasing regularity as the trial dragged on and on, the tempers became heated, and acrimonious charges and innuendoes were bantered between government counsel and the attorney for the defendants.

It was only a short time later that Cooper again appealed to the court to put a halt to the leading questions, which were nothing more than statements reflecting on the defendants, but which brought forth incriminating answers from the witnesses.

"If the court please," Cooper appealed again, "I know how difficult it is for a lawyer to try a case without once in awhile indulging in some leading questions. We are all guilty of it. I think so far as possible that in a matter of this kind, we ought to try to stay away from leading questions."

The Court was in agreement, "I think both sides ought to make an effort to stay away from leading questions."

However, Teitelbaum was insistant, "The only time I do that, your Honor, is where I feel in one question it gives the answer to fifteen, and it speeds it up. I can always do it the long way, but I thought maybe that would help the court and the jury.

"I ask leave to show these two pieces of, two exhibits to the jury, Exhibits 174 and 112.

"One hundred twelve is the ledger sheet of the bank showing the date of the mortgage, and 174 is this judgment note, 'Pay to the order of Charles L. Sober $5,234.48.' "

The exhibits were then passed to the jury.

The questioning of Kelosky was continued, "Now Mr. Kelosky, later in May of 1947 your mortgage was increased to $30,000 with the Freeport Bank, was it not?"

"Just a moment," Cooper fairly shouted.

"I haven't asked the question," retorted Teitelbaum as he turned to Cooper.

"I object to that question as something that happened after the subject matter of this indictment, has no relevancy to it, and has no part in this case, and this question should—I object to it," said Cooper in his defense.

Teitelbaum was insistent, "Your Honor, it is all part of the same design and plan. It is evidence to indicate just what is going on here. I think the Circuit Court of this Circuit has held that you can show, even if the bank had been involved with a different person; now we are showing they are involved with the same person approximately a year later. It's a follow-up to bring this thing to its conclusion and show the plan that was carried out here."

Cooper then pleaded with the court that the indictment spoke for itself, declaring that his opponent had left the matter at hand

and was delving into something else and bringing the same matter before the jury.

Still Teitelbaum was insistent. "I cite," he said "*United States v. Stirone*, with which we are all familiar, in which the court says you may even raise inter alias acts among other people for the purpose of pointing out the intent was there. I feel therefore this is a logical development, rather than leave this thing in the air in the middle of the transaction."

Judge Miller pondered for a moment, "At the moment I am going to sustain the objection."

Teitelbaum acknowledged the judge's ruling by saying "All right." He then launched into the next question, "You," turning to Kelosky, "subsequently to giving this note for $5,000, replaced it by another note in a larger sum, did you not?"

Cooper's face became florid. He again was on his feet. In spite of the judge's ruling given just a few minutes prior, the government's attorney had successfully brought before the jury the idea of unsavory actions, which were not in the indictment. "Again if the court please," Cooper remonstrated, "I again object to that question."

"Objection sustained," ordered the court.

But it was only a few minutes later that Teitelbaum had brought out that Kelosky's mortgage had been raised from the $14,000 to a higher figure, and again Cooper was objecting to bringing out a transaction which was not included in the indictment.

The questioning of the witness on the part of the government attorney continued with frequent objections on the part of Cooper. Sometimes the objections were sustained and at times they were not. Teitelbaum delved deeper and deeper into the affairs of Kelosky. At one point he brought out the ownership of the property. Turning to the witness, he asked, "Do you still own that property?"

"No sir, I do not."

"What happened to it ultimately?"

"Just a minute, please. Objected to," Cooper stated.

"Why?" questioned Judge Miller.

"Immaterial, irrelevant. Whether he owns the property now or not is immaterial," Cooper countered.

"He's already testified without objection from you that the property is now owned by the Freeport Bank," the judge replied to Cooper.

The defendant's attorney acknowledged this with a "That's right."

"I want to find out how it got there," Teitelbaum persisted.

"If that's the deed for it—" but the judge was interrupted.

"That is not the deed for it. That is exactly the point I am making. This is an unrecorded instrument," Cooper stated as he turned to the bench.

"It is still valid," Teitelbaum claimed.

At this point the judge again injected his voice into the argument between the two attorneys, "Let me see it."

After a few moments, while Judge Miller scanned the legal document, he turned his head towards Teitelbaum, "Mr. Teitelbaum, this is a deed, the name of the grantee is not asserted, consideration is not inserted, and the deed could not be recorded because it has not been acknowledged."

"It could not be recorded is right," Teitelbaum consented. "I'm just curious, I want to know how this property got from this man to somebody else."

Again the heat of a previous anger worn off, Cooper returned to his former polite practice which he had forgotten in the bitterness of verbal combat, "If the court please, criminal cases are not being tried to satisfy the curiosity of the United States Attorney."

Teitelbaum was ready for rebuttal, "Well, it's a public curiosity; it isn't my personal curiosity."

The testimony of Rudy Kelosky was interrupted frequently due to the verbal battles between counsels. Teitelbaum insistently would make efforts to bring in other transactions between Kelosky and the elder Sober, while Cooper would battle to keep these matters out of the record. At one time when the arguments became heated, Teitelbaum turned to Cooper after the latter had objected to a question and said, "Of course Mr. Cooper knows the answer," implying that the defendant's attorney was trying to hide something that should be brought before the jury.

Cooper retaliated with, "What did you say, Mr. Teitelbaum?" and his voice rose to a higher pitch than was normal when asking a question.

Judge Miller intervened, "Just a minute, gentlemen."

But Teitelbaum paid no heed to the judge. He turned to Cooper and with a sarcastic tone muttered, "I say, you know the answer."

As the testimony was continued, with frequent interruptions on the part of the attorneys who bickered over points of law, the story was finally drawn from Kelosky. He testified that he needed additional money. The equity he had at that time in his business would not allow him to borrow more on his mortgage. So he had appealed to Sober, who in turn had loaned him money from his personal funds. Each time he would borrow money in this manner he would sign a note to Sober for the amount of the loan.

After some improvements had been made, Kelosky needed still more money. So the note to Sober was satisfied (although nothing had been paid on it) in order for the Keloskys to increase the amount of their mortgage. The legal maneuvering continued throughout Kelosky's testimony, with Teitelbaum trying to bring out transactions between Kelosky and Sober, while Cooper objected strenuously that the matters were not involved in the issue at hand.

The court overruled Cooper's objection and Teitelbaum continued with his questioning. His questions led to this answer by Kelosky, "If I tell you what the purpose is, it is going to mislead everybody, so it will take a little time to explain this."

Teitelbaum urged him on, "You take your time, explain it your way."

"After I built this business in the trailer park," Kelosky continued, "I had great plans, big ideas, and I had decided and had talked to Mr. Sober frequently about it that I did want to build numerous amount of cottages in the trailer park which is bordering on a stream, because I had so many requests to build these cottages, and people wanted to rent them. As a matter of fact, I even had the opportunity to sell, so I went to Mr. Sober and tried to sell him the idea, and he told me then that my financial statement was not enough to obtain enough money from the bank, or I never had enough equity, so we decided to sign the note for the amount of $25,000. I believe that is the correct figure and in turn my understanding was if there was any possibility to have anyone buy that note and go in a partnership or business with me to build those cottages, that was the reason for the $25,000 note, which later was destroyed when the trailer park had been sold."

"All right now; was that $25,000 note to include this $5,200 note?" the U. S. Attorney questioned.

"No, sir."

"It was not. All right; and you ultimately signed one for $35,000 didn't you?"

Kelosky looked toward the ceiling as if trying to collect his thoughts, "That was destroyed also."

"Now did Mr. Sober ever advance $25,000 or $35,000 to you out of his personal funds?"

"No, sir, he did not."

"And did you sign any additional mortgages at the bank for the purpose of paying off this $5,200 note?"

Again Kelosky answered, "Not to my knowledge, sir. I don't believe I ever signed any mortgage to pay off that note. My understanding about that note, maybe I am out of line here, by my understanding about that note —"

Teitelbaum interrupted. The answers of the government's witness were not fitting into the picture he was trying to build of the cruel, cold-hearted banker. He ordered, "Let's proceed."

"Let him finish," pleaded Cooper.

"Go ahead, explain," Teitelbaum authorized his witness.

There was some more testimony concerning the transactions between Kelosky and Sober. At no time, however, did the government attorney find any place were Sober had accepted a fee for securing a loan. The records didn't show anything of this kind, nor did Kelosky's testimony reveal at any place where Sober had profited from the transaction. From the records it was apparent that Sober had, through his efforts to help, lost over $5,000.

The government was thorough. Playing the game with a "stacked deck" the roll call of witnesses grew ever longer. Next called to the stand and sworn was Betty Jean Kelosky, the wife of the preceding witness.

Teitelbaum questioned her for a time. Finally, he brought out a paper, "Do you know whether this note which I have shown you, Government Exhibit 174, was paid?"

"That note wasn't even in existence," snapped Mrs. Kelosky.

"At the time you sold the trailer park?"

"As far as I was concerned, I thought Mr. Sober had lifted it. That was all there was to it."

"You don't know though, do you?"

"No." Again Mrs. Kelosky's voice showed disgust.

"You didn't look at the distribution sheet?" Queried Teitelbaum.

[130]

"Yes, I have a settlement sheet of my own."

"Do you know whether this $5,000 —"

Mrs. Kelosky cut the government attorney short, "That is not it."

Cooper relished the exchange between his opponent and Mrs. Kelosky. He spoke from his place at the defendant's table, "If the Court please, I object to this. Counsel is cross-examining his own witness instead of asking questions."

It was Teitelbaum's turn to appeal to the bench, "If your Honor please, I think this is a hostile witness. I might be entitled to, but I'm not doing it. I merely asked if this was paid at the time."

"Just a minute," Cooper injected.

The Court, however, ordered, "All right, ask her that."

Teitelbaum's questioning of his witness did not go well. Later on he asked, "Of '58; and what did you sell to Mr. Datillo?"

"The trailer park and the house and all the land."

"Do you recall how much you sold it for?"

Cooper was on his feet, "Now if the Court please, that is objected to, this line of questioning, for the various reasons we have assigned before."

Judge Miller agreed "Objection sustained."

So Teitelbaum reverted to an old trick, "I don't want to show this in front of the jury. I think we'd better come to a side bar, to say what I am going to say."

The attorneys for the government and for the defendants moved to the bench. An occasional word was caught as they argued a point of law.

Sober strained from his place at the defendant's table to hear the exchange. "Hump," thought Sober, "this law is a funny thing. It seems you just let the jury hear what you want them to hear— especially the government attorney does." He settled back in his chair in disgust. The truth might come out in a case but if attorneys could prevent it, certainly the whole truth wasn't to be heard.

Teitelbaum was undaunted by the fact that the last witness had been "hostile." He had made sure that numerous counts had been placed against the defendants, and in some of these he could obtain a conviction. There was no thought at the time of being a "defender" — his sole purpose was for a conviction. Is that not on what reputations are built?

So the next government witness was called. He was Gustav C. Heyman of Saxonburg.

After establishing the identity of the witness, Gavin the assistant to Teitelbaum continued the questioning. "You talked to Sober at the bank, did you?"

"Yes," answered Heyman.

"What did you talk about?"

"I had several debts that I wanted to consolidate, and that was the essence of our talk," Heyman lowered his voice as he answered.

"If the Court please, this witness has dropped his voice. I lost the last part of his answer." Cooper stated.

The judge instructed the reporter to read the answer.

Through the question and answer process Heyman unfolded his story. He told from the stand that he had told Sober that he wanted to borrow $23,000, but he had been informed that it didn't look like the bank could lend him that much. Later on Heyman said that Sober told him the bank could go to $13,000, which was approximately $10,000 short of what he wanted. Heyman said, ". . . and I asked him at that time if he knew anyone that might be able to help me, that might go my note or something for the extra $10,000, and he suggested I might see . . ."

At this point Heyman was ordered to keep his voice up.

*See Heyman sworn statement on Documentation page 18.

He continued with his story, which was broken into occasionally with a question from Attorney Gavin.

"He suggested that I might see Dr. Heineman, which I did. Dr. Heineman said that he would come out and see us, which he did in a day or two. He came out to our place of business and in our kitchen, he sat down and talked to us, and he at that time said that he could but that he —"

Again there was a prodding question from Gavin, "Could what, sir?"

"He could help me with the $10,000 but he couldn't give it to me all at one time, that it would be easier on him if he gave it to me a couple of thousand dollars at a time. At the same time he said it would cost me less interest because I wouldn't have the full amount as long, and he said that he would see, maybe I could get it for five percent interest and I would make my payments directly to the bank because he wasn't in the finance business and he didn't do clerical work."

"Did he say how much," Gavin asked, "he would want to be paid back?"

Judge Cooper rose from his chair quickly, "Just a minute, please. Just a minute. I object to that question, leading."

Gavin turned to Cooper, "I will withdraw that question."

Judge Miller said, "It is."

"The danger of questions of that kind," continued Cooper, "after they are put before a witness are a suggestion. This witness so far has given no indication as to the substance of the question that Mr. Gavin put before him."

"I withdraw the question," Gavin repeated.

"Did you discuss terms of repayment with Dr. Heineman?" the assistant to Teitelbaum questioned.

"Yes, in our kitchen," was Heyman's reply.

"And what was the discussion?"

[133]

Again Cooper pleaded, "Just a minute please. I object to this question. Object to the question, request that the answer be stricken from the record."

"Why?" Asked Judge Miller from the bench.

"Because no loan was ever made by Dr. Heineman. It is not embraced within this indictment, has nothing to do with the question involved in this case," Cooper replied to the bench.

"Well, that's true, strictly speaking, Mr. Gavin."

At this point Gavin requested a side bar.

The Judge, government attorneys and attorneys for the defendants argued the point of law involved. Both Gavin and Teitelbaum tried to point out, even though admitting that Dr. Heineman was not charged in this particular count, it was a part of a grand scheme involving the defendants. At this point Judge Miller ordered the discussion off the record and no further remarks were recorded for a time. Later on Schwartz requested that the remarks be placed in the record.

"You are wanting to go on record?" Queried Judge Miller with a note of surprise in his voice.

"Yes, sir. I seriously object to any testimony concerning any discussions with Dr. Heineman as to whether or not Dr. Heineman would loan this witness any money, or any terms discussed between them, since the indictment doesn't contain it. Furthermore the argument presented by Mr. Teitelbaum and Mr. Gavin show a scheme and a course of conduct relating to Burkett and Gallagher counts is to me not plausible, because the Burkett and Gallagher loans occurred two years prior to the time that we are now involved in with this witness."

Teitelbaum had his say, "I think we have had that before, haven't we, Judge?"

"You can put it on the record," stated Cooper with some heat, "Are you going two years after a deed to show a plan?"

Teitelbaum countered, "We have offered it for two reasons, and the question is whether it is relevant or not. That is the relevant questions. If it is relevant, then it is up to the court to reach the further decision as to whether or not the prejudicial effect overweighs the probative value, and the probative value here is considerable . . ."

The argument continued. Even though Dr. Heineman was not involved with Heyman, other than having a conversation with him about a loan, Teitelbaum was intent on bringing this phase of the conversation into play. He well knew the effect that it would have on the jurors regarding the other counts with which Dr. Heineman had been charged.

Cooper was just as insistent that this line of questioning be forbidden stating, ". . . I will object to any questions that do not go to the essence and substance of the count, and after this witness has given this story and what he did and what loan he made, who loaned him the money, everything else at this stage of the game is not relevant and not admissible."

"You are trying to build that wall around counts again that you have tried throughout the trial. We don't try cases that way. Each count is not departmentalized. A witness isn't necessarily testifying about a particular count; he is giving testimony as to the indictment," Teitelbaum retorted to Cooper.

At this point Judge Miller intervened by saying, "At the moment the objection will be overruled, and I caution you about the way you put your questions."

Apparently the caution issued by the judge was to have little effect. As the trial went on and on, time after time counsel for the government propounded leading question after leading question in spite of objections on the part of Cooper. Thus were Dr. Heineman's and Sober's names tied into the "plan" as Teitelbaum called it, even though Heyman later testified that Sober had said, ". . . and he told me that if Dr. Heineman was financing five percent interest that was his business, but that he wouldn't or that the bank wasn't going to loan any money at five percent..."

The questioning of Heyman continued and in his answers he revealed that he had contacted several people for money so that he could consolidate his debts. Among the people contacted was John E. Cypher. In Heyman's words the story before the court ran, "The main reason was, after seeing some of the people I just happened to remember — I have known him ever since I was a little kid, or he's known me ever since I was a kid. I figured he might be able to help me."

"Did you know at that time he was associated with The Old Freeport Bank?" Gavin questioned.

"No, sir," replied Heyman.

Heyman continued to tell how he had gone back to the bank and of his subsequent conversation with the elder Sober. "So after that I in turn went back to see Mr. Cypher again, and I made him an offer of ten percent and gradually each time I seen him, he always left the case pending by telling me that he would let me know after he goes to the bank. That is when I found out he was something at the bank, but I didn't know what, I didn't have the least idea what. I thought maybe a depositor. Each time he said he'd see what he could do for me at the bank he'd call me up or I'd call him, and he'd give me the answer, but he always left it in a way that it left a door open, and I'd offer a little more each time, I'd offer him a little more. For about two months that is the way that went, so I finally decided I'd offer him what Dr. Heineman said I'd have to pay him for a risk loan."

"What was that?" the attorney prodded.

"Two for one, and two days later I was down at the bank signing papers."

So Heyman added to the words of the other government witnesses in testimony of striking similarity. The jury was notably impressed.

Heyman's testimony continued with a revelation of how the money was distributed.

Cooper's attempt to cross-examine the witness was frequently interrupted by Teitelbaum.

"Mr. Heyman," Cooper approached the witness, "I show you a paper which has been identified as Defendant's Exhibit D-9, and ask you to look at it."

"Just one minute, please," injected Teitelbaum.

"Just tell us what it is," continued Cooper with the witness.

"If your Honor please, the statement of list of creditors that was shown on that document was not necessarily the list of creditors at that time. The two aren't contemporaneous."

"That is very true," Judge Miller stated, "I don't know whether they are the same or not. They shouldn't be."

"Sir?" Teitelbaum turned to the Judge with a note of surprise in his voice.

Judge Miller repeated, "They shouldn't be."

"Should not be," repeated Teitelbaum.

Even though the game had been played smoothly and the attention had been drawn from the witness, and the jurors had their eyes focused toward the bench and the argument taking place, Cooper tried to return to the witness, "Let me ask the question, then you can object."

"I just want to know whether these are the papers that you signed at the time you went through bankruptcy?"

"Yes, they are," answered Heyman.

However, Teitelbaum was insistent on helping Cooper with the cross-examination, "Did you get the date they were signed?"

Cooper turned to Teitelbaum, "Yes he said he signed them."

"The date?" queried the government attorney.

"Tenth day of February, 1958," Heyman complied.

Cooper, undaunted by the interplay continued with the witness, "I will ask you to please look at a sheet which is marked A-3, Schedule A-3 which is a list of the creditors, ask you to look at it and tell us whether or not, or which one of those did you list as creditors, did you owe at the time you made the application for the loan at the Freeport Bank. Do you need glasses, Mr. Heyman?"

"No."

Again Teitelbaum interrupted, "I think we ought to have something clear here, whether it is the same debts that he owed them."

The Court intervened "Just a minute. That can be brought out."

By now the jurors were thoroughly confused. The issues confronting them were torn asunder by the frequent interjections on the part of Teitelbaum. The seeds of lawful injustice were being carefully sown.

The cross-examination of Heyman continued to delve into the partnership between him and Cypher, but Heyman made no direct statement. His answer regarding the partnership was, "Verbally he might have mentioned that in a round about way that he would be standing there in case I need help."

"When did he come around?" Cooper asked.

"Maybe two or three times. I mean I can't swear to that. Two or three times."

"When he came around he tried to tell you what to do with the business?"

"In some cases, yes."

[138]

"And acted like a partner would who has an interest in the business, didn't he?"

"Well, you might say that," the witness reluctantly conceded.

The testimony on the partnership was held to a minimum. Thus the web was woven with another strand to strengthen the government's position.

Chapter IX

THE FALSE
ENTRY CHARGES

THERE WERE SEVEN criminal counts entered on the docket against Sober, his son, Ira, and Jack Reese. These counts were for false entry in connection with the call reports in two instances, and in one count the false entry charge was placed against Ira and Jack relative to Ira's purchase of a car. In relation to two of these counts, the F.D.I.C. reports, Sober was also charged with criminal action.

Thankful for favors, one, which loomed large at the time, was that a trial motion of acquittal relative to the count of false entry against Jack Reese was granted. At the close of the trial, the jury brought in a verdict of not guilty in favor of Ira in relation to the embezzlement charge. These young men had suffered and will suffer enough as a result of the "justice" metered out at the trial.

To get back to the charges regarding the F.H.A. mortgage loan balance, the entire story will be presented. Once again the reader can judge regarding the verdicts which the defendants were to bare.

There is no need to go into the history of the laws governing the Federal Housing Administration. Basically they were designed to help people with less funds than required for a standard mortgage loan, to get and build houses. The main difference between standard mortgage loans and the F.H.A. mortgages was the amount of down payment required. As a service to customers, the Old Freeport Bank took several of these loans. No one in the bank was experienced in this work. The charges against the bankers in relation to these loans rose out of the fact that these were carried in account columns, the way they were initiated—as F.H.A. loans. There was no other place to put them. Yet the homes were not completed solely under the F.H.A. plan.

The bank granted F.H.A. mortgage loans to the Sheltons, the Nickels, John Spencer, and the Bartells. Under such loans, prior to being made, a commitment had to first be secured from the F.H.A. This prerequisite was taken in all cases and where the plans, papers and the like were approved, the loans were granted. Now, in such cases as these, as the construction progresses, inspections are made by F.H.A. representatives. When the inspection has been approved to that point, the bank makes a payment in a specified amount to the contractor.

In the cases named above there was no final inspection on the part of the F.H.A., because the contractor had gone broke. The matter was turned over to an attorney. At the same time there were no further charges for F.H.A. insurance on the part of the bank.

Let us listen for a moment to the testimony of Mrs. Rita Shelton as she answered the government's attorney, Gavin:

"Well, we had a little trouble with our home, and we had two inspections I would say by supposedly F.H.A. men that came and made their inspection. When so much money was paid they'd make an inspection, but the final inspection was never made, so I inquired at the bank".

Rita Shelton continued, after questioning, ". . . I don't know if

I talked to Mr. Ira Sober or if I asked to talk to him. I asked him who was in charge of the F.H.A. in Pittsburgh, or who the director was, and he said, well he didn't know who the director was, so I wrote a letter to the director of the F.H.A. in Pittsburgh and asked them if they would send the final inspector because we were not satisfied with the job, but when I got the letter back and that went on, that was about March of 1956, when I received the letter they said we did not have an F.H.A. Loan, so they could not send a final inspector, words to that effect."

In the cross examination Rita testified that the house had been completed on schedule or approximately on schedule and that they (she and her husband) had moved in. She also said they had a mortgage then and it was with the Old Freeport Bank.

So the testimony went on and on. The government's attorneys intent on making their case with a multiplicity of charges called John Spencer to the stand. Spencer is a rather quiet person. The surroundings were foreign to him. He was a little hesitant at first, but he answered forthrightly.

After establishing the name and residence of the witness, he was asked, "Did you make a mortgage loan at the Old Freeport Bank, Freeport, Pa.?"

Spencer answered in the affirmative. He also answered that he had made an F.H.A. loan.

Then came the pointed question, "Do you know whether or not you have an F.H.A. insured mortgage?" Gavin questioned.

"I had assumed," Spencer stated, "the last five years that we had an F.H.A. mortgage."

"Do you know, did either the bank or the F.H.A. ever notify you to the effect that you have an F.H.A. insured mortgage?"

Spencer's answer was definite, "No!"

So the "little people", the "little people" whom Sober had tried to help, were called one after another. Their stories were similar.

Charlotte Nickels was questioned about her mortgage. Gavin questioned, "Do you know of your own knowledge whether or not you have an F.H.A. insured loan from the Old Freeport Bank? Did either the bank or the F.H.A. ever advise you that your loan had been approved and insured by the F.H.A.?"

She answered the query, "I have a letter at home. I don't know when it was dated, but it was by Mr. McFarland saying that our loan had been approved and we were to go to our lending institution and apply for it."

So with a faith inherent in the word of her government, Mrs. Nickels applied for and received the loan.

James Bartell also testified. He, too, filled out papers and was granted an F.H.A. loan. Before such a loan could be granted it had to be approved by documented authority from the F.H.A.

No final inspections were made. On one hand the government agency said, "Yes, we approve an F.H.A. Loan." On the other hand, after the bank carried such loans for months, another agency says, "Oh, no, these were not F.H.A. loans. You have falsified the records."

It was apparent that government agencies merely carry out the Biblical injunction, "Let not the right hand know what the left hand doeth."

Forrest D. Stout, who described himself as the Real Property Officer of the Federal Housing Administration, Pittsburgh Office, faced Mr. Gavin on direct examination.

"Did you bring with you certain records?" Gavin proceeded to question his own witness.

"Our records, yes. They are very sparse. Our records are not maintained for a long period of time."

Stout continued his story. He told what happened to the records in the Pittsburgh office, and that they were shipped from the Pittsburgh office elsewhere, and stored in various warehouses

[143]

around the country. He went on to declare before the government's attorney and the court that the firm commitments had been issued. These commitments entitled the mortgagee to go to the lending institution and get the loan. Inspections had been made, but because of no final inspections the commitments had expired. Any records, other than the little cards, were not available.

"Mr. Stout," questioned Gavin, "were you able to locate any records of any insurance ever having been issued by the Federal Housing Administration to Mr. and Mrs. Clarence Nickels?"

"We found evidence," he answered, "that we had an application. The status card such as was shown in the other two cases was not in our office any longer, and the reports from Washington state that they have no files at all on the case."

"There was no, the F.H.A. has no record of any insurance ever being issued by the F.H.A. to Mr. and Mrs. Nickels?"

Again Stout answered, "To the best of my knowledge we have not. There is none in our office."

"In regards to Mr. and Mrs. Charles A. Shelton, were there any records on file with the F.H.A. that would indicate that F.H.A. insurance had ever been issued to Mr. and Mrs. Charles A. Shelton?"

"Only that we had an application." Stout continued, "we have a number for it."

It was briefly after this that Teitelbaum injected his voice into the legal battle: "If it pleases the court, I wish to read into the record a stipulation which has been agreed upon by counsel for the plaintiff and defendant, and I have for the court a copy.

"It is stipulated and agreed by and between counsel for the United States . . ."

Teitelbaum then proceeded to read a legal document concerning the transaction which took place between Ira Sober and Marino A. Piccoli, Jr., regarding the purchase of a car.

Teitelbaum then turned to my counsel, "Is that agreed to, sir?"

"If the court please, it is agreed to," Cooper replied.

Judge Miller said, "Certainly."

"But does this have anything to do with this witness on the stand?" Cooper turned to Teitelbaum as he put the question.

"No, it has not." There was the trace of a smirk on Teitelbaum's face as he replied, "I just read the stipulation out of order. You have cross examination of your witness. I merely put the stipulation in because we agreed to it".

"All right." Cooper had difficulty in controlling his voice from a show of irritation, "I wasn't going to change my mind, but it has nothing to do with this matter."

"Not with this matter," Teitelbaum replied.

"About which Mr. Stout was questioned", Cooper continued.

"No, sir."

"All right."

Cooper then turned his attention to Stout on the witness stand who had, along with the jurors been distracted from the subject at hand, to another phase of the case which had been read into the records by the United States attorney.

As he continued to cross-examine, Cooper asked, "In other words, when the application expires and no renewal was filed all the records including the inspector's reports are lifted and shipped either to Washington or to some place in Washington, the rest of them go?"

"That is right," replied the witness.

"So that on these matters you testified to, there could have been and may have been some inspections and records that you do not have in the office now?" Cooper queried of Stout.

"There isn't any question about there were. There are, there were."

From where the defendants sat watching the jurors one could see that the answers, the pointed answers, that there were and there had been other records not produced in the trial, had little effect on the jurors. Teitelbaum, in his climb for a conviction which might enhance his own name, was doing his work well. He, once again, injected into the trial remarks which threw the train of thought in another direction.

Cooper blithely questioned the action but never the motives. Of course this was all being done in the interests of justice.

To advance Sober's story a little further, regarding the F.H.A. loans and his part in them, for which a charge of false entry was entered, the loans had been taken in good faith. In many instances these loans enabled people to buy or build houses, who otherwise could not have done so. The F.H.A. mortgage permitted them to build with a smaller down payment than a conventional mortgage loan.

It was the duty of the contractor, as the buildings reached certain stages, to notify the F.H.A. who in turn would send inspectors to see that the work was being done according to the requirements of the contract.

In the case of the F.H.A. loans mentioned in the case, the final inspections had never been made because the contractor shortly after the completion of his work, had gone broke. He neither notified the F.H.A. or the bank of the status of the work or of the inspections.

Since these loans had originated as F.H.A. mortgages, they couldn't very well or logically be placed in the column which listed the conventional mortgages. Had this been done the indicted would indeed have been guilty of falsifying the records. So, they continued to carry them in the records as F.H.A. mortgages. Since they were so carried in the records, having no other place in which to put them, they were held guilty of false entry. The charge being that the bank showed greater assets than it should have because these loans weren't insured!

As the long night turns to dawn, when the mind once again begins to function, the ever rising questions begin to plague. Were there not other banks which had similar F.H.A. mortgages, wherein the contractor had not completed the work or where no final inspection had been made? Why was it so difficult for the government's witness Stout, to get all of the records pertaining to the case? Couldn't he, or shouldn't he have gotten them in this case?

So the little man, plagued today and in the days to come, by increasingly heavy paper work in all fields of endeavor, may find that these papers which he will turn over to some bureau in the government will do him little good, should he become involved with another branch of the government — they will be lost in the maze of paper store houses now growing by leaps and bounds throughout the nation.

Yes truly, in government circles, "the right hand knoweth not what the left hand doeth."

Chapter X

EMBEZZLEMENT?

Before getting down to the charges of embezzlement, Teitelbaum had other trump cards to play. Called to the stand was Frank P. Paz, a witness on behalf of the United States. Paz, who had served on the bank's board and had served as legal advisor in some of the transactions. After being questioned concerning some of these matters in re-direct examination Teitelbaum asked, "Up until the time you sat on this witness chair, did I ever question you about this in detail?"

"No, never went over it," Paz answered.

"And we ask you certain questions you hadn't put in the letter?"

Cooper objected.

Teitelbaum reworded the question and for the second time Cooper objected.

"Your Honor," Teitelbaum pleaded, "the point of the question is that while Mr. Paz was writing his own letter as to those facts which appeared to him to be important, there are certain facts which appear to me to be important, which I ask him about at trial, which he had merely not thought of when he was writing that statement. That is what I am trying to bring out. If that is objectionable, I don't know."

The wrangling over the question proceeded for a short time. However, the big question to at least one of the defendants involved was the fact that Paz had written a letter to Teitelbaum. Jack Reese wondered why Paz had advised him not to write a similar letter in his own behalf.

Since the two young attorneys were involved as attorneys for the Old Freeport Bank, there was one point in the trial when the question of their tacit approval and participation in the affairs of the bank did not align them with the defendants. Teitelbaum immediately called for a side-bar. The position of the young attorneys was discussed freely, although the discussion was not recorded. All of the defendants were able to hear the counsels protect their colleagues with the plea that they were young men and through lack of knowledge were participants in affairs which, if they were charged, would likely ruin them in their chosen professions. Judge Miller concurred in this and the young attorneys were never charged.

Sober's head dropped in his hands. He didn't want to see these young men hurt, but he couldn't help wondering what was happening to his son and Jack Reese. By the same token they were young men with futures before them, yet they were being held up before all with criminal charges against them.

It was time for another move. Now to appear on the stand was Alonzo Canaday, senior examiner for the Federal Deposit Insurance Corporation. In direct examination Gavin called Canaday to the stand, and after being sworn, he began to tell his story of how he had been assigned to the Old Freeport Bank case. His testimony in this vein continued for a time.

A little later the Court intervened, "Members of the jury, you have heard Mr. Canaday speak. We all appreciate he is laboring under considerable difficulty, a very severe cold which has affected his throat, and we are anxious that you all thoroughly understand everything that Mr. Canaday says . . . so after I conferred with Mr. Gavin representing the government and Judge Cooper representing the defendants, and having talked with Mr. Canaday, I deem it advisable to adjourn court for the rest of the day so that Mr. Canaday may consult a doctor and perhaps rest up for the rest of the day, probably will be better off tomorrow if he does that."

Judge Miller then urged counsel to confer in respect to the various exhibits, to agree on the number of the exhibits in order to save time.

The trial was then adjourned until Tuesday morning, April 27, 1959, at 10 o'clock A. M.

But Canaday's illness prevented his appearance for a week. When the trial resumed he looked drawn and weary. Everyone in the court was solicitous. Here was a witness appearing for the government who apparently had been suffering from an illness. As he testified under the gentle questioning of Gavin, he constantly reached for a glass of water and pitcher which had been thoughtfully provided.

Canaday reviewed the entire case and charges. He dwelt for a time on the Gallagher, Heyman, Burkett and Kelosky loans. Again the jury was treated to a repetitious review of the acts which had brought the defendants before the bar of justice.

As Canaday left the stand for the noon recess, France, a customer of the Old Freeport Bank, grabbed Sober by the arm. "That guy ain't been sick, like they're saying. I've seen him at the Pittsburgher hotel every evening. And you know where I spend my time." In disgust the man ranted to Sober about the government's principal witness.

Later on Gavin, for the government, said to Canaday, "Mr. Canaday, I refer you now to Government Exhibit 133, which is a check issued by the Old Freeport Bank dated September 14th, 1957, payable to Marino A. Piccoli, Jr., in the amount of $725.02.

"Did your examination include the circumstances surrounding the issuance of this check?"

(It was on the basis of this check that the charge of embezzlement had been placed on Ira Sober.)

"It did," answered Canaday, "This cashier's check for $725 made payable to Marino A. Piccoli, Jr., the cashier's check was signed by Jack C. Reese as cashier. The cashier's check is endorsed in green ink there, Marino A. Piccoli, Jr."

"My examination of the books and records of the Old Freeport Bank, I found that this cashier's check was purchased or offset by an item being placed in the cash items of the bank of The Old Freeport Bank. It is the practice and habit of the bank to prepare a list each day of cash items, in other words, it properly should be items in cash rather than cash items, but they now use cash items. These cash item sheets here from the issuance, on or about the issuance date of the cashier's check to Piccoli, there is an amount that appears of $2,725 . . ."

Canaday went on to explain, using for the most part banking terms that on or about November 12 of 1957, the cash item offsetting the cashier's check, was proceeds from a loan issued to Ira L. Sober. The note was for $1,876.11 and from this amount $725 was used to pay off the cash item, which had been the cause of so much trouble.

Young Sober had told his story many times. He had repeated it to bank examiners long before he was ever charged with embezzlement. If there had been a case of wrong in the transaction it was due to laxity, and not to any attempt to embezzle. Again from the stand, Ira poured forth his story, ". . . but actually Mr. Piccoli wanted $725 over and above what he owed, so he knew the description of the car, the approximate total figure that he was carrying on the lease. Well, that was on a Friday evening. After I left I met Mr. Piccoli, told him I would think it over overnight, that I'd probably go through with the deal, to meet me on a Saturday. Again we were unable to transact any business —Saturday morning is usually a pretty busy time, it was sometime after our noon meeting, Mr. Reese was there, I briefly explained to him what the transaction would involve. I had a lease signed by Mr. John J. Jack as Jack's Auto Sales, the car was described on the lease, I told him the $725 was what was necessary to satisfy Mr. Piccoli; so while Mr. Reese made out a check for the $725 payable to Mr. Piccoli he in turn signed the lease, or signed the title I mean on the back, which was already encumbered to The Old Freeport Bank on his own lease which had come from another dealer. He was satisfied. . . .

"Mr. Reese offset the cashier's check as a cash item which balanced; supporting the cash item was a lease signed by John J. Jack, then I in turn either that afternoon or Monday contacted the insurance agent who had the insurance on my present automobile, give him the numbers, described the car, told him to write the two of them together, and give me the figure. I also told Reese as soon as I had the figures we would complete the lease."

Schwartz continued to question, "What figures do you have reference to now, Mr. Sober, please?"

"I wanted to consolidate the price of the automobile, the premium on the insurance, and as I stated previously there was absolutely very little rubber on the tires, they had to be ordered, and at least minor repairs to the car. . . ."

"Wait now," urged Schwartz, "Let's see if I understand you. Do I understand you wanted to have all of these items included in the loan at the bank?"

"That's right," young Sober exclaimed, "so I had no further reference as to what the complete transaction was involved."

"How long did it take after that day before all of the items that you wanted to include of that loan were completed?"

[152]

"Well, I don't mind," Sober answered, "but sometime later Reese reminded me of it and I stated that the insurance agent for one had not given me a figure to give him. Also, I don't know what the price of the tires were but I felt that he had the lease supporting the cash item. Then along about that time the examiners came . . ."

"Which examiners?"

"Well the State and the F.D.I.C. came together."

"All right."

"I don't mind which two of them, but they were itemizing and listing the various items in the cash items, which would be any number—sight draft, could be government bonds, return item checks, exchange checks; at any rate, they ask me about this cash item."

"Which cash item do you have reference to?"

"The cash item of $725 regarding the automobile lease which we had intended to process and complete."

"How soon after the date of issuance of this check?"

"The original lease was signed on or about, or dated as of September 14. The reason, as I said, when he reminded me of it, I contacted the agent, I said "I definitely must have those figures today." I got those figures up to November 12; I got those figures. I told Reese to process them. I did not have the figures on the tires yet. I said, 'I will pay for those, I will pay for the insurance, I am reducing whatever the total is.' In other words I had possibly six, $700 in the transaction; so he processed the lease. There was nothing more said at the time so I presumed that the examiners were satisfied. There was no question raised then until the examiners came in which their initial date was July 14. When they actually decided to change their mind on it I don't know, but after my removal from the bank—"

So the charge of embezzlement was to cling to young Sober until the end of the trial. Even the verdict of not guilty on this charge was lost in the many findings of guilty against the others. While the newspapers blaringly headlined the charge, the findings of the jury were in small body type. There are those, to this day, who never knew that Ira Sober was found innocent of this charge.

Chapter XI

DEFENSE – WHAT DEFENSE?

W<small>ORDS SPOKEN</small> remain in the minds of those who hear them — words written remain forever inscribed on paper or parchment and are seen again a thousand times by those who read them.

Alonzo Canaday, an examiner for the F.D.I.C. did a lot of talking. Somehow, someway his words told two stories. The records show this.

Canaday during the trial began to tell of the nature of his work. He declared under oath that he was on special assignment — "Naturally the special assignment work, when I'm assigned I know that I should do special work, and if there are any irregularities at all I'm supposed to find them. I imagine there are cases where they exist where I don't find them. In this case in The Old Freeport Bank, I did find irregularities."

"How did you know where to get started, what happened when you were there, what did you do?" Sober's attorney questioned.

Canaday continued his dissertation on how he had met with the FDIC examiners and the state bank examiners, and that they didn't know exactly what the nature of their work would be, whether in this phase or that phase of the bank's departments. He continued by telling that he met with Sober and that they had talked for some forty-five minutes. He told how Sober had revealed some of the history of the bank, and of how he had talked generally about various items and then he said, "Here's a fast —"

Attorney Cooper halted his recital, "Wait a minute, please."

Of course the district attorney could not keep himself out of the repartee, and said, "As I understand, he wants to know why he did what he did. He is telling him (Cooper)."

The Court upheld Attorney Cooper's point that what a man says to himself is not testimony.

Then Canaday continued his testimony that he went to work on the loan accounts. He volunteered the information that the bank had some big real estate mortgage loans. He stated that he was checking out the disbursements of proceeds on the mortgage loan accounts and that the first one he worked on was the Gallagher account. It had been closed out but the sheet was, according to Canaday, still in the ledger book.

Then sure of himself, he continued, "I saw the disbursements on the back side listing one of the director's names, and I tried to find out, I mean determine why a director of the bank, The Old Freeport Bank, would get any money out of the loan proceeds, somebody with a different name."

Attorney Cooper placed himself before the witness. He removed his glasses and tapped them in the palm of his hand. "I want you to look at the jury when you answer this question, Mr. Canaday." The statement was followed by the question, "Will you tell this court and jury how you happened to get to the account of Leo Gallagher the first thing when you got to the bank?"

The general buzz in the court room became silent. The spectators were intent upon the witness. It was even noticed that some of the jurors, who had at times seemingly paid little attention to proceedings, were focusing their attention on Mr. Canaday. Canaday cleared his throat, "I didn't get to the account the first thing, I mean, the first day when I got to the bank. It was a few days later after the examination was started."

Attorney Cooper began driving his points home in question after question, "Why did you just now, when I asked you a question how you got started and you said, 'I got started on the Leo Gallagher account.' How did you happen to get to that Mr. Canaday?"

"I opened up the ledger book," Canaday cleared his throat "information sheet book, and I just flipped the sheets over, and I come to this Leo Gallagher where it had the disbursements of the proceeds. I saw the name "Heineman" there opposite $2,000. I quite naturally stopped and traced the proceeds of that loan."

"Yes," said Attorney Cooper, and he became plaintive in his request for more information, "Where is that book with the Gallagher account, that mortgage? Do we have it here? Will you just show the court and jury how you happened to hit on the Gallagher account first?"

"The Gallagher account wouldn't be in the discount register."

"Was it the same kind of book as this?" Attorney Cooper continued questioning.

"No," answered Canaday, "it was a loose-leaf book about this size." He indicated the size by holding his thumb and fingers apart.

"What do you call that book?"

"Mortgage loan ledger. I think it is a mortgage loan information sheet."

"You were just leafing through the book?"

"I have done that many times in banks, just leafed through the ledger."

"Then by accident," continued Attorney Cooper, "you stopped at Gallagher, is that right?"

Canaday drew a deep breath, "Well, it wasn't by accident. When I saw the disbursement on the back I naturally stopped. It is very unusual that a director of the bank gets proceeds, part of the proceeds out of somebody else's loan."

"On that day did you know how many directors of the bank there were?"

"Yes, I knew at that time."

"How many?"

"I think at that time 24 directors."

"Was Dr. Heineman one of those directors?"

"He was one of the directors when we started the examination."

Cooper continued to lead Canaday on. "On that sheet," he asked, "did it show that Heineman who was paid that amount of money, was then listed as a director?"

Canaday answered that there was no designation of "Director" listed by his name.

In subsequent questioning, Attorney Cooper asked Canaday if he knew the names of all the directors at that time and if he memorized these names. Canaday in his reply did not state that he had memorized all of the names, but did say that he had looked over the list bearing the directors names.

The questioning went on and on and on. Attorney Cooper had Canaday show the jury how he had leafed through the ledger and how he had come upon this particular sheet.

Building up to the climax, Attorney Cooper put the question, "Now you worked at the bank for a number of months before you concluded your examination, didn't you?"

"I did," answered Canaday, "I worked in the bank from July 14, 1958 until December 18. I believe it was in 1958. I wasn't there every day, but I mean that was the, my work spread over that period of time."

"Could you tell this court and jury," pleaded Attorney Cooper, "Who the board of directors were in 1958 for the Old Freeport Bank?"

"No. I couldn't right now, because that happened several months ago, when I worked out there. I have been on other jobs and I don't remember. I can't remember, retain in my mind a list of directors in every bank I examine."

"Would you tell this court and jury that on that day that you discovered the Gallagher account, that you knew the names of the 24 directors of the Old Freeport Bank?"

"Yes, I knew the names of the directors and also the officers of the bank," Canaday replied.

The questioning continued. Canaday, the examiner at large for the Federal Deposit Insurance Corporation, could when he had to, remember the names of the directors, but with the trial coming up he couldn't name the directors then. However, a convenient memory is one of the principal assets of certain witnesses.

Cooper tried another track. "Weren't you," he asked, "told by your superiors exactly what to look for when you came here?"

"I got it," Canaday answered, "not from Mr. Hirning but from Mr. DeHority in Washington, I got something, maybe there was some loan in the name of one of the directors that the bank might be carrying the security as other real estate. The conversation was rather garbled. I mean the connection was bad and that was the only inkling that I got —"

What caused Canaday to pause at that moment, no one could say. Cooper said, "Pardon. Go ahead."

"That was the only inkling what type of job that I might be going on. You see, some of those jobs, there is a suspicion of a shortage in the deposit account, you concentrate on that. In other cases there may be some fast work around the loan account, and if, that is, if you got your information leads, or anything like that, your bosses may see surface indications, and they will say "Here is a surface indication that everything is not on the up and up in this bank, the particular loans are in the bond account or in the deposit ledger."

Cooper was solicitous. "I want to know when you stop. I am not going to interrupt you; did you stop?"

Canaday affirmed that he was through.

"Are you now, Mr. Canaday, changing your story about instructions you got when you came to examine The Old Freeport Bank on July 14, 1958?" Cooper asked.

"No," Canaday said somewhat testily, "I am not changing my statement. Earlier I told you that there was a bad telephone connection when I talked to Washington. Actually it was somewhat garbled. Out of that conversation, that attempted conversations — "

"Go ahead," ordered Cooper.

"Mr. DeHority mentioned something. I thought he mentioned about the loan account, maybe one of the directors, maybe some kind of real estate being carried by the bank. It wasn't clear at all. I couldn't after I hung up I tried to figure out what DeHority was talking about. I couldn't."

So the government's principal witness, the examiner at large for the F.D.I.C., testified under oath that he wasn't sure what he had come to the Old Freeport Bank to look for, that the telephone conversation was garbled; he tried to figure out what a Mr. DeHority was talking about; he couldn't — yet he went right to the ledger containing the Gallagher account; he found the Burkett account — and these accounts had been closed out.

Mr. Alonzo Canaday was a smart man, a very smart man to find something for which he didn't know he was looking!

Our attorney wasn't through with him. After numerous questions in which he brought out that Canaday had met Mr. Irvine of the First National Bank of Tarentum (also a member of the Federal Reserve Board from January 1, 1957 to December 31, 1959), he returned again to the subject of the acquaintance between Canaday and Irvine.

"Go back to Mr. Irvine, the president of the First National Bank of Tarentum. I understand you to say you met him just once?" queried Cooper.

"As I recall I met Mr. Irvine just one time."

Again came the question, "Was it in his own, or The Old Freeport Bank?"

"It was never in any bank." The courtroom spectators became unusually still. Canaday continued, "I never set foot in the First National Bank in Tarentum, nor any other bank in Tarentum, nor in the First National Bank in Freeport. I never entered the premises of any of those banks I just mentioned."

"Where did you meet with Frank Irvine?" pleaded Cooper.

"It was one, I believe one Saturday or Sunday afternoon I met with him. He has a country cottage over on the river, and I believe it was in the afternoon. I believe it was on Sunday, and that was several days, or several weeks after the examination was started."

Cooper continued to lead the government's witness on. "Well, tell us about that meeting; tell us what took place and where it was."

"I was seeking investigative leads, if any of the customers of the Old Freeport Bank were complaining that they had been treated unfairly by the bank." Canaday paused for a moment.

"And you went to a competitor to find out about leads of the Old Freeport Bank?" Cooper asked.

"I get my leads from various and sundry places. I don't restrict them to people that are not competitors of that particular bank under examination. All investigative leads are good for is to help you determine if there is anything — I mean, put you on the avenue to verify and check their records to see if there are any irregularities that took place," Canaday answered as he began to show signs of weariness.

"How did you and Mr. Irvine get together?" Cooper plodded on with the questioning.

"Through Attorney Alexander Lindsay."

"And who made the arrangements for that meeting?"

"Well, actually, I presume it was Mr. Lindsay."

"Then you went to Mr. Irvine's home for a social affair was it, a dinner or a cocktail party, or what was it, Mr. Canaday?"

"No, we had no cocktails. We were out there in the middle of the afternoon and —"

Cooper broke into the statement, "Who is 'we'?"

"John Brown, Examiner John Brown of the F.D.I.C."

"And yourself?"

"And myself," Canaday replied quickly.

But Cooper was not to be stopped from this track, "Who else?"

Canaday cleared his throat, "And there was Mr. Irvine and Mr. Lindsay was present and also Sam Kauffman."

"Who was Sam Kauffman?"

"He is the executive officer of the First National Bank in Freeport, Pennsylvania." (This bank is directly across the street from the Old Freeport Bank.)

"He was there for the purpose of furnishing you leads for your examination of the Old Freeport Bank?"

Canaday again cleared his throat, "I asked him, of course I asked him in front of all three of these men, Mr. Lindsay and Mr. Irvine, and Mr. Kauffman, if they knew anything that we should know, like any irregular transaction, or if any customers had complained that, they heard them complain or complained to them. I was after investigative leads."

[162]

What was the truth. Mr. Canaday swore that he met Irvine only once; he swore that it was several days or weeks after the examination started (he wasn't sure whether it was several days or weeks), he admitted going to competitors for information—yet his own partner John Brown of the F.D.I.C. later swore that they had met with Irvine two or three times. Still later in a sworn statement the unheard witness, William Rhodes says that Mr. Irvine brought Canaday to his office of the Allegheny Valley Steel Company early in July. Canaday couldn't remember whether he met Irvine a few days or a few weeks after the examination started—but Canaday swore that he knew the 24 members of the board of directors of the Old Freeport Bank by name when he went over papers pertaining to the Gallagher loan.

In his closing argument before the jury, Teitelbaum cried: "Oh, what a tangled web we weave when first we practice to deceive."

A number of persons observing the trial agreed with the illustrious prosecutor. The question is, "Who wove the web?"

*　*　*　*　*

In spite of the fact that the principal government witness had been trapped in the cross-examination; that he could remember certain things but was not clear on other things, the daily papers in the area had little to say regarding this phase of the trial. Sober knew a reporter on the Post-Gazette and contacted him one day when he felt that the defense was scoring well. Nothing had been said in the columns of the paper. Sober's plea was simple, "I'm not asking you to do anything wrong, just give us a fair break."

The reporter maintained that many of the stories which he had written had been edited to the point where he didn't even recognize them as his when they were published. He then added that if he didn't report the news releases as issued from the government attorney's office, this news source would be closed to him.

The defendants were not satisfied. Sober, accompanied by his son, Ira, and Jack Reese, went to the Pittsburgh Press. Sober proposed to representatives of the Pittsburgh Press that he purchase an ad. Of course, the officials wanted to know what was to be placed in the ad, and Sober readily told them that he wanted an ad "to show our side of the case." This was something new. Here was a man willing to buy space to tell his side of a news story? There was a hurried conference of the "powers-that-be." The answer was not long in forthcoming — the Pittsburgh Press would accept no such ad.

This was the same paper which only two years previously had lauded the bank for its progressiveness and had featured it in a story entitled "Money for Sale."

* * * * *

The trial continued day after weary day. The questioning was long and for the most part repetitious. Sober was called to the stand. Again the part he played in the Gallagher, Burkett, Kelosky and Heyman loans was rehashed. At one point in the questioning, when Sober was being questioned concerning the Burkett loan, Teitelbaum asked, "Did you ask what the $800 for Dr. Heineman was for?"

"No", Sober replied, "when you are writing down there and they are naming something off, you just write down what is said."

"When they said—"

Sober interrupted, "I knew it wasn't for a load of coal because the doctor didn't sell coal."

"What does he sell?" came the next question.

"Services, medicine."

"Is that what he was getting the $800 for?"

Sober answered, "I don't know."

Such questioning was to continue on and on, over and over, with Teitelbaum trying to elicit an answer which would trap the principal defendant.

The charge of false entry in one count or rather on three counts was leveled against Sober because he had signed an F.D.I.C. call report, which had been prepared by the cashier, Jack Reese. Young Sober was involved in this count, too.

A call or a statement of the bank's resources and liabilities is issued twice a year. Sometimes a call will be ordered at odd times; that is other than at the close of business June 30th or at the close of business December 31st. This charge was made on the basis of the examiners' reports which stated that the Old Freeport Bank was showing assets over and above what was actually in the bank. In back of this finding was the fact that the commitment on the F.H.A. loans had expired and they were still being carried under the F.H.A. column. There was no other place to put them. Had they been removed from the F.H.A. and placed in the conventional mortgage column, then the bankers would indeed have been guilty of falsifying the records.

The government attorney, Teitelbaum, was successful in making a strong issue of this count. During the direct examination concerning these reports, the feeling ran high and the debate was long and bitter over the term "correct-attest."

Cooper, in his effort to prove that "correct-attest" was just a signature verifying the report as made by the cashier, brought out these points:

"Mr. Sober, in the 14th and 15th counts of the indictment against you, your son, Ira L. Sober, and Jack Reese were charged with making false entry into the records of the bank in connection with certain F.H.A. mortgages. I ask you to please look at Government Exhibits 222 and 223, tell us if you know what they are?"

Sober's quick reply was, "A call report."

"Tell us what a call report is."

"Well, it's a report to the F.D.I.C., or to the State Banking Department. We are a state bank, so there'd be two."

This line of questioning went on to bring out the various figures which a report contains and what they mean. As the attorney proceeded down the columns, he asked, "Now then, under this column of assets, Mr. Sober, will you please tell us what it does contain?"

Reading from the report, which he held in his hands, Sober answered, "Well the cash in the bank and in the correspondent banks of that day, government obligations, obligations of states, bonds, bank premises, furniture and fixtures and liabilities."

"Now then," questioned Cooper, "after you show the total assets as of that date, what is the next item which is summarized on the sheet?"

"Liabilities," was the quick reply.

The attorney led Sober through a listing of the liabilities which included the demand deposits (checking accounts), time deposits (savings accounts) and as Sober was about to continue Cooper broke into the testimony . . .

"Pardon me for breaking in. In under this 'Time Deposits' would you include certificates of deposit if you know?"

"I am going to tell you," Sober answered, "that this is the first time I ever read one of those reports."

"Well . . ."

"I might as well be truthful about it."

At this point Teitelbaum broke in, "I wonder if there is any point to this thing, your Honor. This is the first time he ever read one."

The questioning continued with the attorney going into some detail as to what the various figures represented. Finally Mr. Cooper came to the point of asking who prepared the reports.

"Who signed this report, Exhibit 222?"

"Jack Reese," Sober answered, because Jack's name appeared on the line which stated: "Signature of officer authorized to sign report."

"All right. Now then, right to the left of his name appears what; what does it say there?"

"Correct-Attest."

"And then whose names appear there?"

"C. L. Sober," came the reply.

"Who else?" continued Cooper.

"John B. McCue, another director."

And the next question came as the attorney read the report which Sober held, "That is Shearer?"

"Hugh Shearer."

Handed a similar report, the same line of questions was presented. Signing in the spaces for "Correct-Attest" were, besides the elder Sober, Hugh Shearer and Leno Fratta, both directors of the Old Freeport Bank at the time of the call reports.

After questioning the capacity in which Jack Reese acted to sign these reports, Cooper continued to question, "And I noticed that you signed both of these. Have you ever signed any other reports of this kind besides these?"

There was a little hesitation. Sober had begun to realize that some questions even so simple, and answers given in the utmost sincerity could come back to haunt and plague you. How often had he signed such reports? Three times, five times, only these two, were Sober's signature on the exhibits? Finally, drawing a deep breath, he said, "Not very often. I think in those two cases they were late in getting them up, there was no other directors around and I signed them."

"Did you check the records of the bank for each one of these items to see that —"

"Absolutely not," was his quick reply.

"Did you go through all the books to see whether or not what is reported here as assets was a correct statement from the books?"

"No," he stated, "I'm no bookkeeper, wouldn't have known how to find it."

The questioning in this vein continued as the attorney brought out that Mr. Sober did not check the records, nor had the signatures of the other directors been made at the same time. It was also brought out that approximately four to five days was the time allowed to prepare a report from the time it was received until it had to be returned to the proper department.

With this line of questioning being completed, court was adjourned until ten o'clock on Tuesday, May 13, 1959.

Sober moved to the aisle of the courtroom. He had planned to go into the corridor to relax, when someone grabbed his arm. It was the late Mr. Martin Jamison, former president of the First National Bank now the Apollo Trust Co., of Apollo. He had heard a portion of the testimony regarding the call reports, while waiting to have a conference with Judge Miller with whom he served on the board of Westminster College.

"My God, Charlie, if they hang that charge on you every banker in the country is guilty. I've had my directors sign those reports for the last forty-five years, and not one of them could actually verify what was in the reports." With these words the elderly banker moved toward the judge's chambers, muttering to himself.

The ordeal was not over. After jumping from one phase of the case to another, Mr. Teitelbaum brought out a paper and had it identified. It was one of our exhibits. While in charge of the bank Sober had a seven year comparative statement issued and printed. The exhibit was one of those statements.

Then the question came, "Mr. Sober, do you of your own knowledge know whether any figure on this exhibit is correct?"

"I don't understand your question," he replied, because he actually didn't know what the question was at the time.

"Well, you remember yesterday," Teitelbaum continued,

"When you were looking at call reports you said you never saw one before?"

"I never said that".

"You never read one before. I don't remember what you said." the government's attorney continued to try to twist the answer of the previous day, "what I want to know is this—"

Sober interrupted, "Pardon. Let's get that straightened out right now."

"You answer my questions," roared Teitlebaum, "then Mr. Cooper will bring it out."

At this point Sober's attorney, Mr. Cooper, injected his soft voice into the verbal fray, "You answer the questions Mr. Teitelbaum asks."

Teitelbaum strode forward, carrying the exhibit in his hand, he thrust it within a few inches of Sober's face, "Did you," and he paused for dramatic effect, "personally verify any figure on this booklet?"

"To the books you are talking about?" Sober asked.

"Yes."

"No," was the quick rejoinder.

Then came another question which was typical of many that were asked during the trial. They are known as "leading questions". One could easily see how they would create an impression on the jury, composed of people who were not acquainted with banking regulations.

"You don't know," Mr. Teitelbaum stated as he questioned, "whether any figure on here is correct or isn't correct, do you, to your own personal knowledge?"

His reply was, "As a bookkeeper, no."

"Somebody else prepared this, that is all you know about it, is that right?"

"That is right."

[169]

"Is this, Mr. Sober, a paper that was prepared from the records of the Old Freeport Bank?"

"Yes."

Thus the questioning went on. He asked how Sober knew it was from the records. Then he would inject such a question as to put Sober in such light as not knowing very much when asked, "You were the officer in chief, weren't you?"

Perhaps the process of reasoning is not sound, but the government's attorney wanted to object to the "seven-year" comparative statement, showing the growth of the bank, yet on the other hand one of the government's exhibits which was being used as a document to back up the charge of "false entry on F.D.I.C. call reports" was being played to the very hilt to substantiate the charges against Sober, his son and Jack Reese.

After undergoing the rigors of a trial in federal criminal court, Sober would respectfully suggest that either the rules for procedure be increased or that the rules be abbroged to the minimum. To illustrate some of the things that work to harm a defendant, especially in a case such as the one experienced, Teitelbaum continued going after the principal defendant with his cross-examination. He moved nearer to Sober. He had a pen or pencil between thumb and index finger, and as he asked the question, he pointed the pencil at him. "When was the last discussion you had with Mr. Heyman?"

"I think a couple of months ago," was Sober's reply.

"Where?" Teitelbaum was questioning in a low voice. The defendant could now tell by this time that the government attorney was ready to try to trap him.

"In his home." The answer was easy. This was when Sober took Cooper's investigator to Heymans. He remained in the car until invited into the house.

"Is that the last discussion you had?" the attorney's voice was a pitch higher.

"I think we talked, he came into Webster Hall one evening when he was going to school, with a piece of paper that told me I had backed into some woman's car and broke a headlight."

Teitelbaum then went into his dramatics, "Mr. Sober, didn't you invite Mr. Heyman about four weeks before this trial out to Webster Hall, have him as your guest for a steak dinner and discuss with him the possibility of making him whole on this business by giving him another greenhouse?"

Sober's answer was "No."

In spite of the fact that his counsel immediately jumped to his feet, swung his face before the bench and said, "I object to that question, ask for a side bar conference," Sober realized then that this was another of the profession's tricks. By being truthful, he admitted that he had talked to Heyman at his hotel. After what Heyman had done, Sober was in no mood to make any "deals" or even try to. Burned by fire once, he was loathe to put his hand to the stove again. Why should he try to help a person out, who in a deposition had "colored" his testimony, as he later stated? Would he not try the same thing again?

To go back to this story, the "side bar" was granted. Sometimes these conferences were recorded and sometimes they were not. In this particular instance, this is what went on: Cooper stated, "If your Honor please, I object to that question. I ask for the withdrawal of a juror. It's a prejudicial question. They had Mr. Heyman on the stand here. If anything like this about which this question was asked was known to these counsel they had a duty to bring it out direct."

Teitelbaum countered with "It was not known at that time."

"Oh, it wasn't?"

"No, we did not know it at the time," reiterated Teitelbaum.

Cooper continued his theme, "I believe it is prejudicial."

"We learned it later," Teitelbaum pleaded.

"It is just like asking a man whether he was arrested for a crime he never committed; the only thing a man can do is say yes or no. I believe this is the time to ask for withdrawal of a juror for a prejudicial statement that was brought in this case in order to prejudice the minds of the jurors against the defendant," Cooper reasoned.

Teitelbaum became a little edgy, "It is not for that purpose. It is for the purpose as shown, for the purpose of showing intent, that he calls a witness who he knows is being relied on by the government; he invites him for a steak dinner at Webster Hall, he makes him a certain offer that he is going to get him, he knows where there is a new greenhouse, he can set it up for him, he can make him whole in the whole business. It goes to show intent, it goes to attack his credibility. I think it is a proper question."

Schwartz, Cooper's assistant, entered the legal word battle, "If that were proper, your Honor, that could be used by Mr. Heyman when the time came. This is the most prejudicial remark that has been made in the case."

Judge Miller leaned over the bench, "Of course if it happened it is very serious."

"If it did it might very well be," concurred Schwartz.

"If it happened, they had Mr. Heyman in court for weeks. He knew all about it," Cooper added.

Teitelbaum defended his remarks, "Mr. Heyman first told us about it yesterday when we called him and said, 'Were you arrested for manslaughter?' and if the deal wasn't what this man said on the stand. He volunteered that thing; we never heard it, we called Mr. Heyman and asked him, 'Were you ever tried for manslaughter?' He said 'No'. At that time for the first time yesterday he told us that there had been an effort by Mr. Sober, much stronger than this question I asked, to tamper with his evidence. Now, the same thing happened with Kelosky, and with Kelosky we can prove that, we didn't bring it out. Now, I think it's very serious."

Schwartz said somewhat testily, "That's the problem, Judge. 'We can do this, we didn't do it, now we are going to do it.'"

This bantering continued and Schwartz finally injected these words into the argument, "If we want to talk about tampering ..."

He was interrupted when Teitelbaum said, "Go ahead."

"That proposition can come up in the future of our case too. We will talk about the manner of interrogation by F.B.I. agents. Stuff like that is not a part of the case."

Judge Miller injected himself into the argument, "It has not been denied."

The Bench then had the court reporter read the transcript of the questions and answers which preceded the side bar.

Judge Miller then ruled that the motion for the withdrawal of a juror "be denied."

Still Teitelbaum was not content. He turned to Sober on the stand and asked, " You say, sir, no such conversation took place?"

"The question has been answered, Mr. Teitelbaum. It has been answered 'No'," the court declared.

Still Teitelbaum persisted and again the court stated, "You are precluded from going into it any further."

But the government's attorney was not to be stopped, "I offer in the presence of the court on the record to prove that we have witnesses who will testify, who could testify that there was such a conference and that this did take place. Do you object to my doing it?"

Cooper objected to any further questions along this line.

Teitelbaum turned to the Court, "Are you sustaining the objection?"

The ponderous words from the Bench were directed toward

the government's attorney, "He is objecting to any further questions. You offered to bring in other witnesses to prove it. You are on cross examination now. If you intend to do that, you bring your witnesses in and offer them and then he can make his objection and I will make a ruling."

"The only reason I say this I think the rule . . ."

Judge Miller interrupted, "I am not going to rule in advance as to what I should do if something happens."

The die was cast. Into the ears of the jurors, through no statement of Sober, but on the part of the government's attorney, they had heard of possible collusion between Sober and one of the government's witnesses. Yet at the side bar, the jurors were precluded from the legal arguments which followed.

Even after the Court had admonished him not to go into the matter any further, he persisted in returning to the question which brought the motion for the dismissal of a juror. He was admonished a second and then a third time — that is in the record.

Why then did not the Court accede to the request of Sober's counsel? Was it because it would not do for a government attorney to be guilty of bringing about a mistrial?

There are some very sincere people who will back you and be willing to tell their stories in court. On the other hand, whether they will be permitted to tell their stories or not, will depend on the court, the attorneys and many other factors.

There had been hopes that through the testimony of Allison Tarr of Butler County, the claim of Gallagher could be refuted that the Old Freeport Bank was the first place he attempted to get a loan.

Prior to coming to the bank, he had tried at several banks and even from individuals. Among these was Allison Tarr, who had frequently sold eggs and other farm produce at the Sunlight Inn

[174]

which was operated by Gallagher. Tarr maintained that Gallagher was so eager to get the money that he offered a premium for it.

When Tarr was called on the defendants behalf, Teitelbaum immediately asked, "Can I have an offer please?"

Cooper replied, "An open offer or a side bar offer?"

"I don't care," said Teitelbaum magnanimously, "I just want an offer. You can make it open if you want to."

Cooper proceeded with his statement, "I propose to prove by this witness that he is one of the gentlemen to whom Mr. Gallagher went to try to borrow money, and what the nature of the conversation was between him and Mr. Gallagher and that — "

Teitelbaum rushed toward the Bench, "Wait, I think we'd better go to the side bar, if that is what it is."

So the attorney for the government who a moment or so prior to this said that he didn't care whether it was an open or side offer, now changed his mind.

At the side bar, Cooper stated, "We are going to prove or proved, that this man Gallagher had gone around to a number of people trying to borrow money, which shows the need that he had for the money, the necessity that he had, what he wanted it for, and as a matter of fact this man will testify that he, Gallagher, made him an offer to pay him for a loan if he was able to get the money from him, and I think it has a lot of bearing."

But the Court made a ruling. In effect Gallagher could have offered money to anyone else for a loan or even paid for it for that matter — but "justice" in this case was pointing the finger at the defendants in this particular case.

The ruling was, "It has no effect on this case."

While the lawyers deliberated this point of law, the jury was shut out, and only a word or two of the conversation at the bench could be garnered as it was wafted to the jury. It was meaningless as far as they were concerned.

[175]

The defendants' attorneys were not content to let the matter lie, so Schwartz asked Tarr, "How much did he ask you to lend him?"

Teitelbaum was quick to question the matter, "Your Honor that is beyond the question that you ruled on."

Cooper made an effort to plead for the question, but Teitelbaum interrupted with, "The judge made a ruling."

Cooper continued, "If your Honor please, in order to identify — I don't want to say anything that might be objectionable, but the question as it stands now with the answer has no significance unless it's shown approximately the loan that he asked for."

"All right," declared Judge Miller, "I will reverse myself to that extent, let him answer just how much he requested. I will not permit anything more than that."

So Allison Tarr left the stand — with the words of a proposed "deal" on the part of Gallagher locked in his head and held from the minds of the jurors. Testimony is valueless unless it is permitted to be brought out in full.

It was months later, after Sober's time in the penal institution, that he met Tarr. This incident of the trial was brought to mind he declared vehemently, "By — — —, I should have just blurted out what Gallagher wanted me to do, I should have just blurted it out."

Dr. Heineman and Cypher in their appearances on the stand told their stories. Their stories were to the point. In relating the Burkett transaction, the doctor told from the stand that they owed him a little more than $200 and that he expected something for putting his money up for that period of time for which the loan would be involved. His testimony was, "Another thing too, if I put the money for you then I feel I should be entitled to something for putting it up and putting this money up for the use of my money." Oh, they understood that was right. He — and first

[176]

she looked a little funny, she didn't say anything, he said, "Look, Honey, look what we pay finance companies."

Heineman went on to relate "that there had been a little bickering and that they agreed among themselves that out of the monies loaned to Burketts by a bank, that he would get $800."

Cypher told his story. He had known Heyman for years. He related how Heyman had come to him time after time and how they had had a man to man talk. Cypher said that he finally agreed to back Heyman's loan. His words from the stand were "Now," I said, "the administration of your business has been very poor to my way of seeing it, now I just have this to say. If I was to back you in any way, shape or form, if a man was to back you, I would first have to have the authority to go into the greenhouse and inspect the books and records at any time that I so felt like doing, and the big item would be I'd want to have decisive authority to the financial end of it."

Cypher then told of the plan to put up the money to back Heyman's loan.

Others were called on behalf of the defendants. Uncapher, who had befriended Sober when he was first arrested, appeared on the stand. His testimony was squashed because "he was a friend." Another witness who had become financially successfully because the Old Freeport Bank had helped her when others turned her down was called. She too was given opportunity to speak only a few words from the stand because hers was nothing more than a business transaction.

Several businessmen and citizens traveled to the court during the latter days of the trial. They were sworn in a body as character witnesses for the defendants. That was it — their words were not heard.

Of the thousands who had been helped, none could be heard. Of the few who thought they were victims of more than their own greed, their stories are emblazoned on the records forever. This is justice!

Worn and weary, Sober returned to his hotel one night during the late days of the trial. He found a note telling him to call a number in Indianapolis, Indiana. "What could he lose," he thought, so the call was put through. The voice on the other end of the wire was that of Phil Spiltalney, a noted Pittsburgh orchestra leader.

It was a strange story he had to tell Sober. He said that he had read of the case in the Indianapolis papers, and that he had been in Pittsburgh a few days before making the call. His story was that he had set out from the Squirrel Hill district one cold, windy morning, headed for the Golden Triangle. Standing along the curb, he noticed this gray-haired woman. She looked uncomfortable and cold, so the Pittsburgh gentlemen offered her a lift. This she graciously accepted. On the way to the business district she informed him that she had been staying with friends in the Squirrel Hill area, since she could not get home because of the inclement weather. One thing led to another, and she had finally mentioned that she was serving on the Federal Jury in the case involving the Freeport bankers on "loansharking" and "kickbacks." She talked freely of her duties and of the case, and as she left Spiltalney's car she cheerfully offered the information, "And we're going to find those dirty bankers guilty, too."

Spiltalney told Sober that he would gladly come to Pittsburgh, because he couldn't see how a juror or a jury could have reached a verdict since the case hadn't been completed.

Sober thanked his caller and in haste told Cooper of the call. The Judge was non-communicative.

Several weeks later, after the trial had been concluded and the little gray-haired lady with her eleven compatriots, had lived up to their word, Sober was invited along with others to a lunch at the Penn Sheraton Hotel.

As the group stood in the lobby, who should enter but Phil Spiltalney. He rushed to Judge Cooper, "Why didn't you call me? Your client told me he would tell you."

The Judge waved him aside, "We are busy now. I'll talk to you later."

He turned abruptly from the orchestra leader and led the group to the other side of the room.

The defense rested!

*See Dattola letter page 36 Documentation.

Chapter XII

THE VERDICT
OF GUILTY

THE TRIAL was drawing to an end. It was time for the closing arguments on the part of the attorneys for the defendants and for the government. Judge Cooper made an eloquent plea for his clients. Again the entire case was covered, count by count, point by point. There was a good bit of the emotional in Cooper's address and while most of the address was devoted to a plea asking for the reasoned judgment on the part of the jurors, little reference was made to actual law under which the bankers had been indicted. The speech was long and before Cooper was through, he asked for a recess. It was at this point that Teitelbaum asked for a side bar and during the time he took issue with his legal opponent on one of the matters brought before the jury, which he claimed was not in evidence.

After the recess Cooper continued and it was during this time that the emotional appeals grew to their highest point. He asked the jury to look at Mrs. Cypher and at the daughter of Cypher. This argument was not lost upon Teitelbaum when his turn came for a summary of the case.

As Cooper closed his argument, the defendants were moved to believe that certainly only one verdict could be brought in — and that would be the verdict of "not guilty."

The defendants had not yet heard Teitelbaum.

During his opening remarks the government's attorney said, "I was surprised to hear the rather eloquent plea for sympathy that was made, in fact that has been made an undertone all through the case. That's why Mrs. Cypher was put on the stand, but imagine even young Mrs. Cypher was put on the stand."

He continued, in an impassioned address, to cast the bankers as the lowest of criminals. The terms "blood-money" "kickbacks" and "loansharks" were used frequently throughout his attack.

Teitelbaum was not satisfied to let it go at this. He turned to sarcasm. He spoke of "Good Old Doc" not once but numerous times; he turned his venom on Sober and into the ears of the jurors were pounded the words that he (Sober) had done everything about the bank and therefore was in complete knowledge of everything.

For the jurors, who had not days and days to study a transcript of the words, he even implied what a witness could have said, when he strode before the jury box and declared, "I will tell you what 'Correct-Attest' means. Mr. Cooper gave his statement. He says 'attest' means that it is the signature of the man that signs it. 'Correct-Attest' doesn't mean that at all, because 'Correct-Attest' — if they only want to say whose the signature was, they wouldn't need a bank director to do it, a notary public, anybody could do it; 'Correct-Attest' means that three directors of the bank are attesting what is in the record is correct. That is what it means. Mr. Canaday could have said that if he wanted to, but it wasn't his position."

Teitelbaum was not through. He had to turn his invective on Cypher and Sober and repeatedly used the terms "Big-hearted" Cypher and "C. D." Charley Sober.

[181]

Then in closing he impassionedly resorted to the patriotic theme by saying, "Many in time of war have a very serious duty to their country, and pay the supreme price. If we want to remain, all of us, free, equal Americans, we must not only share the good things, we must share the responsibilities. We must do so whether they are pleasant or unpleasant."

As impassioned as was Teitelbaum's address, Judge Miller's charge was in the opposite vein. He, too, covered every count in the entire case. He dwelt for a time on the intent to do wrong as compared with a motive for an act.

After warning the jurors that he had requested them previously to refrain from reading newspaper articles or listening to radio or television broadcasts pertaining to the case or discussing it among themselves or with others, he then continued the charge:

"As I have told you, these instructions must not be taken by you as any indication that the court has formed an opinion as to the guilt or innocence of the defendants. Disregard any opinion you think the court might have. The court has no such opinion and is only interested in helping you to arrive at a true verdict. It is your responsibility alone to find the relevant facts and decide the case on evidence heard in the courtroom."

Prior to that the Judge had stated: "From what I have said to you so far, members of the jury, it is obvious that the issue of the defendants' guilt or innocence depends greatly upon the credibility of the witnesses in the case who have appeared for both parties."

So with thousands of words ringing into their ears, with one impassioned plea being counter balanced by an address full of invective, frosted over by a dull, monotonous charge from the bench, the jurors retired to consider a verdict.

The trial was brought to a close May 25, 1959. On May 26th the jury returned with a verdict. The defendants were GUILTY!

[182]

There was little solace for the defendants in the jury's findings. Charles L. Sober was found guilty "aiding and abetting" on the Gallagher, Kelosky and Heyman Loans. The charges of conspiracy were found to be true against him, according to the jury, in the Gallagher, Burkett and Heyman loans, and he was also found guilty of false entry on two counts conerning the F.D.I.C. call reports.

Similar findings were against Dr. Heineman and Cypher, however the latter two were found guilty of receiving fees. Dr. Heineman's involved the Gallagher and Burkett loans, while Cypher's had to do with the Heyman transaction.

The young men in the case, Ira L. Sober and Jack C. Reese were found guilty of the "false entry" charges involving the F.H.A. mortgages, the F.D.I.C. call reports and in the charge which involved the automobile transaction.

There was little cause for rejoicing, however a little light did shine through the darkness when trial motions for acquital were granted in the Devereaux, Kallnar charges or counts. The jury returned "not guilty" verdicts in favor of Dr. Heineman on embezzlement charges as it did for Ira L. Sober. No embezzlement charge ever stood up.

In some quarters there were heavy hearts — all men have some friends — and the question on the lips of many was "Do you really think he (Sober) did it?"

In other camps the fires of victory and celebration burned brightly. The banker — that unorthodox banker — had been vanquished.

Chapter XIII

A NEW TRIAL?

After the trial had been concluded, there were rumblings that something was not right. It is a practice, in most instances, where there are questions on technical points of law that have not been fully cleared during a trial, for the attorneys for the defendants to file a motion for a new trial. This was done in the case, since one of the witnesses as early as May 22, 1959 had indicated that he wanted to change his story.

Sober was not permitted to contact the witness. However, Cooper's investigator Thornton, now deceased, was assigned the task of interviewing the witnesses and seeing if there was any basis for a hearing as the result of a change in testimony. Some of Thornton's interviews will be lost forever due to his death, but he had gleaned enough and had these items placed on paper to reveal that some of "the truth" had cleverly been withheld.

The date for a hearing on a motion for a new trial was set for Thursday, August 27, 1959, before the Honorable John L. Miller, Judge. As the principals gathered in the Federal Building in Pittsburgh, there was the usual bustle of activity with attorneys, clerks and various courtroom attachés scurrying back and forth from one office to another. Besides the principals and the witnesses who had been subpoenaed, who should appear on the

[184]

cene but Mr. and Mrs. John Burkett. Teitelbaum looked unhap-
pily at these people who had helped him so much in winning his
case, "What are you doing here. You weren't called!"

The Burketts replied that they had just been in Pittsburgh and
had decided to drop in to see what was going on.

Teitelbaum rushed up the hall. He hadn't time to be bothered
with the Burketts. Apparently they were after something. On his
return trip he came face to face with Jack Reese. Teitelbaum
wanted to know what Jack Reese was doing there as the hearing
did not concern the counts against Reese.

Teitelbaum continued, "I don't know why you're involved in
this thing anyway."

Reese responded, "It wasn't my idea, Mr. Teitelbaum, apparently it was yours."

"You had your chance," Teitelbaum snapped, "if you would
have come into my office when you were invited, you wouldn't
have been involved." With these words he continued on his
errand in preparation for the hearing.

There was no jury to hear the words that would come from the
witnesses' mouths. The spectators were few and in the main,
people who were personally interested in the defendants' cause.

Attorney Cooper addressed the Court:

"Sometime, I believe in May, before we argued the motion for
a new trial, on a Sunday evening, Mr. C. L. Sober came to my
home at 401 Morewood Avenue and told me that in the afternoon
at Webster Hall, where he has been living, he received a telephone call from Mr. Gustave Heyman. He wasn't there. He left
his number. Apparently he wanted him to call. He left his telephone number. Mr. Sober came over to my home and asked me
what he should do about it.

"Frankly, I hesitated for a while and then I said, 'if you have
the number, call it downstairs,' — I have an extension on my

phone upstairs — 'and I will listen in on the conversation,' which he did.

"At that time Mr. Heyman had indicated to Mr. Sober that he wanted to talk to him about a matter involving his property and the testimony that he gave. And that was the end of the conversation that day.

"That resulted at some subsequent date — the Court will remember that in our brief that we filed on the date of the original argument we gave some intimation, although we didn't have the details — as a result of that telephone conversation, Mr. Heyman was brought to the office and told us that he wanted to tell something. And then we turned him into an office and we had a machine and he talked into the machine. And what he said into the machine became a part of the affidavit that was filed in the court, which resulted in this hearing today."

Judge Miller spoke, "There hasn't been any affidavit filed. Merely a signed statement."

"Signed statement with the petition that was filed." Cooper responded as he corrected himself, "Let me put it that way. Whatever was filed."

"Frankly, I want to say to the court that I was in Washington, D. C. on a matter with the F.D.I.C., involving certain business dealings in connection with the bank (The Old Freeport Bank) that have nothing to do with this case, and at that time Mr. Coburn, counsel for the F.D.I.C., wanted me to tell him whether or not we were making any charges against any employees of the F.D.I.C., I told Mr. Coburn at that time, and I say in court right now, that while we filed this affidavit or petition with a statement, I told him then that I am not making any charges and I didn't know when I came into court today what the testimony would bring out.

"I want to turn the questioning of Mr. Heyman over to my associate, Mr. Schwartz."

[186]

Again the formalities were brought out for the purpose of the record. Heyman gave his name, his address and admitted that he was one witness who had testified at the trial of the five defendants then in the courtroom.

"Now, Mr. Heyman prior to us getting into this statement that you gave, I'd like to ask you some questions concerning the background of the statement. Now, for the record, did Mr. Cooper or myself or anyone from our office solicit your giving of this statement?"

"No, sir."

"Did we in any way tell you what you should say in this statement?"

"No, you didn't," Heyman answered.

"So that anything that you put into the statement was done on your own, without our request?"

"Yes, it was."

Teitelbaum could stand this line of questioning no longer, "If it please the court," he appealed, "I object to leading questions. This is rather important and I ask that they be made in the proper fashion."

"That is true, Mr. Schwartz," the Court confirmed.

"Your Honor," Schwartz faced the bench, "I thought I'd try to facilitate this hearing a little bit, but if we are going to get into that problem I will try to avoid the leading questions. I didn't know that we were in a position of one individual in this type of hearing—"

Judge Miller interrupted, "All right, Mr. Schwartz. I have ruled on the leading questions. Please ask the proper questions."

Mr. Heyman in his statement declared that the F.D.I.C. agents and bank examiners told him and his wife "that if we would give statements that would hold up in court or would be strong enough to convict the men involved that we would get our greenhouse and flower shop back."

Schwartz continued, "Mr. Heyman, did you consult with anyone in the United States Attorney's office concerning this statement prior to your giving it to us? Did you go down and talk to anyone in the United States Attorney's office about this problem?"

"Yes, I did," answered Heyman.

"Who did you talk to, sir?" continued Schwartz.

"Mr. Gavin," Heyman answered again.

"Was that prior to dictating this statement?" questioned Attorney Schwartz as he held up the paper which held the affidavit by Heyman. "Is that correct?"

"That is correct," replied Heyman.

The questioning of Heyman continued to the point where he was asked to tell of the conversation between him and the government agents.

"At the time you gave the statement, was anyone present other than Mr. Canaday, Mr. Brown and yourself?"

"My wife," answered Heyman.

Attorney Schwartz posed his question, "Your wife was present. Now prior to giving the statement when Mr. Canaday and Mr. Brown were there, was there any discussion between you and Mr. Canaday and Mr. Brown concerning what they were investigating?"

"Yes, there was."

"What did that discussion reveal to you?"

"Can I tell you the discussion or—"

"In your own words, yes. Go ahead."

So Heyman launched into a discourse of the conversation as he remembered it concerning the visit of Alonzo Canaday and Mr. Brown, examiners for the F.D.I.C.

"I asked them," he stated, "after they showed their identifica-
ion, I asked them what they were really there for, what they
vanted. And they told me that they were getting statements
rom people like myself that had fallen on the wayside, or what-
:ver you want to call it, had been done wrong one way or the
ither. I don't remember the exact words. But to the effect they
vere trying to do something to help us people that got hurt.

"I asked them how this, making the statement, how that would
uffect in any way us getting our greenhouse, florist shop back.
Fhey told me, Mr. Canaday, and I'm not sure which one exactly
;aid all the words but they were more or less together, that if the
nformation we would give would be of such a nature that they
would get a conviction, that we would stand a very good chance
of getting our place back. And I said, 'Well, how would that go
ibout?' They said, well, they knew two or three lawyers that
would be only too glad to take my case in securing, getting my
place back, I asked them right then and there, before I made any
statement, if he could give me their names. And he says he
couldn't, that he wasn't at liberty to do that at that particular
time, but at the right time they would become known to me."

"All right," continued Attorney Schwartz in the questioning,
"after that you gave them a statement. Is that correct, sir?"

"Yes, I did," answer Heyman.

"Now," Attorney Schwartz put his next question, "did you and
Mr. Canaday discuss who these lawyers would be at any time
after that?"

"No," replied Heyman, "except that I asked him—the day, the
last day that I was on the stand as a witness, in the District
Attorney's office, I asked him if he would give me one of those
lawyers or both of those lawyers' names, being as I was excused
from the hearing. And he said that he couldn't at that time, but
that he would call me in a day or two. And I wrote down my
telephone number and address, where I live now, because I

wasn't living out there no more. He said he'd get in touch with me in a day or two. Of course, I never heard nothing from him since."

A little later Attorney Schwartz asked Mr. Heyman why he went to see Mr. C. Malcolm Andersen, a former U. S. District Attorney.

It was with a sigh of relief, like the awakening from a bad dream, that Mr. Heyman let the words flow from his lips, "I went down to see him and talked to him," Heyman's words came faster, "and asked—he told me right then and there, when I told him, if my conscience bothered me and if I had in my mind honestly thought that any of my testimony helped or convicted an innocent man, that it was my duty to talk up. That's why I did."

Heyman's cross, although he was relieved of a portion of it, was not an easy one to bear. With a viciousness, Attorney Teitel-baum, the government's counsel, attacked the statements made by Heyman. By leading questions, he intimated that Heyman, providing he changed his testimony at Sober's behest, could get his property back. He implied in questions that the government agents had promised nothing, even though examiner Brown had testified "I had no particular interest in them getting their property back, except I thought it would be nice if they could."

Words and their meanings are confusing. What is said by one is often taken to mean something else by another. Sometimes the words carry deceptive ideas, and are spoken intentionally with the purpose of carrying such ideas. At other times the words are spoken in pure innocence, and the meaning is misconstrued by the hearer. While it is the business of attorneys to bring out what was said and the true meaning of such words, truth is often buried under an avalanche of words.

Somewhere, someplace in events preceding the trial and during the trial the whole truth never prevailed. Even Canaday in his testimony at the hearing did stray from his previous statements to the effect that he had not offered to get Heyman's house, greenhouse or anything else back.

The government's counsel called Canaday to the stand. As he did so, Cooper injected this statement, "Before Mr. Canaday takes the stand, I take it from what the court told us this morning that you do not want us to call Mr. Burkett for any testimony."

The Court replied, "That is correct."

"Do you recall when you went out to see Mr. and Mr. Heyman?" Teitelbaum queried Canaday.

"I do."

After a few more questions regarding this visit, Teitelbaum put this to his witness, "Mr. Canaday, was Mr. Brown with you at the time?"

"Mr. Brown was with me on two occasions, when we went to the Heyman home," he answered.

Delving more deeply into the conversations during these visits, the next question came, "Was there any discussion about obtaining lawyers for them?"

"During the interview of Mr. Heyman and his wife—Mr. Heyman did most of the talking—Mrs. Heyman, as I recall, asked if we knew of any lawyers that he might be able to see to help him out in his difficulties, that he would like to, if at all possible, to recover his greenhouse property. That was the discussion in general, or his comments in general," Canaday replied.

"And what did you tell him?"

"Well, I told him that I was a stranger in this area, that I knew no lawyer, therefore I couldn't suggest the names of any lawyers. And during the conversation, when he did ask or was talking about recovering his property, talking about lawyers, I'm quite sure that I suggested to him that any litigation that he

might have or any relief that he might seek that he could consul
or get in touch with an attorney."

However, Canaday apparently forgot that he had testified dur
ing the trial that he had been in a meeting which included
Attorney Alexander Lindsay. He might have testified that he
knew of no lawyers who would help the government's witnesses

The examination continued and during this time Canaday did
not change his story basically from any statements made pre
viously. He maintained from the stand that he had held no
inducements to the Heymans.

During Canaday's cross-examination, Cooper asked, "Do you
remember that there was any discussion between you and Mr
Heyman about his getting his greenhouse back, regardless of
whether you brought it up or whether he brought it up?"

"Mr. Heyman naturally asked what would be the chances of
getting his greenhouse back, his property back."

"And that was before the statement, before he gave the state
ment?"

Canaday hesitated a moment, "Well—oh, yes. That was before
he gave us the statement, sure."

Cooper had elicited the answer he wanted. Canaday had ad
mitted that a discussion concerning the prospects of the prop
erty being returned to the Heymans had taken place before he
got his statement.

The repartee continued for a time and then Cooper mentioned
the other witnesses, "And when you took statements from the
Burketts and the Gallaghers, was there any discussion between
you and those people as to whether they were going to get
their property back, after the trial was over?"

"Mr. Gallagher, in the conversation, he asked, wondered if he
could get his property back, if he could ever get it back, and
gave him the same answer that I gave Heyman, Mr. Heyman

[192]

hat that would be a civil matter, in my estimation," Canaday
eplied.

"And did Mr. Burkett also ask you whether or not he was
going to get his property back, when the case was over?"

"I don't recall whether it was Mr. Burkett, Mr. John Burkett,
o much as it was Mrs. Burkett."

"All right," was the response from Cooper.

Canaday continued, "She, I am quite sure that she asked if
here would be any chance that they could get—that she could
get her house back. She always referred to it as her house."

"That was before she and her husband gave you a statement?"

But Canaday was not to be caught in this trap again. While he
could remember some things quite vividly, he answered Cooper
as follows, "Well, in that particular case, I don't just recall
whether it was before or after the statement was given."

"But that discussion took place before the trial of the case?"

"It took—yes, sir."

From the questioning one truth was established. There had
been discussions with four of the government's witnesses regarding the prospect of getting some property returned. Later on during the hearing John D. Brown, called as a witness on behalf of
the government, testified.

In response to a question during the cross-examination, as to
whether he would help them (Heymans) after the case was over,
Brown answered, "I did not. There was no way I could help them
get it back."

"I am not asking you that," Cooper retorted, "I am only asking,
did you say anything to them, did you lead them to believe that
when the case was over you would be of assistance to them in
getting their property back."

"Of course I don't know what they thought, but I said nothing
that would lead them to believe it, that I know of."

"Would you try to give the court your best recollection of what you might have said to them, which would lead them to believe that?"

Teitelbaum was on his feet, "Objected to. He didn't say he said anything that might have led them to believe that."

Cooper turned to his opponent, "That is exactly what he said."

"No, he did not," countered Teitelbaum.

The Court intervened in the verbal exchange, "All right. We'll let Judge Cooper ask the question."

Brown continued with his testimony, "It is my memory that I said to them that I couldn't help them get it back."

"I'm sorry," Cooper apologized, "I thought you said regardless of what you said they may have believed—"

"They evidently did, from this hearing."

A few minutes later Brown was excused from the stand.

It had always been somewhat of a puzzle to persons who followed the case as to why Mrs. Maria Heyman was not called to the trial proper as a government witness. She had been present when Canaday and Brown had questioned and had taken statements from her husband, Gustave. It has been thought that because of her difficulty with the English language, she was spared the ordeal of examination and cross-examination. However, Mrs. Heyman who had worked with the underground in Germany during the early reign of the Nazis, at one time wondered why she had not been called.

In spite of the language barrier, Mrs. Heyman was not a witness to be intimidated. She knew what she had heard and she spoke effectively.

In direct examination, Attorney Teitelbaum asked, "Did you Mrs. Heyman, think that the government was going to get your greenhouse and house back for you?"

"To tell you the truth," she replied, "I think nobody cares so much about if we get our greenhouse back or not."

"Unfortunately."

"Unfortunately, yes."

"But you didn't think the government was going to do it, did you?" was the next query put by Teitelbaum.

"No, actually not."

"Ever, is that right?"

"Because there was—we were made to believe that we have a good chance of getting it back," Mrs. Heyman answered.

"But you never thought," Teitelbaum continued his repetitious questioning, "the government was going to get it back for you?"

Mrs. Heyman's eyes snapped, then with a seeming inner knowledge that she and her husband were just pawns to be moved at will in the interplay of conflicting forces, she answered quietly and with conviction, "No, I don't know. The gentlemen that was there taking statements from us,—see, I'm not an American, and I'm not so good acquainted with the laws and everything, and I thought they did make suggestions to us that we have a good chance of getting our greenhouse back."

In the cross-examination by Attorney Cooper, Mrs. Heyman reiterated that it was Mr. Canaday who had made the statement that sounded like the promise of getting their property back which was now fading into oblivion.

In the redirect examination by Teitelbaum, the question was put, "What did he say?" (In reference to Canaday.)

"He said," Mrs. Heyman answered, "You have a very good chance of getting your greenhouse back."

"Is that all he said?"

"And your house," she answered, "He said to my husband, he said,—my husband said, 'Now you think, after we make that

[195]

statement—' He said, 'Yes, if you make it stick, that they are convicted, you have a very good chance.'"

"Did Mr. Canaday say that, Mrs. Heyman?" Teitelbaum asked with even a note of surprise in his voice.

"Yes, he did." Mrs. Heyman was positive in her answer.

"And you heard that?"

"Yes, I did."

"And you so state under oath?"

Mrs. Heyman drew herself erect. The weariness was gone. The prodding, the questioning, the ordeal of the past days was over. Now before God and man she could answer with telling effect on all but the calloused souls of those who do not seek justice but only to further their own interests—whatever they may be— "Yes, I do. It's no lie."

After the testimony of Mrs. Heyman, her husband was questioned by Judge Miller.

"Mr. Heyman, in your statement which has now been offered in evidence and which you have identified as your statement and which you have signed, you state as follows, in the last paragraph of the statement: 'I would also like to say at this time that due to the pretense of the Examiners that took statements from us, this whole case, the whole thing everything that I have said since the beginning when we first made our statements, has been colored on purpose by me because I have felt after working for a place so hard, that I want to make sure, like they said, if we can make this stick, we would get our place back.'

"That is part of your statement. What do you mean by your statement that you colored your testimony?"

"Well, your Honor," Heyman answered, "maybe the word 'colored'—maybe I just, for the lack of using another word, maybe I used the wrong word."

"Did you tell the truth when you were testifying at the trial?" he Judge asked.

"I felt I told the truth, but I felt I didn't tell all of it."

"What do you mean?"

"I mean the way I said certain things, it made a reflection, and t had implications that made it look like something that I don't eel that, myself, that I should run around the rest of my life feelng that I am the cause of sending a man that I know in my case lidn't have anything to do with it. That I felt that I implicated him in a way that I shouldn't have."

"How did you do that?"

Heyman took another deep breath, "By different ways I made statements. I said running back and forth so fast, in the same room, and that we weren't partners, Jack Cypher and I weren't partners, because I figured as partners you had to be a partner."

"All right."

"And that actually," Heyman continued, "he was backing me up financially, and also that I never got a chance to explain all the dealings that I had with Jack Cypher, I didn't—Mr. Sober never conferred, never suggested I go see Jack Cypher, never in no way make any suggestions that I have to do this. Jack Cypher never suggested it either."

The Judge looked at Heyman intently, "Now Mr. Heyman, I handed to Mr. Donaldson, who has volunteered to look after your interests today, a copy of your testimony, and I take it you have discussed that with him since ten o'clock this morning."

"Yes, I have, sir," responded Heyman.

"And the testimony as transcribed, is that true or correct? Is it true and correct, is what you meant to say."

"Yes, as far as it goes, sir."

"You were, of course, examined at some length by government counsel and you were cross-examined at some length by counsel

[197]

for the defendants, and you say that there was something that could be brought out that they didn't bring out."

Heyman shook his head slightly, "I don't believe I understand that, sir."

"I mean," Judge Miller explained, "was there something that you have to say? Was there some testimony that wasn't brought out on your direct examination or cross-examination, at the trial of the case before the jury?"

"Yes, as far as what Mr. Canaday and Brown, what our discussion was pertaining to getting the statements. Another fact that I told them, that they didn't take down, was that Jack Cypher had offered to, if I could find another bank that would take the loan, that I, if I could get $23,000 from another bank that he would be willing to forget about everything, plus after that I went to see Mr. Kaufman at the First National Bank in Freeport and he told me that one of these days he's going to slip up, they are going to catch him. And he was referring—"

The Judge interrupted, "Well now—"

"I made that statement, but they never wrote it down."

So, finally, truth began to reveal itself. There were still a number of questions arising out of the hearing. The Burketts were not called to testify. Judge Miller had ordered that. Even their statement that they had answered "in a run-about sort of way" told the truth, was not questioned at the hearing.

Friends of the principals in the case held to hopes that something would transpire from the hearing, but their wishes were to be denied. The recanting witnesses had done their work well the first time. The appeal for a new trial was denied.

No stone was to be left unturned. The firm of attorneys representing the Old Freeport Bank officials, with the approval and urging of the bankers, carried the case to the United States Court of Appeals for the Third Circuit. In the brief prepared Attorneys Cooper, Schwartz and Sikov presented three questions involved.

The first had to do with the facts proven by the government. In the brief the attorneys for the appellants maintained that the proven facts did not constitute a violation of the law regarding the commission for securing a loan nor were there any false entries. In the second premise set forth the conduct of the government counsel was questioned, as was the highly confusing method of introducing evidence. The introduction of evidence outside the scope of the indictments was detailed, and should the testimony of a recanting witness require a new trial?

The attorneys also looked and appealed with favor for the two young men in the case, Ira Sober and Jack Reese, claiming that they should not have stood trial with the other defendants on unrelated charges.

While the brief related the charges and the testimony which had already been heard, it pointed out that Mr. Canaday had become ill for a week during the trial and the trial was in recess. Because of the multiplicity of charges and the fact that the government examiner was involved or was to testify on all counts against the defendants, the attorneys for the appellants maintained that the interruption was prejudicial because the testimony on each count had not been completed prior to the recess and that thereafter Mr. Canaday testified relating to all counts. The brief states, "This would tend to place more emphasis on his testimony than should have been accorded it."

Brought out more plainly was the reference to the conduct of the counsel for the government when he made the summary before the jury. The brief referred to his use of stories concerning the dead man and the casket, and the impropriety of statements when he used the reference of armed robbery and smoking guns as analogous to the present case.

The summation of the case on the part of the government counsel reached the peak of vindicativeness when he repeatedly referred to the three principal defendants in the case as "Old

Doc" and "Good Old Doc" in a sarcastic and facetious manner. Nor did he leave any of them out. The principal defendant was scathed with the terms "Big-Hearted Charles Sober" or "C. D. Charles Sober." Stinging comments were also leveled at Cypher. To the jury he was referred to as "Sympathetic, Big-Hearted John Cypher."

The brief went on and did not skip the inflamatory phrases as "loan-sharking," "loan shark deal," "C. D. racket," and "Blood Money" and various other terms which were intended to prejudice the jury.

Cited was the motion, at the close of the government attorney's address, for the withdrawal of a juror which was denied.

As the attorneys argued before the august panel of judges of the Third Circuit Court, there was an air of hope. Surely, thought the defendants, after hearing the arguments and plea on the part of Attorney Cooper, no man or woman should be subjected to the verbal abuse and innuendoes in a court of justice in the United States.

Victory was to be denied. The opinion of the court filed June 24, 1960 upheld the verdict of the lower court. In the opinion by McLaughlin, Circuit Judge, the following was stated:

"We have examined appellants' other points i. e. questions and remarks of the District Attorney other than at closing; manner in which the government presented its evidence; evidence allegedly improperly admitted; restriction of Tarr testimony; allegations re testimony of the Burketts and Mrs. Heyman. Regarding all these, a close examination of the voluminous record convinces us that no substantial error has arisen out of this trial because of them.

"The judgment of the district court will be affirmed."

Even though this august panel of jurists did agree on one point, there must have been some question.

Biggs, Chief Judge, with whom Hastie, Circuit Judge, joins, concurring.

"Though we concur in the ruling that the judgments of conviction against the defendants must be affirmed, we cannot join with our Brother McLaughlin in praising the manner in which the United States Attorney summed up to the jury. The appellations and examples which he applied to the defendants and to their acts fall just short of that degree of impropriety as would require a new trial. It is true that the summation of the defendants' counsel was just as to offer a temptation to rebut in kind but the prosecuting attorney should not have succumbed to such a temptation. Cases brought on behalf of the United States should be conducted with a dignity worthy of the client. This is particularly true where a jury is present and an individual is on trial on a criminal charge. It is the duty of the trial judge to make sure by the ample means at his disposal, whether citation for contempt or some less drastic expedient, that the trial is conducted with due propriety by both prosecutor and defense counsel."

Of what use is admonishment of a higher court after the act has been done and the words have been spoken?

The defendants and their attorney did not stop. There was one step higher — The Supreme Court of the United States.

A petition was prepared for this body. It was the last hope. The Supreme Court, it had been said, would hear anyone from the highest to the lowest.

The Supreme Court refused to review the case.

The defendants' last ray of hope faded into darkness.

Chapter *XIV*

INTO THE UNKNOWN

Sober aroused himself from a fitful sleep. The night had been short. There had been many things to complete and arrange at the last moment, but even though he got to his bed in the early hours of the morning, the rest was not peaceful. His dreams brought forth a small man with a leering smile. The small man was saying, "You're guilty! You're guilty! You're guilty!" At the same time there was a parade of faces — the prosecuting attorney, who snarled, "They say there is something behind all this — there is something behind all this — there is something behind all this." He walked down a long aisle. Here were people he had helped and befriended. As he approached them, they would turn their faces and say, "We wash our hands of the whole affair. We wash our hands of the whole affair."

Sober awoke in a cold sweat. He glanced at the hands of the clock. Through the gloom the luminous dial stood out distinctly. The hands pointed to six and twenty. He tried to return to sleep. A thousand and one faces and thoughts entered his mind. He finally decided that there was no point in trying to sleep. He arose slowly and shook himself to full consciousness. As he sat on the edge of the bed, he wondered if he wouldn't awaken again and find the whole sordid story of the past year and a half a dream — nothing but a bad dream.

There is in the process of human reasoning that which tells reality from hallucination. This wasn't a dream. He was awake. Every last resource had been tried and explored. This was the day he was to appear to begin serving his sentence. Sober closed his eyes. He opened them again, only to find that he was in the same small room. Everything was real — too real.

He dressed himself slowly and deliberately. There was no need to hurry. It was still three hours before he was to report to the Federal building at Grant Street in Pittsburgh. He had made arrangements to close out his room the night before. He remembered the look on the face of the clerk, who, half in embarrassment, tried to jest about saving his room. There was no one to bid goodbye to. The good-byes had been said previously.

He had his suitcase packed and walked to the elevator. An elderly woman greeted him with a cheery "good morning" as he entered the elevator. He had never seen her before. He wondered if she knew that he was on his way to begin a prison sentence. On the elevator, the two rode down together, with comments concerning the weather predominating the conversation.

Sober walked to the desk and turned in his key. The clerk took the key and started to say something about "We'll be seeing you soon." He cast his eyes downward, and his words soon became a mumble of incoherent sounds.

"Save me a room; I'll be back," Sober related as he smiled at the clerk. He walked to the dining room for breakfast. The waitress came to the table. She made an effort to act nonchalant. "Well, what'll it be this morning? Same thing? Poached eggs, bacon, toast, coffee?"

Sober looked up into her face, "Yea, same thing!" She looked at him for a moment, and then dropped her eyes. She reached out and pressed his hand for a moment, then quickly hurried away.

They knew. She knew. All knew. He was going to prison.

Having made arrangements for storage of his car, Sober hailed a taxi and ordered the driver to discharge him at the U. S. Building. As he stepped from the taxi, a cloud floated over the sky obscuring the last rays of the sun. It was a dull, chilly, cheerless morning. Sober pulled his coat collar up and buried his chin. He picked up his suitcase and walked into the building, and arrived at the Marshal's office at 10 o'clock on that morning of November 28, 1960.

There were no formalities. The greetings were perfunctory. Shortly afterward he was handcuffed, for the first time since his ordeal had started, to another prisoner. As he left the Marshal's office, newspaper photographers jumped in front of him to explode their flashes; so that all could see a human in humiliation. After all, of such things were newspapers made; the unpleasant things in life were displayed and sold. His enemies could revel in his downfall, and gleefully assert that they had helped to put him "where he belonged."

The prisoners were walked up Grant Street to Sixth, and then up Sixth to the County Jail. Following a brief preliminary examination, all cash was turned in except three dollars and such silver as a person carried. Sober was unceremoniously taken to a cell. The handcuffs were removed, and the lackey stepped out, the door clanged shut and the first step into the unknown became a reality.

It was not long until one of the prisoners in an adjoining cell asked Sober if he wanted some ice cream or candy. Sober inquired as to how this could be, since they were all shut in their cells.

"Just give me three bucks," said the man in the adjoining cell, "and you'll see."

The three dollars were dutifully handed over and in about a half hour Sober was presented with an ice cream and a candy bar. "Where's the change?" he inquired.

"Oh, you don't get any change," his provider answered. "The other guys gets something out of this too."

Sober received his first initiation into the workings of prison life.

During the day, one could hear the various tales of exploits and escapes. Prominent among these were the stories that this prisoner or that prisoner wouldn't be in very long. They explained that all they had been doing was selling numbers and the "big fellow" would have them out soon.

Sober ventured a question, "Don't they ever get the 'big fellow'?"

"You kiddin'?" queried a fellow in an adjacent cell.

"Do they know 'em?" Sober pursued further.

"Damn right they do, but they never pick them up."

Close to five o'clock two men came walking down the cell block. One carried a bucket and the other a dipper. Sober watched the other inmates and when the men came to the front of his cell, he did as he had seen others do and thrust a tin pan between an opening in the bars. The man with the dipper reached into the bucket and sloshed a gob of spaghetti onto the pan. A couple of strands slid over the side and onto the floor. The prisoner looked at the mess and his mind carried him back to the days on the farm. He thought to himself, they served that stuff just like I slopped hogs back on the farm fifty years ago.

The night was one long to be remembered. Sober threw himself on the cot and tried to sleep. A colored man in a nearby cell started to croon an old Negro spiritual, but he was soon hushed by the clamor of others telling him to pipe down. Occasionally there would be a rackety laugh, followed by chuckles and snickers. Toward morning the cell block quieted down, and the snores and wheezes from the prisoners, breaking the stillness, created a discordant symphony of sound.

Between four and five on the morning of November 29, Sober was ordered from his cell. He was given his suitcase and personal belongings and ushered into a car with another prisoner. The second step into the unknown began.

As the car carrying the deputies and the prisoners wound over the hills of western Pennsylvania, Sober began to feel the knawing pangs of hunger. "Say," he inquired, "don't we get something to eat? This is a long trip."

"Yea, we'll stop," answered his guard, "but don't order too much."

At the stop a full and complete breakfast was ordered. The deputies made no move to pay, so Sober reached into his pocket and paid for the four of the party. He knew, however, that the men who were shepherding him to Lewisburg had been allotted funds to purchase meals for their prisoners. Sober chuckled as he was returned to the car after the meal.

"Something must have amused you," one of the guards stated.

"It did," replied Sober, without additional explanation. He thought to himself, "I've been accused of chiseling, kickbacks and a lot of other things, and here are a couple of fellows who would gain a couple of lousy bucks by not buying a meal for a prisoner." He wondered how many prisoners had been taken to Lewisburg from Pittsburgh, who didn't have the nerve to say, "How about something to eat?"

The car in which the four were riding pulled up to the reception building. Before Sober left the officer, whose duty it was to bring him to the Federal prison, he handed him five dollars and requested that he make a phone call for him. He found out later the call was never made.

Immediately upon entering the prison, Sober along with others who had been brought in, was stripped and given a thorough examination. As the line moved forward, one of the guards asked him whether he wanted to give his belongings to charity or have them burned. The guard intimated that these were the only choices. Sober insisted that his clothes be mailed to an address which he had given, and that he get a receipt for them. This request was finally granted, but similar requests that he be allowed to keep his Bible and his medicine were denied.

Sober pondered this refusal regarding the Bible and medicine. So few in busy, work-a-day lives turn to the Book for comfort and guidance. Here was the time, yet this privilege was denied. His medicine, he learned later, was denied him, but replaced from the prison pharmacy, because there are those, who humiliated and defeated, seek to leave this vale of tears through the use of the poison-filled capsule. The authorities take no chances.

During the time at Lewisburg, the prison routine was disrupted at frequent intervals for immunization shots and vaccinations. Within a few days, Sober with other prisoners, was loaded in a car and driven to the minimum security farm at Allenwood, Pennsylvania. After two days at the farm, Sober was summoned before the Superintendent, and asked what he wanted to do in the way of a job. In a facetious manner, the "super", as he was called by the inmates, informed Sober that there were no bank jobs available—the farm didn't have a bank—but he listed the jobs which the prisoners could request. He was a little surprised when Sober stated that he would take a janitor's job. He was assigned to what is known as Number Two building. The "super" had expected a request for an office job, or work in the library.

There was some freedom. The boundaries of the farm marked the outer perimeter to which the prisoners could walk. While there were guards, they were unobtrusive, and the routine varied considerably from that experienced at Lewisburg.

It was not long until Sober became acquainted with many of the others confined because of run-ins with Federal law and law enforcement officers. While the crimes, both real and imagined, covered a wide range, many were incarcerated for violation of Federal tax laws. Among this latter number were several from the mountain areas of the southern states, whose entire life had been centered around the manufacturing of illicit whiskey. Many of them, unschooled formally, ekeing out a living in the harsh scrub land of the Appalachian range turned to the still for a cash crop. They were philosophical about the game of hide-and-seek they played with the "Feds." There was little indication that they would turn to any other avenue upon being released. They knew nothing else, their training fitted them for no other task, and their inherent sense of independence handed down from generation to generation, only whetted the instincts of self-preservation in the only way they knew. When a "cash crop" was needed, the still would provide it.

There were others, too. One was a former banker. While Sober was confined for a "technicality," this prisoner was being held for the embezzlement of $100,000. Within two weeks after being admitted, he began talking about the time he would be released. "Oh, yes," he emphatically declared, "I'll be out shortly. I could be released any time."

His prognostication was correct, because by the grapevine within the farm walls, Sober learned that any number which carried an "A" before it, could be released at any time. So the man who bilked the depositors of $100,000 served less time than the man who had been adjudged guilty of knowledge of "kickbacks," and because he had signed a call statement without knowing for sure that the figures thereon were backed by cash, bonds and other securities. He had followed a practice used by other bankers for years and years.

[208]

As day followed day, and week followed week, the routine into which the inmates lapsed was broken occasionally. Besides the church services, occasional visits by a choir from one of the Amish groups not too far distant from the farm, forums, among the prisoners were held on occasion. Sober was approached one day and asked if he would participate in a forum on "Banking." "Aw, I don't know about banking. If I did, I wouldn't be here." Finally, he was persuaded to participate and instead of dealing with the formal subject of banking, he urged his fellow prisoners to re-establish their credit when they were released.

"Don't let it get you into further trouble," he urged. "If you owe for anything, go immediately to that person or firm and make arrangements to liquidate your debts. You'll be surprised," he continued, "how such action will help you to find your rightful place in society." His talk then outlined some of the pitfalls which one would encounter if credit standing were neglected. From then on the forum centered around this subject, with Sober being plied with question after question.

It wasn't long after this that he was summoned to the Superintendent's office. He was informed that word had reached the "super's" ears, through the grapevine, that his talk had been one of the best the prisoners had heard, and some of those who had slighted the first forum because they believed it to be a dry, uninteresting lecture, were now asking for a repeat performance.

However, many of the days in the camp were marked by dull routine. Sober would rise at the appointed hour, march with the other inmates to breakfast, return to Number Two building to sweep, clean and mop which were his assigned duties.

His associations with the prisoners were on a friendly plane, and he found that, here too, like individuals on the outside, men had their feelings. There were those who were morose and bitter. There were those who took the confinement in their stride and creeping out was the inherent sense of humor that is a distinguishing characteristic of Americans, regardless of the circumstances in which they find themselves.

One day he walked into the portion of the building which was set aside as the barber shop. He found a group centered around Al Barnes, who hobbled around the chair as the scissors went snip, snip, snip. The man destined to wear an artificial leg did not seem to mind his predicament. He had the ability to lift the spirits of others.

"Hey, Sobers," a fellow inmate yelled, "don't you think Al is a good looking fellow?"

"Why, sure," Sober replied as he joined the group.

"Then ask him," the inmate prodded, "why he never got married."

Sober entered into the game. Barnes seemed to be enjoying it as much as the others.

"I'll bet you never had a girl," Sober stated.

In a drawl that placed Barnes as a resident of the southern hills, he answered, "I shure did." There was a twinkle in his eye as he waited for the next question.

"Well, now, why didn't you marry her?"

"One day when I was up to her house, her pappy came in, an' he said to her, you tell that young man you go home and read Proverbs 25:17. She did. I went and I read. Knowin' her pappy, I never went back."

"Well, what's Proverbs 25:17?" Sober asked.

"You kin look that up fer yourself," chuckled Barnes.

Sober lost no time in wading through the snow to the library, only to find it closed. Again, when he knew the library would be open, he sought the answer to be found in Proverbs 25:17.

Sober opened the Book and read, "Withdraw thy foot from thy neighbor's house; lest he be weary of thee, and so hate thee." Sober had his answer.

All were not light-hearted and gay. There were days of mental anguish and torture. Sober awakened one night to hear the terrible retching of one sick. He tried to ignore the sound, but couldn't. He arose and wandered between the rows of cots. He could make out the dim outlines of the figures who were trying to escape their plight in the solace of sleep. There were snores, groans, grunts and an occasional mumble as he made his way to the toilets at the end of the building, from whence the sound of retching was coming.

Upon going into the room he found Cypher leaning over a toilet. Between the spasms of agony, Sober questioned him as to his trouble. Cypher was thinking of his home, his wife who was trying to carry on. It was only another example of the torture inflicted, because one had acceded to the desires of another, who was to later turn against him.

Sober returned to his cot. He could find no sleep. The trial was gone over and over. Other questions arose to bother him. "Why," Sober wondered, "were we the ones chosen to pay a penalty to society? What about the officers in the banks who were part of the television quiz scandal, whose very participation in this quiz show gave authenticity to a deliberate misrepresentation? Didn't they know the answers that were in their safes had already been given to someone else? Where were the bank examiners in these cases, or were these banks too big to handle?"

Question after question went through his mind. There was no sleep. The light of a cold gray January dawn began to dispel the darkness. Sober pulled himself from the cot and sat on its edge. The "whys" of a thousand and one questions went through his mind. His thoughts were broken by the buzzer summoning the inmates to arise and begin another day.

It was only a day or two later that Dr. Heineman who was also a prisoner was seen pacing the floor. He ignored all of his fellow inmates. Sober's curiosity was aroused. "What the devil's the matter with you, Doc?"

"Matter with me? You should know! They take a man away from what has been his life. I can't help but wonder what has happened to some of my patients. Whatever I've done, I'm still a doctor, and Sober, whatever has been said about me — no one has ever questioned my ability or my ethics as far as the medical profession goes. Here I am nothing."

The occasional name of one of his former patients could be heard as he continued pacing the floor.

Dr. Heineman was a doctor whose first concern was his patients at any hour of the day or night.

There was another occasion when Sober was summoned to the office. As he walked in, the Superintendent glared at him, "Sober, you have been informed of the regulations here. What do you mean by this!" He waved his hand at a pile of parcels in the corner of the room. "You know very well that you are only permitted one package at Christmas—2 pounds of shelled nuts and 2 pounds of candy total 4 pounds."

"Well, I didn't ask for them. You know all my mail is read. I haven't asked for a thing," Sober replied.

"Open 'em," ordered the Superintendent.

Sober complied. He began tearing the wrappers off the parcels. There were boxes of cigars, candy, cigarettes, cookies, handkerchiefs and many other small articles which people, who had remembered, thought he might find useful.

At the Christmas season, there had been those who remembered. He was told to leave the cigars in the office, and was given permission to distribute the candy and cookies and other edibles among his fellow inmates.

[212]

The Superintendent relaxed slightly, "Now get this Sober, 1 don't want this to happen again."

"Maybe the same people will remember me next year, and I won't be able to tell them to stop . . ."

"You won't be here next year," yelled the head. Then he muttered as Sober cleaned up the wrappings, "I don't know what you're doing here anyway."

Chapter XV

THE DAWN
OF TRUTH

WHEN A WORK has been disrupted, it is sometimes difficult to pick up the threads where one has ceased to work. With Sober the job of picking up the threads to begin repairing the rent in his life was doubly difficult. A term in prison is not the easiest thing to shrug off as a bad dream. Such an experience is real. In a sense while fully aware of the activities which take place on the outside, the everyday contacts are missing. Sober was to realize this more and more when he returned as an ex-convict. There were those who had passed from this vale of tears; there were those who had been uprooted from the local climes and had settled in other parts; there were those whose interests had changed and then, too, they wanted to have no part of anyone who had a "record." Such is the way of life.

Sober called on a doctor for a physical check-up. The anxiety, coupled with the worry of the trials, hearings, appeals and prison life had taken its toll. Yet, being rather philosophical, Sober later declared to a friend, "You know, I've always believed there is a reason for everything. If I'd have kept working in the bank those long hours — fourteen, eighteen hours a day — I probably wouldn't be here today. Anyway, always said I'd take time for a check-up, but I never did. I think the Almighty had a hand in things. I have been spared to do something — I'll never believe anything else. It may be to show what really goes on in the banking business."

To say that no bitterness existed, would be false. However, Sober's main theme dwelt on his own and the vindication of his associates.

Sober began making his residence in a Pittsburgh hotel. He found that his first days of freedom were occupied with myriad small tasks. His son had cared for many matters for him. Lawyers had taken care of others, but still there were those things which he alone could do. It had been a trying day. He had in some instances felt the aversion toward him as he returned to face people with whom he had done business previously. There were times when he felt good. There were those who welcomed him warmly and in their various ways showed that they wanted to help.

The question confronting him at the time was what useful and gainful occupation should be followed. He knew that as a result of the conviction, that banking business would be barred for years — perhaps for his life. It had been his life. What does a man do who is not versed in other fields?

His shoulders drooped as he returned to his hotel. He was tired. Automatically he walked to the desk and asked for his mail. He chuckled inwardly to himself. What mail would he be getting? The clerk turned to his box and brought forth a letter which he placed in Sober's hand. Sober looked at the corner return address. It bore a familiar name "Burkett, 1039 Nelson Ave., Brackenridge, Pa." His hand shook as he re-read the address. What in the thunder do these people want with me, thought Sober. Haven't they done enough damage already?

He slowly tore the end off the envelope, and pulled out a letter

[215]

on fine paper. Even before he opened it, he could see through the back that it had been typed. This was added reason for concern. The Burketts did not have a typewriter. What kind of a legal form could this be? There is always a questionable attitude when mail, prior to the prison term, consisted mainly of legal documents. "Well," thought Sober, "I might as well face this too." He unfolded the letter. The imprint bore the name of Irving Sikov, Attorney at Law. It was dated August 4, 1961.

Sober read on:

Rolf L. Larson, Esq.
Room 1002 Sherwyn Hotel
Pittsburgh 22, Pa.

Dear Mr. Larson:

I have your letter of August 2, 1961, to Dr. Richard W. Heineman, in re Mr. and Mrs. John Burkett.

I have been directed to advise you that there is no money due by Dr. Heineman to the Burketts. I might also add that I am personally well aware of what transactions these people have had which involve Dr. Heineman. They have, so far, managed to defraud everyone in the community with whom they have had any business dealings and have earned for themselves a reputation for being notorious prevaricators.

With full knowledge of the case, it is not hard for me to understand Dr. Heineman's shocked reaction to this new piece af brazenness on the part of these people, who, in a sworn statement, admit they testified under oath falsely to convict Dr. Heineman in hopes of getting money.

Very truly yours,

(Signed)   Irving Sikov
IRVING SIKOV

At the bottom of the letter, was this penned note:

1039 Nelson Ave.
Brackenridge, Pa.
August 6, 1961

Dear Mr. Sober:

We are sending you this letter and asking for Mr. Canaday's address, as he was the government man from F.D.I.C. along with Mr. Gardner that promised us that we would get our money back if the statement we made along with testimony convicts you.

(Signed) Mrs. Sylvia J. Burkett
John Burkett

See Documentation Section, pages 14, 15, 16, for actual reproduction of this letter.

Sober was a man of action. He hadn't lost the incentive to move and move quickly. He sat in thought for a moment or two, and slowly tapped the letter against the back of his left hand. "If," he pondered, "the government agents had made offers to the Burketts to the extent that they were seeking his address to be rewarded for their part in the trial what was said to other people?"

Without stopping for something to eat, although it was late in the afternoon, Sober strode through the hotel lobby to the parking lot. He climbed in his car and headed for Freeport. He had little thought as to the party he might see or talk to as he drove the highway that borders the Allegheny River. The sun was glaring down mercilessly. The pavement shimmered in the heat before him. He drove on, unmindful of the discomforts of the weather. The sun was a golden ball which seemingly rested on the top of the western hills as he entered Freeport. One person's name came to mind. It was that of Richard J. DeSalvo. He had known that DeSalvo had been questioned by either FBI personnel or F.D.I.C. examiners before he had been brought to trial.

Sober went to DeSalvo's home on the outskirts of Freeport. He was welcomed warmly. After the usual inquiries concerning his well-being, DeSalvo then launched into a theme Sober was to

[217]

hear in a variety of ways for the next several months. DeSalvo expressed the wish that Sober could return to the bank. He continued by telling Sober that he couldn't get any help from the financial institutions he had gone to, and as a result had lost about everything he had. As the conversation continued Sober asked DeSalvo if he would make a statement relative to the conversation that had taken place when he was visited by the FBI or the examiners.

DeSalvo readily consented.

"What do you want me to say?" DeSalvo inquired of Sober.

"Wait a minute, wait a minute," Sober laughed, "you'd put me in the same spot those other fellows are in. That's what they did — so I'm told — they wrote the statement and then had people sign it. Nope, I won't have a thing to do with it that way. I'd appreciate a statement, but you write what you honestly want to write and swear to it. Then you can give it to me some time again."

"Come back tomorrow evening," DeSalvo ordered. "I'll have that statement for you and it will be in my own words and just what happened."

The sworn statement which Sober was to receive read in part:

That during August 1958 Mr. Higgins and Mr. Pudester from the F.B.I. came to my house to ask me questions about the Old Freeport Bank and what connection I had with Charles Sober. I answered their questions to the best of my knowledge, but this did not seem to satisfy them. I asked them to act as gentlemen and I would do the same. They twisted their questions around several times. I asked if I was on the witness stand the way they kept at me. They said that did I know that I could go to jail if I did not cooperate with them in their investigation. So they started all over again. I gave the same answers to the questions. They again said I was lying and said what could happen to me if I did not tell them the truth. They said I could be prosecuted and sent to jail. This made me angry as I was telling them the truth at all times. I asked them to come outside for I could see they were upsetting my wife and daughter. They insisted I was not telling everything so I told them to leave.

See Documentation Section, page 5, for actual reproduction of this letter.

The word soon spread through the area that Sober had been around and had been seen. Requests for visits on his part began to multiply. It was with trepidation that he began to make some calls, but in most instances his fears were allayed. There were literally hundreds of "little people" who found that with Sober removed, banking facilities were inadequate or that banks did not want to bother with them. At the same time these people, small as they were in the scheme of our lives, were big enough to recognize the strength in truth and justice. They had not sold their birthright for a mess of pottage as offered by the agents of their government. They had and they did stand for truth.

While sworn statement after sworn statement began to come to Sober, one glaring thing stood out. The statements not only showed the makers' belief in Sober's integrity, but many of them detailed a pattern of intimidation used by government representatives in many instances.

Among the many who believed in the right to defend integrity was Richard Becker of the City of Lower Burrell, near New Kensington, Pa. His sworn statement follows:

I, Richard Becker, was approached in 1958 at a Service Station by an F.B.I. man on questions of a loan at the Old Freeport Bank of Freeport, Pa. I told this man about a $300 loan plus a truck I bought at the same time from the Old Freeport Bank for $900.00. He said that he couldn't understand. He thought I gave the $300 to Mr. Sober. Then later an F.B.I. man stopped at my home. I told this man that I

[219]

was given a loan for $1200.00. This was for a truck (1954 model Ford ¾ ton) which the bank repossessed and was selling the truck at $900.00. My father signed the note for $1200.00. This note was for a $300.00 loan plus the truck of $900.00. Therefore I received the $300.00 above the $900.00 making the loan $1200.00. The F.B.I. said you gave the $300.00 to a Mr. Sober. I said no. He insisted I did. My father was in the adjoining room and he heard this. He came out and said "no one accuses my children falsely." He then told the man to leave the house. My father was astonished that an F.B.I. man deliberately tried to intimidate me.

See Documentation Section, page 6, for actual reproduction of this letter.

Such statements as this has led to the question of what would have happened to the boy had his father not been present to defend him, and to further instill the lesson that "truth is truth" regardless of whom one faces.

As the affidavits multipled, there were more and more in this same category. Clarence Rogers and his wife Thelma faced similar accusations. Their statement regarding the visits from representatives of the Federal agencies reads as follows:

In 1958 two Federal Bureau of Investigation men came to our home (82 N. Canal St., Natrona, Pa.), wanting us to sign a statement, which they had prepared before they came saying we paid extra money or a kickback of one thousand dollars when we borrowed money from the Old Freeport Bank to buy our home. I told these men, in my office (Justice of the Peace) I had people make out statements of their own with their own free will not prepared one like they had. My wife and I told them above men that the above statement wasn't true and that we wouldn't sign anything to that effect. The above men insisted that we weren't telling the truth. So, I told them to leave my home which they did.

A few days later Alonzo Canaday and another man came to our home. When my wife went to the door, these men identified themselves as Federal Insurance Corporation men. They asked if they could come in. My wife said they could if they would be gentlemen and not stinkers like the other two F.B.I. men, who had been here a few days earlier. My wife told these men that we were tired of being bothered and being told we lied by men who are supposed to be officers of the law. Mr. Canaday said we wouldn't be bothered any more and left.

See Documentation Section, page 7, for actual reproduction of this letter.

For some strange reason representatives of the Federal agencies were intent on making a case out of the matter. When the original investigation was taking place, they were not dealing with hardened criminals. They were dealing with "little people," whose crime had been, apparently, dealing with Sober in the Old Freeport Bank.

Satisfaction must have been great when the agents interviewed such people as Dorothy M. and Joseph E. Eck of R. D. 1, Corsica, Pa. Their volunteered statement which came when they discovered that Sober was making an effort to be reinstated reads:

To whom it may concern

During the examination of the Old Freeport Bank, Freeport, Pa., conducted by Alonzo Canaday in 1958, we were approached by two men at our place of business Camp Joan, Box 877, New Kensington, Pa., and asked if we accepted a bribe or paid a bribe on our loan or whether we knew of anyone who did accept a kick-back on loans. And we told them no sir, to both questions that we did not pay anyone connected with the bank or loan. After several months we lost our place of business and home because the bank would not go along with us and refinance or lower our payments.

[221]

And we feel that if Charles or Ira Sober had been at the bank at the time of our troubles they would have gone along with us, and we would have been able to keep our place of business & our home to this day."

See Documentation Section, page 8, for actual reproduction of this letter.

The case of the Ecks was doubly tragic, because at the time they sought help and were turned down by a bank or banks, they had already paid on their mortgage to the extent of $15,000. Such was their equity in their home and business.

But the Federal agents were not satisfied with the Eck answers. The Ecks had purchased the property and business from a Mr. and Mrs. (   ) Bell, who, since the sale, had moved to Arizona.

One day Mr. Bell looked out of the window in his home in Arizona to see the sheriff's car pull up in front of the door. Bell later related that one of the men alighting from the car identified himself as an FBI agent, and had stated that he had come to ask some questions regarding the sale of their (the Bells') property. The agent found the stories of the Ecks and the Bells were similar, but the visit of the sheriff to these comparative newcomers was not lost upon Bell's neighbors. It was some time after that that the Bells were able to establish themselves in the community. The relentless efforts to find evidence against Sober did have the result of planting seeds which produced bitter fruits for the innocent.

Even more startling was the statement of James Sawyer, who at the time of Sober's arrest and conviction, was the Sales Manager for the Allegheny Steel Spring Company of Springdale. Sawyer's words reiterate the story of his employer, William D. Rhodes, who warned Sober that he was being investigated and that something was wrong in July of 1958.

Sawyer declared:

I, James Sawyer, being duly sworn according to law, deposes and says that I am a resident of the State of Ohio; that I make this affidavit on its behalf being authorized so to do; and the facts set forth herein are true and correct; and that I make this statement of my own free will. During May, June and July of 1958 I was the Sales Manager of the Allegheny Valley Steel Company, Inc., and was present on several occasions when Frank Irvine, Sr., President of the First National Bank of Tarentum now known as the Union Bank of Pittsburgh, came to see Mr. William D. Rhodes and told him that Mr. Alonzo Canaday, an investigator for the Federal Deposit Insurance Corporation, was going to examine our records in connection with the company's account at the Old Freeport Bank of Freeport, Pennsylvania and Lower Burrell, Pennsylvania. The said Mr. Irvine told Mr. Rhodes in my presence, "any help that he could give Mr. Canaday would be a personal favor to him." Also in my presence the said Mr. Canaday and Mr. Frank Irvine, Jr., son of the above bank president, had in their possession photostatic copies of the Old Freeport Bank Records, which Mr. Canaday had placed in custody with Mr. Irvine, Jr.

During the investigation in my presence, Messrs. Canaday, Irvine, Sr., Irvine, Jr., and John Brown, an investigator for the F.D.I.C., tried to convince Mr. Rhodes to testify that Mr. Charles Sober, then President of the Old Freeport Bank, of being guilty of misconduct in his bank transactions with Mr. Rhodes and our company. The truth of the matter was both Mr. Rhodes and I knew of our own personal knowledge, that Mr. Sober was not guilty of the misconduct they accused him of.

Also in my presence, Mr. Canaday, on several occasions told Mr. Rhodes to change his account from the Old Freeport Bank to the First National Bank of Tarentum if he wanted to stay in business.

[223]

On countless occasions I was present when Mr. Canaday called Mr. Rhodes, usually late at night, from Pittsburgh, Pennsylvania, trying to convince him to perjure himself in testimony against Sober.

The above statements were made in my presence, in the presence of Mr. Rhodes and also in the presence of his Secretary, Mrs. Evelyn Gamble, who was secretary and comptroller, had been happy to give above testimony under oath to proper governmental agent or agencies.

See Documentation Section, pages 9-10, for actual reproduction of this letter.

The Mr. Rhodes referred to in Sawyer's sworn statement, had more to say concerning the activities of Canaday and the Irvines, Sr. and Jr. He, too, was caught in the web of legal injustice and as a result had to close his plant. The financial help offered when efforts were being made to convict the unorthodox banker, was withdrawn when the conviction was secured.

Rhodes, like many another young man of the period, had served his country. At one time he was a member of the United States Marine Corps and during his course of action had been decorated for meritorious service. Like many other veterans, he was loath to talk of his activities while in the service. He returned to his native land and after a few years as an employee of others, organized the company mentioned in the previous statement. With a dream of starting on a shoestring and building a business, he had laid the groundwork for such a venture five years prior to the time he had met Sober.

It was sometime during the early part of January in 1958 that Rhodes, accompanied by a Dr. McClowery, approached Sober relative to making a loan. As the story unfolded they had previously gone to the First National Bank in Tarentum and had been turned down. The story seemed plausible to the Old Freeport Bank officials, and at the same time such an account looked

[224]

like good business for the bank. Dr. McClowery offered to put up ten thousand dollars in U. S. Treasury 90 day notes, while Rhodes submitted 350 shares of stock in his company with a value of fifty-five thousand dollars. Before granting the loan, an examination of the Company's assets was made and the loan was granted. It consisted of one ten thousand dollar note and three notes of five thousand dollars each.

The arrangement was working satisfactorily for all parties concerned until about the first of June when Dr. McClowery told Rhodes that he would like to get off the note.

Rhodes visited Sober in the bank during the latter part of June and told him of Dr. McClowery's request and at the same time informed Sober that a C. L. Schmitt and Frank Irvine, Jr., manager of the Lower Burrell Branch of the First National Bank of Tarentum, had contacted him. They had stated that the members of the board of the bank which they represented, would like to take another look at the Rhodes plant, so that industrial growth and development could be forwarded in the area.

Even though it was a direct reversal of an attitude displayed by the bank some six months earlier, Rhodes turned from the Old Freeport Bank to the First National Bank of Tarentum.

In his sworn statement he writes:

> He (Irvine, Sr.), told me at that time in the presence of my Sales Manager, James Sawyer, that a fellow by the name of Canaday from the Federal Deposit Insurance Corporation, was coming to examine my records in connection with my account at the Old Freeport Bank. The gentleman I referred to is Mr. Alonzo Canaday, an investigator with the F.D.I.C. Mr. Irvine told me, "any help I can give Canaday would be a personal favor to him."
>
> Shortly thereafter, the said Mr. Canaday came to visit me and tried to have me testify against Mr. Charles Sober, whom

he had under investigation at the time. And in the above named Mr. Sawyer's presence, Mr. Canaday, on several occasions told me to change my account from the Old Freeport Bank to the First National Bank of Tarentum if I wanted to stay in business.

On at least 50 occasions thereafter Mr. Canaday called me either at my home or office from the Pittsburgher Hotel in Pittsburgh, Pennsylvania, usually very late at night, trying to convince me to testify that Sober was guilty of misconduct in his bank transactions with me and my company in connection with a loan I had obtained from Mr. Sober. The truth of the matter was that Mr. Sober had not been guilty of any misconduct in his dealings with me, nor did I know of any incident in which Mr. Sober was guilty of misconduct in his dealings with anyone and I so told Mr. Canaday.

During the F.D.I.C.'s investigation of Mr. Sober, the aforesaid Mr. Canaday, Mr. Frank Irvine, Sr. Mr. Frank Irvine, Jr., and Mr. John Brown, also an F.D.I.C. investigator, tried to convince me to testify against Mr. Sober. . . . Also during this investigation, Mr. Canaday and Mr. Frank Irvine, Jr., son of the above named bank president and in the presence of Mr. Sawyer, brought into my office photostatic copies of the Old Freeport Bank's records which Mr. Canaday had turned over to Mr. Irvine, Jr., to have photostated.

It was apparent to me that Messrs. Irvine, Sr., and Irvine, Jr., were extremely good friends of Messrs. Canaday and Brown.

In late May, 1958, I was taken to the Lower Burrell branch of the First National Bank of Tarentum to attend a Board meeting in connection with my application for a loan from that bank. Present at this meeting were the Messrs. Irvine, Sr., Irvine, Jr., and other officials of the bank. They told me at that time they were out to get Mr. Charles Sober, because they wanted to stop him from putting a branch bank in Lower Burrell, which would be in competition with their branch bank at the same place. I had applied several times before for a loan with Mr. Irvine's bank, which he had turned down until the time he wanted me to testify against Mr. Charles Sober for an alleged misconduct.

The government subsequently subpoenaed me as a witness in Mr. Sober's trial but never let me tell the above story.

(Signed) William D. Rhodes

See Documentation Section, pages 11, 12, 13, for actual reproduction of this letter.

Rhodes story was interesting in other ways too. He told Sober, after the latter was released from prison, that the First National Bank in Tarentum gave him the required service for a time, and then withdrew that service. One of the withdrawn services was that of factoring accounts. (When a bank factors the account of an individual, company or corporation it receives the account of work completed, and advances funds against this completed work until it is paid for by the customer. When the customer pays, the bank will receive the payment of the note, and charge for the service given.) Factoring of accounts provides working capital for a firm.

Anyway, this service was withdrawn. Rhodes always felt that the offer of the service in the first place was an attempt to get him to be a witness against Sober.

It was a bitter and disillusioned Rhodes who after having closed his plant told Sober, "You know, Charlie, I was subpoenaed by both sides. I was never called. Perhaps I should have, on my own, gone in and told my story. I didn't know whether this would be the thing to do. I was trying to hold the business together. I didn't want to see all my work go down the drain, nor did I want to see my stockholders lose everything. I'm like a lot of people, Charlie, I sat back when I should have gotten up and yelled."

There were some others who should have gotten up and yelled at the same time. Among the affidavits which came in were those from the people who have been numbered as the principal witnesses for the government.

The Burketts swore:

> To whom this statement may concern. I Sylvia J. Burkett and John Burkett, were promised by Alonzo Canaday examiner from the F.D.I.C. that the statement we would make to convict Charles L. Sober and others, that if they were convicted we would get our money back.
>
> Mr. Alonzo Canaday also told us he personally would see to it himself, that he would bring it up to the Board of Directors of the F.D.I.C.
>
> During the Court Trial I was asked by the Defendants Attorney Alexander Cooper if we were promised our property back. I Sylvia J. Burkett said no. But if Mr. Cooper would of asked me if we were promised anything, I would of answered him yes we were promised our money back.
>
> We were told to study our statements and say nothing more by the Government Attorneys. The statements we are referring to, were worded by Alonzo Canaday, and typed by Mr. Gardner from the F.D.I.C. Corp.
>
> (Signed)   John Burkett
Sylvia J. Burkett

(Dated) 20th day of January
      A. D. 1962

See Documentation Section, pages 14, 15, 16, for actual reproduction of this letter.

Sober was showing the statement to a friend. "How in the world did you get that?" he was questioned.

"Well, now," Sober replied, "I got a call one night that the Burketts wanted to see me. You know, I was almost afraid to go. It turned out that they wanted some help. Me? I couldn't help them. The trial and troubles I've had just about wiped me out. I told them so. I said that the best thing they could do was tell the truth. Of course they wanted to know how that could be done. I told them to make a statement and just tell the truth. It came to me a couple of days later."

Sober paused, and then more to himself than to his companion, continued, "Most of them that turned against me when I was in trouble, can't seem to find help now, even from the ones they were supposed to help."

The surprise came when a statement was handed Sober by Al Tarr, who had been a witness for the defense, whom the government would not let tell his story.

Sober glanced at the bottom for the signature. It was signed by Leo Gallagher and Mrs. Leo Gallagher.

"How'd you get this?" Sober asked Tarr.

"I'se in there one day and Gallagher asks me how you're getting along. I told him that you were trying to be cleared. He told me that he hadn't seen you since the trial and he wondered if you was still mad at him. Sobers, I said to him, the best thing you can do is to tell the truth. He wanted to know how and I told him to make a statement and swear to it. He gave it to me a couple of days later. Here it is and I sure hope it helps you Sobers," and with the conclusion of his words Tarr handed Sober a legal form.

In part it reads as follows:

"We knew Dr. Heineman and went to him and offered his $2,000 as we had offered to other people, if he would put up security for us. He put up $8,000 in the form of a Certificate of Deposit, which was assigned to the Old Freeport Bank as security.

We didn't pay on our loan at the bank for nine months, because we were putting too much money in our business, improving the property and furnishings. About a year later we were able to get the money from another bank, because of these improvements which increased the value of our property.

In 1958 a Mr. Canaday, an F.D.I.C. agent came to us and said that if we would make a statement, we could get our $2,000 back. This $2,000 involved a deal between us and the doctor concerning some construction machinery which included a bulldozer. The government agents kept coming to us until we got scared and did what the government men told us to do. We signed several statements written by them, one being signed during the trial of Mr. Sober. Such a long time has passed between the time we made the loan at the Old Freeport Bank and these statements that we may have said things at the trial that weren't true. Also at the trial, when we were testifying, no one questioned us or brought out the deal concerning the construction machinery which involved the $2,000. We never did know why we made so many statements."

See Documentation Section, page 17, for actual reproduction of this letter.

Even the man who had tried to make things right with his conscience during the hearing for a new trial, produced this statement:

During the late fall of 1957 when we were trying to secure a loan to pay off the Old Freeport Bank in Freeport, Pa., and additional money to expand our business we went to Mr. Samuel Kauffman who was an officer of the First National Bank of Freeport, Pa. After hearing our story he told us he could not handle our loan at this time. He told us that Mr. C. L. Sober an officer of the Old Freeport Bank would not be there long as his (meaning Mr. Kauffman) connections with Frank Irvine, Sr. a member of the Federal

Reserve Board and President of the First National Bank of Tarentum now known as the Union Bank of Pittsburgh, had connections and political power with the controller of currency who was a director in the Federal Deposit Insurance Corp., and also a friend of Attorney Coburn counsel for the Federal Deposit Insurance Corp., were going to get charges against C. L. Sober an officer of the Old Freeport Bank. C. L. Sober and others were arrested in late 1958 and came to trial in early 1959. I was a witness at the trial and did not have an opportunity to explain the answers I gave. Also my wife was never called to testify at the trial. However, my wife was called to the stand at the hearing for a retrial but again was not given a chance to testify before a jury. Also the court appointed lawyer that I talked with told me that I should not change anything I had said at the trial.

(Signed) Gustave C. Heyman
Maria Heyman
6491 Iroquois Trail
Mentor, Ohio

See Documentation Section, page 18, for actual reproduction of this letter.

Even the government could not refrain from using tactics that would be frowned upon had they been tried by other people. Canaday took records from the Old Freeport Bank and turned them over to Irvine, Jr., to have them photostated. It made no difference that bank records are supposedly inviolate; these records could and possibly were perused by a competitor.

Jack C. Reese, one of the convicted bankers, swore to this statement:

> . . . that during the examination of The Old Freeport Bank of Freeport, Pa. in 1958, the officers of the bank were told that some records of The Old Freeport Bank were being photostated at Edwards Studio in Tarentum, Pa., by an officer of the First National Bank of Tarentum, Pa. We

were concerned and began trying to find out if this was true and how they were getting the records.

On Tuesday, August 5, 1958, Ira L. Sober and I confronted Mr. John P. Brown, Chief Examiner of the F.D.I.C. in my office and questioned him about taking bank records out of the bank without notifying the officers of the bank. He admitted to us that records had been taken out of the bank and said "What did we do that was so bad." He also admitted at this time that the F.D.I.C. Examiners had had several meetings with Frank Irvine of The First National Bank of Tarentum, Pa.

On Saturday, August 9, 1958, I went to see Mr. Schenk, the owner of Edwards Studio, however, I was unable to locate him at that time. At 8:30 the same evening, Leonard J. Rychlik, a Justice of the Peace in Lower Burrell Twp., Pa. and I went to Mr. Schenk's home and waited until 11:30 but he did not return home.

On Sunday, August 10, 1958, I made three trips to Mr. Schenk's home and finally found him on the third trip. I immediately returned to New Kensington to get Mr. Rychlik and went back to Mr. Schenk's home, hoping to get a sworn statement. Mr. Schenk admitted to Mr. Rychlik and myself that Frank Irvine, Jr., of The First National Bank of Tarentum, Pa., had come into his studio within the past ten days with another man whom he did not know (his description of the man fitted Mr. Canaday of the F.D.I.C.) to have records of The Old Freeport Bank photostated. He said that he did not know what records they were, but could identify them if he saw them. We asked him who paid the bill, and he stated he had not yet been paid. He would not give us a sworn statement.

See Documentation Section, pages 19-20, for actual reproduction of this letter.

Thus principles and minors in the case of the "lollypop" bank came forward with story after story and letter after letter to defend Sober, and hope for his reinstatement.

While Sober was busy hearing the story of many of these people and getting them to put their thoughts on paper, his son, Ira, was carrying petitions.

In brief, the petitions which were signed by hundreds of residents in Freeport and the immediate area, appealed to the powers that be to have the Sobers and Jack Reese reinstated in the bank. The reasons for signing were many. There were some few who carried in their hearts a deep hatred of Sober personally and of the methods he employed. These would not sign. However, their influence went unheeded by others.

Kenneth Miller a resident of Freeport expressed the thought of many when the topic of Sober's conviction was discussed. Miller said, "I don't know whether the man was guilty or not. He's served his sentence and in my book after a man has paid his debt to society, it isn't right to keep him from his work." A second thought came as he walked away from the group. He turned, and continued speaking, "Look at your town — our town — look at it now. One thing Sober did was to put some life into it." Miller walked slowly past the darkened window of an empty storeroom.

Even the matter of circulating petitions was not without its difficulties. Ira turned a petition, bearing several names over to a friend, who in turn promised to get some additional signatures. A few days later the friend approached Ira. He averted his eyes and shuffled his feet. Finally he muttered, "You aren't going to like what I've to say, Ira, but someone stole that petition from my desk. I don't know who or why. Listen, Ira, I'll carry another one, I'll make it right, I'll . . ." The victim was at a loss for words to express his feelings.

One other petition was lost. No one knows where it went or

who had it. It just disappeared. It too carried many names of people who favored the return of the bankers.

As the summer months roled on, Sober was jubilant, that most of the people he had contacted and even those who had heard of his efforts and had contacted him, expressed a strong desire to see him return to the bank. As he pondered this turn of events, he thought about the letter that the former U. S. Attorney had sent him.

August 11, 1961

Mr. Charles Sober
Hotel Webster Hall
4415 Fifth Avenue
Pittsburgh 13, Pennsylvania
Dear Mr. Sober:

In accordance with our discussion, I met with the General Counsel of the Federal Deposit Insurance Corporation in Washington, D. C. recently and discussed with him the possibility of your requalifying for employment in a bank insured by that corporation.

I was advised that the proper procedure is to request the appropriate form and data from the supervising examiner of the corporation, Mr. Mounts, at Columbus, Ohio. This form must be secured by the bank desiring to employ you. Generally the bank should submit that form through Mr. Mounts along with accompanying data, the nature of which Mr. Mounts will suggest.

Generally, the General Counsel suggested that along with a certified copy of the indictment and sentence of the court, information should be submitted from people who are knowledgable in the banking field. It was suggested that bankers in this general area would be best qualified to judge whether such re-employment would be advisable and the Board would give greater weight to letters from such individuals.

As I orally advised you the General Counsel suggested that such reinstatements are not generally considered favorably until a period of five years has elapsed so that rehabilitation can more effectively be determined.

I will be pleased to discuss this matter with you further at any time you may desire.

Very truly yours,

HIT/rmp   (Signed)   Hubert I. Teitelbaum

See Documentation Section, page 21, for actual reproduction of this letter.

Sober paid a visit to the Attorney at his office in the Frick Building, he was ushered into Teitelbaum's office. Teitelbaum extended his hand. Sober hesitated a moment and then took it. There was some probing on the part of the former U. S. Attorney who had been instrumental in putting Sober behind the bars. Here were two men who had played a serious game—one had been the victor and the other the loser. The vanquished—at the moment—had lost a great deal. Even though to his own satisfaction and to the satisfaction of his friends he had proven his innocence, the stigma of "convict" hung to him. The prejudging as the result of news stories and thousands who had read these stories saw only a law violator.

Now, the two men sat face to face with only a desk separating them.

Teitelbaum cleared his throat, "Well, Sober, how are you getting along?"

"Oh, I'm making out all right. I just came in for a little help." Sober replied.

"Help! What do you mean? How can I help you?" was Teitelbaum's startled question.

Sober launched into his story. He told the man who had prosecuted him how he was trying to be re-instated in the bank, and finally made his wants known. He wanted a letter.

"What do you want in the letter?" Teitelbaum again questioned.

"I'm not telling you what to put in," Sober said. "You handled

[235]

the case against us and you know all the details. Just put in what you want to."

Teitelbaum looked Sober directly in the eyes. Sober returned his stare. "I'll do it," volunteered the attorney. "Wait right here." He then disappeared into the outer office. Within a few minutes he returned to Sober and handed him an envelope. Sober drew a piece of heavy bond paper from the enclosure. It crackled as he unfolded it. He read:

To whom it may concern:

I am writing on behalf of Charles L. Sober, Ira L. Sober and Jack Reese. All three were convicted for certain violations of federal law during the time when I was United States Attorney for the Western District of Pennsylvania and in charge of the prosecutions. The offenses which they committed were for violation of banking laws but to the best of my knowledge did not involve any personal dishonesty since I do not believe that any of the three received any personal financial gain. Their violations were for a sort that involved breaches of regulations which had been codified into criminal offenses without involving any necessity of receiving moneys for their own benefits.

I have since had frequent occasion to talk with Mr. Charles Sober, and I am personally convinced that his rehabilitation has been complete.

The bank with whom they were connected prior to their convictions remained in excellent financial condition and was not in any way hurt by the offenses which they committed.

Very truly yours,
(Signed)   Hubert I. Teitelbaum

See Documentation Section, page 22, for actual reproduction of this letter.

"Is that all right?" the attorney queried.

"That is fine, just fine. Thank you very much." Sober rose, shook hands with his one-time opponent and walked out of the office.

Chapter XVI

THE BATTLE
CONTINUES

THE MATERIAL — sworn statements, petitions, letters and the like — gathered by the recent defendant convinced him more than ever that there had been a grave injustice. The fact that he had been found guilty, along with his son and Jack Reese, of false entry because he had signed an FDIC call report, led him to believe that every banker in the country would therefore be guilty of the same offense. Since law is based on previous findings of the court, and since this had been the first time that individuals had ever been tried on such a charge, then all who signed such reports without first verifying that every cent of cash, all of the bonds, items for collections were as represented by those in charge of the books would be guilty.

Perhaps, some of those who through giving vent to the baser emotions of human nature and had been instrumental in having Sober put in prison and withheld from reentering the banking business, might someday be caught in the web of their own weaving. This was not the primary purpose Sober had in continuing the battle. First, he desired to be vindicated, and second, he began to foresee the control which could be exercised over little and big bankers throughout the nation. To him, it was a battle well worth the efforts. By his very nature, he was not a quitter, and having paid a penalty to society, even though an unjust penalty, Sober made plans to face those in the high echelons who had been a part of the unseen and unidentifiable power to grasp him in forceps designed to bring individuals into a set pattern that stifles initiative, individualism and progress.

Sober decided that in fairness to all of the departments, which had been interested in his case and subsequent conviction, should be advised of every move that he had made since he had been released from prison. When he received the following communication, he started to move:

Dear Mr. Sober

The records of this office indicate that you have completed the period of Federal sentence on which you were released for supervision.

Sentence began 11-28-60

Supervision ended 11-27-61

Therefore, this letter is forwarded to you as evidence of your discharge from supervision.

(Signed) Joseph N. Shore
Parole Executive

See Documentation Section, page 23, for actual reproduction of this letter.

The material was gathered, photostatic copies were made. There were petitions bearing hundreds of names of people who had been and many of whom still were customers of the Old Freeport Bank. These petitions had been signed for various reasons. Some of the signers frankly admitted that they never did understand the trial and all of its technicalities; there were others who firmly believed that Sober was innocent and had been framed, and still others who exercised that ideal of ideal citizens.

The first stop on a tour that was to include that first weekend in December of 1961, took Sober to Harrisburg and the State Department of Banking. Here he met some of those with whom he had had conference while he had been an official of the Old Freeport Bank. At first on the part of them, there was some reticence as Sober approached them. He had brief conferences with representatives of this department and left with them photostatic copies of the material which had been gathered since he had been released from prison. The agency men with whom he visited at first, with one excuse or another, claimed they hadn't much time being engaged in conferences and the like. However, as they began to peruse the sworn statements, they asked their visitor to remain for a time. The final answer, while in a variety of words, was always the same. It would run something like this, "We're sorry, Charlie, but you know we've always been with you and never held that you were guilty of wrong doing. You'll have to get this matter straightened up in Washington."

The next step of the journey was to Washington, D. C., where on December the 4th, 1961, Sober sought and was given permission to see some of the officers of the FDIC. Again he told his story. Again he left copies of the material. Again there was the attempt at the free friendliness which had existed before the trial, but this was clouded with shadows of reticence on the part of the officials now. Sober could almost see them thinking, "The nerve of this man. He has been tried and convicted. Why does he bother us now?"

Attorney Coburn of the FDIC was gracious and pleasant, yet he would give his visitor no answers to certain queries. Another man, Neil G. Greensides, greeted Sober pleasantly, but he too was guarded in his statements as to what might be done relative to the reinstatement of the banker in his business.

The next stop was at the Justice Department and here too Sober faced that formal politeness and heard the meaningless words that sounded good but in reality meant nothing.

The fighter for justice did not stop. He turned his step in the direction of the office of Congressman Dent, a resident of Westmoreland County. At the time of Sober's visit Dent was busily engaged in hearings as head of the Subcommittee on the Impact of Imports and Exports on American Unemployment. However, Congressman John A. Dent was receptive to Sober's request to be heard, and giving what time he could on that day reviewed in part the statements carried by the one-time banker. He then invited his guest to accompany him as an observer to the hearings scheduled for that day.

Sober relished this opportunity. He would be able to see our government at work. He listened with interest as representatives of labor and industry revealed their plight, the loss of jobs and the loss of revenues, the subsequent closing of plants resulting from the impact of goods produced in the foreign plants with such a difference in divergent costs of materials and labor. As the witnesses droned on telling how their particular groups were being affected adversely, with questions being interspersed here and there, Sober became reflective. Here was a committee fighting to retain jobs and business for its citizens, yet other agencies seemingly strangled business and initiative, thus increasing the unemployment situation. He wondered how the two groups, both representing the same government—the people of the United States—could justify opposite actions.

Sober had retained an attorney to look into his interests in Washington. He reported to his office and what he had done and then returned to the Pittsburgh area. Now, he must try to patiently await the results of his visit.

In the meantime as word spread that Sober was seeking reinstatement and vindication, there were those who sought to help him. His folio of sworn statements grew. People, whom he had befriended and helped as a banker came forward with additional statements. The clouds, so heavy and dark, seemed to be parting and letting shafts of light through to dispel and clear the machinations of deceit and collusion of the previous two years.

Another week revealed that the winds of justice were not going to carry away these clouds easily. There were forces on the other side—just as powerful—which seemingly didn't want the glare of light on certain actions. It wasn't said so in so many words, but by letter the inference was made that action couldn't be taken until certain items were on file. Sober found that this subterfuge was to be used more and more as the fight continued. He would no more than satisfy one request, until another appeared for additional statements or letters.

The awakening to this mode of "putting aside" his appeal was first revealed in a letter from the FDIC. The communication was as follows:

December 14, 1961

Dear Mr. Sober:

On December 4 you visited my office and informed me that photostats of certain material relating to your ambition to become a director of an insured bank had been left in Chairman Cocke's office. I now have reviewed the material and note that this does not constitute an application on the part of the Old Freeport Bank, Freeport, Pennsylvania, or of any other bank and therefore we have no occasion for taking action on the subject of your ambition.

I note also that your attorney, in a letter dated August 11, 1961, advised you of the procedure which would have to be pursued were (sic) any desirous of employing you either as an officer, director, or employee and therefore it will not be necessary for me to go into details as to the requirements of Section 19 of the Federal Deposit Insurance Act.

In absence of further word from you we will hold the photostatic material, which you left, in our general files.

Sincerely yours,

(Signed) Neil G. Greensides

Chief, Division of Examination

See Documentation Section, page 24, for actual reproduction of this letter.

Surely thought Sober, the Justice Department will have some encouraging news. Almost at the same time a letter arrived from the Justice Department and its contents stated that as far as it was concerned, the case was closed. There was no further action to be taken by them.

This material was turned over to Sober's attorney in Washington, J. Anthony Moran.

Sober wondered what legal red tape had to be unscrambled in being reinstated as a director or officer of the bank. Searching his files he found a copy of the following letter written six months previously:

June 7, 1961

Chairman and Board of Directors
Federal Deposit Insurance Corporation
Washington, D. C.

Gentlemen:

We, being all of the directors of the Old Freeport Bank of Freeport, Pennsylvania, wish to advise you that we have full confidence in the honesty, integrity, and ability of Mr. C. L. Sober. In the best interests of the bank, we should like to utilize Mr. C. L. Sober's ability in some capacity, where he can make his greatest contribution to the future success of the Bank.

We are familiar with your regulations governing Mr. C. L. Sober's position on account of his case in the United States District Court for the Western District of Pennsylvania.

[242]

Under the circumstances, we realize that we may not make any move to employ Mr. C. L. Sober unless we obtain your permission and consent. It is for this reason that we write this letter in the hope that you may decide to set aside any restrictions that you may have against Mr. C. L. Sober's association with this Bank. We firmly believe that Mr. Sober is entitled to consideration, and we definitely believe that if we are permitted to have him associate with the Bank, that it will be beneficial to the stockholders of the Bank.

Sincerely,

See Documentation Section, page 25, for actual reproduction of this letter.

The letter was signed by all of the directors of the bank, and heading the list was the signature of H. J. Israel, the president. Israel became the president of the bank shortly after Sober was forced to resign, and it was only through the sale of Sober's stock that he could be in the position which he then held.

As Sober scanned his copy of this letter, he wondered what was necessary to constitute a letter of application for reinstatement. Reviewing his communications the FDIC intimated that for reinstatement, he (Sober) would have to have a bank willing to employ him. Here was a letter which confirmed a willingness, yet the FDIC refused to act. There was a big question to be answered.

It was during the summer of 1961, that Sober met one of his former customers, J. J. Sample, Jr., a former Justice of the Peace, who lives approximately three miles from Freeport. Sample informed Sober that he had been quite interested in his case and had written the Federal Deposit Insurance Corporation in his behalf.

He informed Sober that he was under the impression that he (Sober) had been seeking reinstatement in the Old Freeport Bank through the FDIC.

[243]

Sober replied that he had.

Sample drew a letter from his pocket. The letter was read by Sober. It was as follows:

July 26, 1961

Dear Mr. Sample:

Your letter of July 13, addressed to the Corporation has been referred to me for attention and reply.

You are advised that the Corporation had no matter pending before it concerning the eligibility of Mr. Sober to serve as an officer or director of an insured bank. Mr. Sober has been fully advised as to the procedures that should be pursued in the event that any bank desires to make application for permission for Mr. Sober to serve.

Sincerely yours,

(Signed) Royal L. Coburn
General Counsel

See Documentation Section, page 26, for actual reproduction of this letter.

The communication was on a letterhead of the Federal Deposit Insurance Corporation, Office of the General Counsel.

Something didn't jibe. A letter from the Old Freeport Bank Directors had been directed to this department June the 7, but the FDIC had no matter pending before it regarding Sober.

Perhaps it was the "red tape," anyway it seemed that no Federal Agency wanted anything to do with this case. Again it might have been that the approaches for the rehiring of Sober were not on official forms, or it could have been that one official of the bureau didn't know what had been or was taking place in another part of the bureau.

As the months of 1961 drew to a close, more and more statements were going to J. Anthony Moran, Sober's Washington lawyer. A petition was being prepared for submission to the Federal Deposit Insurance Corporation.

Every new statement regarding the affairs at the bank during Sober's regime, seemed to draw aside the curtains of adversity. The statements were favorable. Many of them came without being sought. Now, it seemed, there was only the wait until the wheels of justice were put in motion.

On April 16, 1962, Moran submitted the petition to the Honorable Erle Cocke, Jr. Chairman, Federal Deposit Insurance Corporation.

In a letter accompanying the petition, Attorney Moran wrote:

"Because of the serious nature of this matter, it is felt that this petition warrants special handling by the members of the Board of the FDIC who, I am sure, would insist upon a fair and impartial investigation of all of the facts. Any FDIC employees who are alleged to have been improperly involved in this matter should be disqualified from any connection with a new investigation and hearing. In this respect, it is requested that the FDIC reopen this matter and cause a fair and impartial investigation to be made, and thereafter, a hearing. If this request is not granted may we be advised if any other administrative remedies are available."

If the wheels of justice grind slowly, even the gears of a bureaucracy grind more slowly. Nothing was heard for a time.

Then a letter from Moran to Sober revealed the holdup. It was dated May 16, 1962.

Dear Charlie:

Received your letter of May 14.

Pleased be advised that your friends at the Old Freeport Bank pulled a fast one on us of which we had no knowledge at the time we prepared and filed the presentation for your reinstatement. In a letter dated August 25, 1961, a majority of the Directors withdrew their signatures and rescinded the action of June 7, 1961. As you recall, we submitted a photostat of the June 7th letter as an exhibit to the petition.

In view of the above, the FDIC has raised a technical question concerning that technicality which I hope we can overcome. However, if it is possible for you to obtain a request for yourself and the other petitioners from any other bank in any other capacity, I would suggest that you do so and let me know as soon as possible.

Sincerely,

(Signed) J. Anthony Moran

See Documentation Section, pages 27 to 33, for actual reproduction of this letter.

Sober was startled as he read the letter. What directors he wondered had betrayed him. All had signed the letter being forwarded to the FDIC, and now this. He began to make inquiries. No copy of this letter could be obtained, yet there were directors who maintained that they had never signed such a communication as was referred to by the counsel in Washington.

Again the files were searched and the only thing which could add to the maze of "red tape" was a letter to Moran signed by William A. Dobkin and Alphonse J. Gelorme, directors of the Old Freeport Bank, dated March 27, 1962.

It read as follows:

During the time C. L. Sober was in prison, we thought it would be nice to have Ira L. Sober and Jack C. Reese reinstated in the Old Freeport Bank. Mr. William Dobkin contacted Mr. G. E. Mounts of the F.D.I.C. and Mr. Fred Wigfield of the State Banking Department, and arranged for a meeting in Pittsburgh with Ira L. Sober. This meeting took place in the early part of 1961. At this meeting, they explained the procedure that had to be followed.

When C. L. Sober was released in May 1961, Mr. Herman Israel, President of the Old Freeport Bank, agreed to hire C. L. Sober, Ira L. Sober, and Jack C. Reese and send the necessary papers to the F.D.I.C. At the regular monthly

[246]

meeting of the Board of Directors, Mr. Israel made a statement to the effect that he would make arrangements to hire C. L. Sober, Ira L. Sober, and Jack C. Reese providing the stock owned by C. L. Sober and Ira L. Sober be put in trust with him having the voting rights.

See Documentation Section, page 34, for actual reproduction of this letter.

Nothing was said of this "stock in trust" in the original letter to the FDIC asking for the reinstatement of Sober in the bank. But later some other communications were forwarded to the FDIC, rescinding a previous request. Again, what plays were put in motion to prevent a man from holding a place in the business community that was rightfully his? How would Israel have gained his eminence as the president of the bank, had not Sober been forced to sell some of his stock to carry the burdens of costly hearings, trials and investigations? Was the whole thing a plan to not only discredit an individual, but to bleed him of all resources so that he could not be the "bother-some fly" around agency heads?

Was the second letter from the bank directors, rescinding the action of the first, a true act on the part of all the directors? Why do some of the directors maintain that they never heard of the second action and deny having affixed their names to such a document?

There was a lull in the battle, and the various forces fell back to regroup material and supplies.

In the meantime the innocent seek justice, and the bureaucracies blithly move along seeking only to protect their own positions — after all, who is Sober? He's only a little speck in the teeming mass of millions.

Throw in a technicality here, another there, disclaim knowledge of this paper or that — who can find them anyway?

The triumphant army of bureaucracy marches ever forward.

[247]

Chapter XVII
THE EPILOGUE

THERE IS AN END to nothing. Material things may change form, but what once was is and will be. In abstract matters, an idea is not just an idea for a time. It grows and develops. In law, a ruling does not end with one particular case. That ruling oft time forms the basis for subsequent rulings and judgments in similar matters, where there is a question of law. So this little case in the Federal Court of the Western District of Pennsylvania may in the end have a decided effect on banks and banking for years to come. If the motives of those who had Sober placed behind the bars were pure, then it is time to begin on practically every banker in the United States. If it is the purpose of law and justice to single out one or two as an example to the remainder, then where is justice? Are the law enforcing agencies in this government so steeped in the foreign ideologies that individuals must be destroyed for the good of the masses? Only the individuals themselves can decide, whether they be bankers, farmers, merchants, manufacturers, laborors or in whatever field of endeavor, which path to follow. To follow the path of least resistance and say, "This can't happen to me," one will only be repeating what Jack Reese thought when the FBI agents appeared at the bank and arrested Sober.

The law has been decided by a jury of citizens, good and

true. Now the heavy hand of guilt lies upon many. The principal charges in the case of Dr. Heineman and Cypher were based on the law which reads that "Whoever, being an officer, director, employee, agent or attorney of any bank . . . stipulates for or receives or consents or agrees to receive any fee, commission, gift, or thing of value from any person . . ." Both Cypher and Heineman readily admitted that a charge had been made for securing the loans, but the big question was this: Cypher and Heineman put these monies in the bank in the form of Certificates of Deposit to secure these risk loans. Sober's part in these loans brought a charge of "Aiding and Abetting," which was to say that he worked with the directors in this plan. Since these charges were made, it also resulted in additional charges being made against him titled, "Conspiracy." The latter charge as defined by the dictionary is a "combination for an evil plot."

Both Heineman and Cypher lost—not only reputations—but several thousands of dollars. Since the chief witnesses for the government, except in one case (Gallagher), had become delinquent in their loans, the bank was forced to liquidate the assets of the mortgages and the security that backed these loans, the bank took the Certificates put up. So there were no commissions nor fees nor gifts nor anything of value received by these men.

The tragic part of this story deals not so much with banks and bankers, but with obligation to humans. The bank which has been described as cold and heartless will have little to do with customers like the Burketts and Heymans and Keloskys. This type of individual is considered a poor risk. So they often become pawns of the unscrupulous finance companies which charge up to 42 percent annual interest. These finance companies, not regulated by the law which doesn't permit a banker to do the same, can blithely milk the unfortunate and down trodden. The banker, on the other hand, must for other than a small personal loan, have sufficient security to aid such people. They do not have security

[249]

in bank terms, so if someone else puts up the security and charges a fee for it—providing he is not a director, officer, employee, agent or attorney of a bank—it is perfectly legal. If this does not reveal a discrepancy in law, it certainly reveals a discrepancy in logical reasoning.

The District Attorney, Teitelbaum, went to great efforts during the trial to bring out how much stock Sober and his son, Ira, owned. The purpose, since there was no testimony that revealed that Sober or his son had received any of the alleged "kickback" funds, was to show that both of the above named defendants had profited through stock. Apparently, the jury was swayed by this line of reasoning.

Thus any officer of a corporation, who also serves as a bank director, had better go to another bank than the one in which he is interested, if his firm needs funds. By using his good offices as a director in the bank to secure funds for his company or corporation, he stands to gain through being a stockholder. If a reasoning is to be carried to a logical conclusion, then a number of outstanding industrialists are guilty because they seek funds from a bank in which they are interested as directors, and thus tend to profit as a director.

There have been known cases where an attorney, who is also a member of a bank's board of directors, has sent his clients to the institution in which he is interested, to get a loan. The attorney may or may not go security for the loan, but he will advise his clients how much will be needed to carry out their aims. This amount will include the fee charged by the attorney. Under the findings of the court, this could be interpreted as a gift "for securing a loan." Therefore the danger is quite apparent, for if any member of a bank's official family urges clients, friends or even strangers to patronize his bank, there is the possibility that he would profit from the transaction as a stockholder. This is what Teitelbaum said of Sober and his son. Would not the same hold true for anyone else?

A great deal was made over the certificates of deposit put up for security. Nothing has been said or was said about the bankers who require additional deposits on mortgages or loans. An individual went to a commercial bank to secure ten thousand dollars on a first mortgage to get a home. It was a conventional mortgage, with one third down. The bank was receptive, only the bank would not loan the individual ten thousand. If he wanted that particular bank to take the mortgage, he must borrow twelve, place the additional two thousand in the bank as a savings account (upon which he could not draw) until the mortgage was paid. This two thousand was labeled as additional "security." So the individual paid interest on twelve thousand, received ten and was paid a smaller interest on the savings account. The Old Freeport Bank issued certificates of deposit which paid the guarantor of a loan more than a straight savings account.

There are literally thousands of practices in the field of finance, some condoned by law and others not. But in many instances the laws has never been defined. There are banks which herald far and wide their treatment of customers as being just and honorable. However, these same institutions will sell mortgages to individuals, when such a mortgage becomes financially precarious. Such action is prefectly legal, even if in the mind of the individual selling the mortgage it is known that the buyer will foreclose because he wants the property.

Throughout the country there are people in business who at one time or another become directors of a bank. If a banker is in the furniture and appliance business and offers credit to his customers, it is only natural that the papers of credit be directed to the bank in which he is interested. The papers are discounted at the bank, and this merchant receives a portion of the interest paid to the bank as his own. This is a kickback, but according to law, this is a legal kickback. In numerous instances, a customer for such items as require credit, are told to deal at a certain bank, or the credit will not be granted. Conspiracy? No, a thousand times no—just business.

The ways of finance are strange. The dealer in major items where long term credit is needed, may sell an item and give up to any time for the customer to pay. Added to the original price, besides the interest may be a service charge. The dealer can discount the note at the bank and receive two additional profits besides the profit on the discounting of the note. There is no set charge as far as the dealer is concerned regarding the "service" and his third avenue of profit comes from being a director and stockholder in the bank.

If a bank or banker desires to give the same terms as a dealer, he is legally bound not to do so. The limit on such loans for banks is thirty-six months, and for a banker to urge an individual to borrow money for a car from his bank, would be wrong, for that banker would surely profit from the additional earnings as reflected in his stocks. Illogical? That is exactly what the district attorney said of Sober and his son in connection with loans made by the bank.

Among the questions coming to the fore as the result of this trial are many which could cause the men who deal with money some sleepless nights. The elder Sober, his son, Ira, and Jack Reese were found guilty of false entry relating to the "call reports." The basis according to the trial for these charges arose out of signing reports as witnesses, in the case of Sober and his son, and for making the report on the part of Reese. Sober maintained that he, as an officer of the bank, was witnessing the signature of Reese who prepared the report. Since the report was allegedly wrong, then Sober was found guilty of witnessing his signature, at a place on the report where it says "Correct-attest." Even the principal government witness, Canaday, testified that "I have not been too clear, Mr. Counselor, on that myself."

However, Teitelbaum knew the answer and he gave an answer that all bankers or directors who have to deal with "call reports" might well study. He said, "Correct-attest" means that three directors of the bank are attesting what is in that record is correct."

Since the close of the trial to the present time there have been numerous instances where embezzlement on the part of bank employees has been found. Even some of the larger banks are not immune from this weakness in human nature, and they too have been startled to find a trusted member of their "family" dipping his fingers into the sugar bowl. Sometimes this tasting of the forbidden sweets has been going on for years, sometimes for just a short period of time. In the meantime, the call reports are issued and signed under "Correct-attest" by three directors. If these directors have not made a personal examination of all funds, paper, bonds, notes and the like, then they, like Sober, are guilty of "false entry." It would be the height of the ridiculous to claim such directors are guilty, but that is what the court found in one case and is not justice commended for all?

Laws designed to thwart injustice, can sometimes be foolish. A bank, large or small, has about ten days to prepare a call report — sometimes even less time. It is the practice for an officer of the bank, usually the cashier or assistant cashier, to get these figures from the "General Control Ledger." It would be humanly impossible for such a bank official to personally check every item which the report calls for; so he fills out the report from the records at hand. This makes every banker who has filled out a call report and affixed his name to it, guilty of "false entry." He could not personally swear that all items were as represented. In the case of the big banks with their hundreds of branches in some instances, how would an individual in a few days time, visit every one of the branches and check every item which has been listed? When will the return be made to the principle of faith in our fellow man, which certainly must be exercised if commerce is to proceed for the well being of people?

If the small individual banker is required to be so accurate in

[253]

his reports, should not the government which represents him be just as accurate. On frequent occasions various departments of the government will issue reports concerning the growth of deposits in the various savings institutions in the country. The Old Freeport Bank, like many of its contemporaries, had deposits with other banks in the metropolitan area that served Freeport. When a government bureau issues a report on the growth of savings in the United States, does it bother to subtract what the small banks have deposited with the larger banks? Are such accounts grouped together, thus reflecting a duplication of the same funds? If such funds are not carried separately, then is not that government agency guilty of "falsification of reports?" What justice exists in law designed for the individual, but not for the agency under which he labors?

The other charges arising from the FHA loans have in them something of the questionable. The loans were not insured, it is true, because the commitments had expired. The contractor for these homes in question went broke. The bank did not know what action to take, so two attorneys on the Bank's board of directors were put to work to straighten the matter out. In spite of the efforts to agree with the edicts of a bureaucracy, the personnel involved in handling the matters will bear scars for a lifetime. The bank did not lose any money, the government did not lose any money, the individuals who had FHA did not lose money— they have their homes—but the label of criminal will be borne by three men because of this.

Sober felt that, surely, the bank he represented was not alone in facing this problem in FHA loans. He made inquiries. Yes, it was true that other banks were carrying FHA loans in which the final inspection had not been made. They, like Sober and his fellow workers, guardedly admitted that they couldn't move these loans to the column carrying the conventional loans. Originally, the people who had made the FHA loans had not paid the one third down payment required of a conventional mortgage loan.

Thus, it would have been falsification of records, had the FHA loans been moved to the conventional loan column. Since the trial, however, a ruling has been issued in like cases and the banks faced with a problem, similar to that faced by the Old Freeport Bank, can place such loans in the conventional mortgage column. This does not remove the wounds of injustice!

There are other questions concerning this trial which will probably never be answered. Is it true that a concerted move was on foot to rid the country of little banks? Reports have it that the then Comptroller of Currency declared that any bank under ten million was too small to exist. During his tenure of office there had been a rash of bank mergers, not only resulting in big banks becoming bigger, but forcing the small banks to become branches of the large ones. Thus, in spite of the words of those in high places who proclaim their fealty to individual initiative and small businesses, at the same time the little businesses are hampered and harassed until they become smaller, and the big thus become bigger.

The community thus loses its individuality. It is but a part of the forces controlled from some metropolitan center miles away. The presidents, the vice presidents, cashiers and hundreds of other individuals with the interests of these at heart, are removed or demoted. They are powerless to provide and promote, except as such moves behoove those sitting in their castles of steel and marble miles away. When such an area no longer serves the purpose of the bigs, when the last resources are drained away, the branch will be closed and such a place will move closer to the grave of obsolesence, decay and ruin. There are none within it to help promote and bring it back to life.

There are still stronger conclusions to be drawn from the trial of Charles L. Sober and his associates. If he was guilty, he has paid for his crime against society. However, the question of guilt is brought to the fore when Frank Irvine, Sr. a competitor, and also a member of the Federal Reserve Board, at the time of the arrests and trial, was active in bringing Canaday, the chief-examiner-at-large for the FDIC into the picture and guiding him to those who might serve as government witnesses. Was this conflict of interest, which has been frowned upon in the government, for a competitor to use his good office to embroil another banker?

If the methods used by Sober were so outrageous, why have other banks adopted the longer hours, and the deposit plan which pays more than the regular savings account? Besides the longer hours and additional services, now banks are offering the "friendly" services, implying that they are the places to go for financial help. What security would they demand from such people as the Burketts, the Heymans, the Keloskys and others. Would the average banker, because he is hemmed in by laws and rules of what security must be obtained, turn down the type of person which in many cases the Old Freeport Bank did help?

A friend questioned Sober after his release from prison, "What are you going to do to these people who lied about you during the trial?"

Sober reflected on the statement for a time, and then answered, "Who do you mean—the little people involved in this case?"

"Yea, you know, the people to whom you loaned money, and then turned against you."

"Nothing," replied Sober, "you know these people were scared. Chances are a lot more would be scared if government agents came pounding on their doors and told them a man did them wrong; that they had better answer what the agents wanted to hear, or they'd go to jail. Then too, whether it was outright or implied by the statements the agents made, these people thought they were going to get something. After all doesn't the government have something for everyone today? It would be pretty easy for these people to believe, because they wanted to, that they were going to get their homes and greenhouses and money and everything else back. Nope, I'm not going to do anything

gainst them, and as for helping them I can't. As for anyone else
elping them, I doubt if that will happen. Funny," Sober mused,
oo many think they can get something without paying some
ay, some place, some how. Just can't be done."

There are other questions concerning this trial which will re-
ain forever buried. One can still wonder why the attorney for
e defendants did not seek a new trial when he was advised that
woman juror had told a citizen, "We are going to find those
irty bankers guilty," before the trial had ever been concluded.

Charles Sober   December 22, 1961
    c/o Webster Hall Hotel
    4415 Fifth Avenue
    Pittsburgh, Penna.

Dear Charlie,

I have been doing a lot of thinking since I was with you
last night to see Mr. Maurice Spitalny the orchestra leader in
his apartment in the Penn Sheraton Hotel in Pittsburgh.

The big question is why your attorney Mr. Cooper did
not do something about this. I think when Mr. Spitalny was
nice enough to tell Mr. Cooper about picking up one of the
jury women who told Mr. Spitalny to leave her off near the
Federal Building as she and the other jury members were
going to send the bankers from the Old Freeport Bank to jail.

I believe this was enough to get you a new trial but I am
not an attorney therefore I think you should do something
about this, see another attorney or some one.

Your friend,
Christopher J. Dattola

*See Dattola letter, page 36, documentation.

Reports were made following the trial that some of the jurors,
hemselves, didn't know what it was all about, and that it was
explained to them" by fellow jurors. There is still a technicality
egarding the question of furnishing security for a loan. Even the
overnment's attorney admits this in a letter for the defendants.
Iowever, he won his case. The humiliation of prison and a record

[257]

that will live with these men for the remainder of their natural lives cannot be wiped from the memory, in spite of the letter.

Some good may result from this case. It won't help Sober, his son, Reese, Dr. Heineman or Cypher. It might help other bankers before they are subject to rulings and interpretations of an edict, before they are caught in battering rapids of conflicting rulings. The new Comptroller of Currency in February of 1962 issued the following letter to the Presidents of all National Banks. It states in part:

> So that there may be no misunderstanding with respect to the policy of this Office concerning the service charges of banks, I am issuing these formal instructions to all national banks.

> Agreements, arrangements, undertakings, etc., among banks, through clearing houses or otherwise, concerning service charges are not permissible in any form. It is the responsibility of the Board of Directors of each national bank to terminate promptly any of these practices which it may now be following.

The letter goes on to spell out what steps should be taken, and it also recognizes that identical charges may occur where there are no agreements. However, when there are identical charges individual banks must be prepared to demonstrate conclusively that there was no collusion.

The letter is brought to a close with this paragraph:

> Our examiners have been instructed to explore, regularly and in detail, the methods by which the existing scale of service charges was determined by each national bank. At the time of the next examination of your bank, inquiry shall be made to determine whether appropriate action, has been taken, where necessary, to conform to these instructions.

There are numerous other rulings, aside from the one above which need to be clarified. Saxton, the new Comptroller of Currency, appointed late last year, is on the right path. Additional clarifications of rulings on various phases of the banking business are needed, so they are not subject to the whim of some official seeking self aggrandizement by prosecuting a hapless banker as the spirit moves. Then, too, with the laws defined and the rules spelled out, a banker will be able to give better service to all.

The questions regarding this trial continue to plague the reader. Three of five of the government witnesses showed a desire to "recant" regarding statements made during the trial. The statements given at a hearing for a new trial, were not heard by a jury. Thus the impressions given during the trial would remain with the jurors, but these same jurors would not be called to hear additional testimony which might in effect, change the decision.

The Honorable Judge Miller, who presided at the hearing for a new trial, intimated that the statements of the witness, who admitted "coloring" their stories, could be of no value because they were not reliable. However, the jurors never heard this. The trial was over.

If some hapless individual is slandered before many, of what value is it for the slanderer to go to that individual and say, "I'm sorry. What I said was not true."

The words of untruth are repeated by the many who originally heard the story as a truth. Where was the justice?

Then there are tragedies which lie even deeper. They are not the tragedies which are inflicted upon the lives of defendants in the case. They come from the uprooting of the firm beliefs held by others in sacredness and justice of a democracy. They are as a thousand tiny darts creating invisible wounds in the hearts of those who fled from the persecution of others, only to see another type of persecution. No, it was not the persecution of the whip or lash; the persecution of the hot cigarette held before the eyeballs, or the persecution of needles threaded under the quick of the finger nails. It is the persecution of character, the assassination of everything a man stands for—carried by word of mouth to grow and fester in the decadent moral swamp. It is the seed implanted in the minds of those who sought in this country justice, only to wonder what manner of "law" this is.

So people—the so called little people—without backing and influence can join with Mrs. Maria Heyman, who was not called to testify before the jury, who said:

"What you do to this man is wrong. Why do you not call me? While I can't speak so good, I tell what happen in our place. I tell that these government men say we can get our shop and house back, if we say right thing."

Mrs. Heyman stretched forth her hands. The palms were deeply scarred. She continued, as the memories of the days of tyranny flashed through her mind, "I help people escape from the Nazis in Germany. I am caught. These hands," again she held them up and the scars seemd to grow afresh with new pain, "are held against a hot stove to make me tell. I no tell, because I believe in truth."

Her head dropped.

"What you do to this man is wrong."

Mrs. Heyman was not called before the jury.

Now the burn and scars lie deeper then on the palms' surface.

Now there are scars on the hearts of the "little people" for whom there is seemingly no help.

Over—buried! No—never. As long as there are those who seek justice through truth, this case will never end. The awakenings of a people who have lost their moral fiber, are already showing signs of being rekindled into fires of justice once more. The complacency of a people who feared to become involved, is giving way to reseeking the heritage of proud, courageous forebears. Already there are cracks in the protective sheath of the bureaucracies who can pick first this individual and then that to whip others into line, while the bureaucracies themselves are a festering cancer of self-perpetuating robots feeding at the public trough of an already burdened people.

DOCUMENTATION

All the Documents

in the following pages

were submitted to:

THE HONORABLE ROBERT F. KENNEDY
Attorney General of the United States

THE FEDERAL DEPOSIT INSURANCE CORPORATION

THE PENNSYLVANIA DEPARTMENT OF BANKING

U. S. CONGRESSMAN JOHN DENT

U. S. CONGRESSMAN JOHN P. SAYLOR

STATE SENATOR ALBERT R. PECHAN

Comparative

THE OLD FREEPO

	June 30, 1952	Jur
Cash and Due From Banks	$ 191,940.83	$
U. S. Government Securities and Other Bonds	510,725.97	
Loans and Discounts	515,048.37	
Building, Furniture and Fixtures	31,516.68	
Other Assets	823.20	
TOTAL	$1,250,055.05	$1,

		L
Deposits	$1,130,974.10	$1,
Unearned Interest	None	
Capital	50,000.00	
Surplus, Undivided Profits	69,080.95	
Other Liabilities	None	
TOTAL	$1,250,055.05	$1,
Dividends Payable at % of Par Value	5%	

OFFICE

FRANKLIN V
Chairman of t

IRA L. SOBER	C. L. SOI
Executive Vice-President	*Presiden*
HUGH L. SHEARER	JAMES G. FI
Vice-President	*Vice-Presi*
C. HOMER CRAIG	LOUIS F. LI
Vice-President	*Vice-Presi*
WILLIAM R. SUTTON	NICHOLAS 2
Assistant Cashier	*Assistant C*

Outstanding Capital—20,000 Shares, Par V

Member Federal Deposit Insurance Cor

The above is a statement showing the condi

with resources of $1,250,055.

nt of Condition

NK, FREEPORT, PA.

E S

	June 30, 1954	June 30, 1955	June 30, 1956	June 30, 1957	June 30, 1958
	18,019.61	$ 605,165.54	$ 942,257.54	$ 844,235.19	$1,453,170.21
	26,509.35	608,619.20	657,126.80	1,110,573.50	1,046,476.45
	71,603.00	2,042,281.53	2,842,984.57	4,272,489.60	5,505,915.33
	50,035.36	66,588.24	73,778.35	83,326.29	85,796.68
	None	13,447.38	12,851.01	12,160.35	12,439.52
	56,167.32	$3,336,101.89	$4,528,998.27	$6,322,784.93	$8,103,798.19

E S

	June 30, 1954	June 30, 1955	June 30, 1956	June 30, 1957	June 30, 1958
	28,723.36	$3,167,373.52	$4,190,133.09	$5,792,619.91	$7,384,303.19
	5,147.00	29,260.85	73,582.27	143,863.52	176,394.21
	50,000.00	50,000.00	100,000.00	143,330.00	200,000.00
	32,296.96	86,362.44	162,177.83	242,971.50	343,100.79
	None	3,105.08	3,105.08	None	None
	56,167.32	$3,336,101.89	$4,528,998.27	$6,322,784.93	$8,103,798.19
	½%	7½%	10%	12½%	**Current Dividend** 15%

JACK C. REESE
and Secretary to the Board
ORGE A. MARSHALL
ant Secretary to the Board
RD W. HEINEMAN, M.D.
Vice-President
JOHN W. STALEY
Assistant Cashier

bank when Charles Sober took over in 1952
wing resources of $8,103,798.18 in 1958.

SUITE 1 PLAZA 5
NATRONA HEIGHTS. PA.
TELEPHONE ACADEMY 4-5545

BERGER BUILDING
PITTSBURGH 19, PA.
TELEPHONE COURT 1-1935

IRVING SIKOV
ATTORNEY AT LAW

August 4, 1961

Rolf L. Larson, Esq.
Room 1002 Sherwyn Hotel
Pittsburgh 22, Pa.

Dear Mr. Larson:

I have your letter of August 2, 1961, to Dr. Richard
W. Heineman, in re Mr. and Mrs. John Burkett.

I have been directed to advise you that there is no
money due by Dr. Heineman to the Burketts. I might
also add that I am personally well aware of what
transactions these people have had which involve
Dr. Heineman. They have, so far, managed to defraud
everyone in the community with whom they have had
any business dealing, and have earned for themselves
a reputation for being notorious prevaricators.

With full knowledge of the case, it is not hard for
me to understand Dr. Heineman's shocked reaction to
this new piece of brazenness on the part of these
people, who, in a sworn statement, admit they
testified under oath falsely to convict Dr. Heineman
in hopes of getting money.

Very truly yours,

[signature: Irving Sikov]

IRVING SIKOV

IS/fef

Dear Mr. Saher
We are sending you this letter
and asking for Mr. Candlay's address,
as he was the government man
from F. D. I. C. along with Mr. Gardner that promised us, the
we would get our money back if the statement we made
along with testimony convict you.

1039 Nelson Ave.
Brackenridge, Pa
August 6, 1961

Mrs. Sylvia J. Burkett
John Burkett

[4]

Commonwealth of Pennsylvania, ⎱
County of Westmoreland ⎰ ss.

Before me, the subscriber___ a Notary Public_____

in and for the County and Commonwealth aforesaid, personally appeared Richard J. DeSalvo_____

who being duly sworn, according to law, doth depose and say. that I (we) are giving this sworn
statement in the interest of justice and that I (we) have not been promised anything for giving this statement nor have I (we) been coerced into giving it. If
required I (we) will give this statement personally before any appropriate federal
or quasi-federal board. That during August 1958 Mr. Higgins and Mr. Pudester
from the F. B. I. came to my house to ask me questions about The Old Freeport
Bank and what connection I had with Charles Sober. I answered their questions
to the best of my knowledge, but this did not seem to satisfy them. I asked
them to act as gentlemen and I would do the same. They twisted their
questions around several times. I asked if I was on a witness stand from
the way they kept at me. They said that did I know that I could go to jail
if I did not cooperate with them in their investigation. So they started
all over again. I gave the same answers to their questions. They again
said I was lying and said what could happen to me if I did not tell them
the truth. They said I could be prosecuted and sent to jail. This made
me angry as I was telling them the truth at all times. I asked them to
come outside for I could see they were upsetting my wife and daughter.
They insisted I was not telling everything so I told them to leave.

and further deponent saith not.

Sworn and subscribed before me this 16th

day of February_____ A. D. 19 62

_____ Richard J. DeSalvo
Notary Public_____

My Commission Expires____ ARMSTRONG, Notary Public
STRONG CO., PA.

[5]

Commonwealth of Pennsylvania,
County of WESTMORELAND } ss.

Before me, the subscriber PAUL D. LUCAS

in and for the County and Commonwealth aforesaid, personally appeared RICHARD BECKER

who being duly sworn, according to law, doth depose and say that I (we) are giving this sworn statement in the interest of justice and that I (we) have not been promised anything for giving this statement nor have I (we) been coerced into giving it. If required I (we) will give this statement personally before any appropriate federal or quasi-federal board. I Richard Becker was approached in 1958 at a service station by a F.B.I. man on question of a loan at the Old Freeport Bank of Freeport, Pa. I told this man about a $300⁰⁰ loan plus a truck I bought at the same time from the Old Freeport Bank at $900⁰⁰. He said he didn't understand the thought that I gave the $300⁰⁰ to Mr. Soles. Then later an F.B.I. man stopped at my home, I told this man I was given a loan for $1200. This was for a truck (1954 model Ford 3/4 ton) which the bank repossessed and was selling this truck at $900⁰⁰. My father signed the note for $1200. The note was for a $300⁰⁰ loan plus the truck of 900⁰⁰ therefore I received 300⁰⁰ above the 900⁰⁰ making the loan 1200⁰⁰. the F.B.I. said you gave 300⁰⁰ to a Mr. Soles. I said no. He insisted I did. my father was in adjoining room and heard this he came out and said "no one accused my children falsely." He then told the man to leave his house. my father was astonished that an F.B.I. man deliberately tried to intimidate me.

and further deponent saith not.

Sworn and subscribed before me this 24

day of January   A. D. 19

Paul D. Lucas

PAUL D. LUCAS, Notary Public
New Kensington, Westmoreland Co., Pa.
My Commission Expires

         Richard Becker

ADDRESS
CITY OF LOWER Bu...
NEW KENSINGT...

[6]

Commonwealth of Pennsylvania,

County of Alleghey } ss.

Before me, the subscriber Wellington B. Craft

in and for the County and Commonwealth aforesaid, personally appeared

Clarence Rogers and Thelma Rogers

who being duly sworn, according to law, doth depose and say that I (we) are giving this sworn statement in the interest of justice and that I (we) have not been promised anything for giving this statement nor have I (we) been coerced into giving it.

If required, I (we) will give this statement personally before any appropriate federal or quasi-federal board.

In 1958 two Federal Bureau of Investigation men came to our home (82 N. Canal St. Natrona Pa.), wanting us to sign a statement, which they had prepared before they came, saying we paid extra money or a kick back, of one thousand dollars, when we borrowed money from The Old Freeport Bank, to buy our home. I told these men, in my office (Justice of the Peace), I had people make out statements of their own with their own free will not prepared ones like they had. My wife and I told the above men that the above statement wasn't true and we wouldn't sign anything to that effect. The above men insisted that we weren't telling the truth, so I told them to leave my home which they did.

A few days later Alonzo Canaday and another man came to our home. When my wife went to the door, these men identified themselves as Federal Deposit Insurance Corporation men. They asked if they could come in. My wife said they could if they would be gentlemen and not stinkers like the other two F.B.I men who had been here a few days earlier. My wife told these men that we were tired of being bothered and being told we had by men who are supposed to be officers of the law. Mr. Canaday said we wouldn't be bothered anymore and left.

and further deponent saith not.

Sworn and subscribed before me this 24 th

day of January A. D. 1962

Wellington B Craft (SEAL)

My Commission Expires First monday 1966

Wellington B. Craft, Justice of the Peace
Harrison Township, Allegheny Co., Pa.
My Commission Expires
First Monday in January 1966

Clarence Rogers
Thelma Rogers
82 N. Canal St.
Natrona, Pa.

[7]

FORM No. 149-L—Affidavit   For Sale by P. O. Naly Co., Law Blank Publishers, 415 Grant St., Pgh. 19, Pa.

Commonwealth of Pennsylvania,
County of _Clarion_ } ss.

Before me, the subscriber _a Notary Public_

in and for the County and Commonwealth aforesaid, personally appeared _Dorothy M. Eck_
Joseph E. Eck

who being duly sworn, according to law, doth depose and say _that I (we) am (are)_
giving this sworn statement in the interests of justice
and that I (we) have not been promised anything for
giving this statement nor have I (we) been coerced into
giving it. If required I (we) will go both statement
personally before any appropriate federal or
quasi-federal board.

To Whom it may Concern)

During the examination of The Old Freeport Bank
Freeport, Pa., conducted by Alonza Canaday
in 1958, we were approched by two men
at our place of business Camp Joan Box 877
New Kensington, Pa., and were asked if we
accepted a bribe or paid a bribe on
our loan or whether we knew of anyone
who did accept a kick-back on loans
And we told them no-sir to both questions
that we did not pay anyone connected with
the bank or loan After several months
we lost our place of business and home
because the bank would not go along with
us and re-finance or lower our payments.
And we feel that if Charles or Ira Sober had
been at the bank at the time of our troubles
they would have gone along with us, and
we would have been able to keep our
place of business & our home to this day.

and further deponent saith not.

Sworn and subscribed before me this _26th_

day of _January_ A. D. 196 _2_

[signature] (SEAL)

NOTARY PUBLIC
Clarion (Clarion Co.) Pa.
My Commission Expires My Commission Expires Jan. 29, 1963

Dorothy M. Eck
Joseph E. Eck
RD #1
Corsica, Pa

[8]

STATE OF OHIO)
             (ss
COUNTY OF TRUMBULL)

I, James W. Sawyer being duly sworn according to law, deposes and says that I am a resident of the State of Ohio; that I make this affidavit on its behalf being authorized so to do; and that the facts set forth herein are true and correct; and that I make this statement of my own free will. During May, June, and July of 1958 I was the Sales Manager of the Allegheny Valley Steel Company, Inc., and was present on several occasions when Mr. Frank Irvine, Sr., President of the First National Bank of Tarentum now known as the Union Bank of Pittsburgh, came to see Mr. William D. Rhodes and told him that Mr. Alonzo Canaday, an investigator for the Federal Deposit Insurance Corporation, was going to examine our records in connection with the company's account at the Old Freeport Bank of Freeport, Pennsylvania and Lower Burrell, Pennsylvania. The said Mr Irvine told Mr. Rhodes in my presence, " any help that he could give Mr. Canaday would be a personal favor to him." Also in my presence the said Mr. Canaday and Mr. Frank Irvine, Jr., son of the above bank president, had in their possession photostatic copies of the Old Freeport Bank records, which Mr. Canaday had placed in custody with Mr. Irvine Jr.

During the investigation in my presence, Messr. Canaday, Irvine, Sr., Irvine, Jr., and John Brown, and investigator for the F.D.I.C., tried to convince Mr. Rhodes to testify that Mr. Charles Sober, then President of the Old Freeport Bank, of being guilty of misconduct in his bank transactions with Mr. Rhodes and our company. The truth of the matter was both Mr. Rhodes and I knew of our own personal knowledge, that Mr. Sober was not guilty of the misconduct they accused him of.

Also in my presence, Mr. Canaday, on several occasions told Mr.

[9]

Rhodes to change his account from the Old Freeport Bank to the First National Bank of Tarentum if he wanted to stay in business.

On countless occasions I was present when Mr. Canaday called Mr. Rhodes, usually late at night, from Pittsburgh, Pennsylvania, trying to convince him to perjure himself in his testimony against Mr. Sober.

The above statements were made in my presence, in the presence of Mr. Rhodes and also in the presence of his Secretary, Mrs. Eveyln Gamble, who was secretary and comptroller, had been happy to give the above testimony under oath to the proper governmental agent or agencies.

James W. Sawyer

Sworn and subscribed to before me this 22nd day of October, 1962.

Ruth Esther Riffle
Notary Public

(My Commission expires March 20, 1963)

COMMONWEALTH OF PENNSYLVANIA)
)   SS:
COUNTY OF ALLEGHENY   )

      William D. Rhodes being duly sworn according to law, deposes and says that I am a resident of the Commonwealth of Pennsylvania; that I make this affidavit on its behalf being authorized so to do; and that the facts set forth herein are true and correct; and that I make this statement of my own free will. In June, 1958, I was a depositor of the Old Freeport Bank of Freeport, Pennsylvania, and Lower Burrell, Pennsylvania; that I personally knew Mr. Charles Sober, who was then president of the bank. During the month of June, 1958, Mr. Frank Irvine, Sr., President of the First National Bank of Tarentum, Pennsylvania, now known as the Union National Bank of Pittsburgh, unsolicited came to my plant and office in connection with an application for a loan that I had placed with his bank in the latter part of May, 1958. The application for this loan, which was a business loan to help me in the conduct of my business, the Allegheny Valley Steel Company, Inc. He told me at that time in the presence of my Sales Manager, James Sawyer, that a fellow by the name of Mr. Canaday from the Federal Deposit Insurance Corporation, was coming to examine my records in connection with my account at the Old Freeport Bank. The gentleman I referred to is Mr. Alonzo Canaday, an investigator with the F. D. I. C., Mr. Irvine told me, "any help I can give Canaday would be a personal favor to him."

      Shortly thereafter, the said Mr. Canaday came to visit me and tried to have me testify against Mr. Charles Sober, whom he had under investigation at the time. And in the above named Mr. Sawyer's presence, Mr. Canaday, on several occasions told me to change my account from the Old Freeport Bank to the First National Bank of Tarentum if I wanted to stay in business.

[11]

On at least 50 occasions thereafter Mr. Canaday called me at either my home or office from the Pittsburger Hotel in Pittsburgh, Pennsylvania, usually very late at night, trying to convince me to testify that Mr. Sober was guilty of misconduct in his bank transactions with me and my company in connection with a loan I had obtained from Mr. Sober. The truth of the matter was that Mr. Sober had not been guilty of any misconduct in his dealings with me, nor did I know of any incidents in which Mr. Sober was guilty of misconduct in his dealings with anyone and I so told Mr. Canaday.

During the F. D. I. C.'s investigation of Mr. Sober, the aforesaid Mr. Canaday, Mr. Frank Irvine, Sr., Mr. Frank Irvine, Jr., and Mr. John Brown, also an F. D. I. C. investigator, tried to convince me to testify against Mr. Sober when I knew Mr. Sober was not guilty of any misconduct. Also during this investigation, Mr. Canaday and Mr. Frank Irvine, Jr., son of the above named bank president and in the presence of Mr. Sawyer, brought into my office photostatic copies of the Old Freeport Bank's records which Mr. Canaday had turned over to Mr. Irvine, Jr., to have photostated.

It was apparent to me that Messrs. Irvine, Sr., and Irvine, Jr., were extremely good friends of Messrs. Canaday and Brown.

In late May, 1958, I was taken to the Lower Burrell branch of the First National Bank of Tarentum to attend a Board meeting in connection with my application for a loan from that bank. Present at this meeting were the Messrs. Irvine, Sr., Irvine, Jr., and other officials of the bank. They told me at that time that they were out to get Mr. Charles Sober, because they wanted to stop him from putting a branch bank in Lower Burrell which would be in competition with their branch bank at the same place. I had plied several times before for a loan with Mr. Irvine's bank, which he had turned down until the time he wanted me to testify against Mr. Charles Sober for an alleged misconduct.

[12]

The government subsequently subpoenaed me as a witness in Mr. Sober's trial but never let me tell the above story.

William D. Rhodes
William D. Rhodes

Sworn and subscribed to before me this 24 day of January, 1962.

John D. Maglisco
Notary Public

My Commission expires:

Dec 7, 1963.

JOHN D. MAGLISCO, NOTARY PUBLIC
NEW KENSINGTON, WESTMORELAND COUNTY
MY COMMISSION EXPIRES DECEMBER 7, 1963

Commonwealth of Pennsylvania,
County of Allegheny } ss.

Before me, the subscriber a Notary Public

in and for the County and Commonwealth aforesaid, personally appeared Sylvia J. Burkett
of 1039 Nelson Avenue, Brackenridge, Pa.,

who being duly sworn, according to law, doth depose and say that I am giving the statement in the interests of justice and that I have not been promised anything for giving this statement nor have I been coerced into giving it. If required, I will give this statement personally before any Federal or quasi-federal board.

The statement I made to Mr. Canaday was worded by Mr. Canaday, and typed by Mr. Gardner.

To my knowledge now, it was false for we were promised our money back. And were told to study our statement and not to say anything more than what was in the statement.

I also asked the first day of the trial in Mr. Gowin office if we would get our money back if they were convicted. He told us that we wouldn't talk about that now but later.

These false statements were made at the trial of Charles L. Solee and others in Federal Court.

and further deponent saith not.

Sworn and subscribed before me this 28th

day of June A. D. 1962.

Sylvia J. Burkett

Julius N. Sopouiga (SEAL)

JULIUS N. SOPOLIGA, Notary Public
PITTSBURGH, ALLEGHENY COUNTY, PA.
My Commission Expires MY COMMISSION EXPIRES
MARCH 5, 1965

Commonwealth of Pennsylvania,
County of _Westmoreland_ } ss.

Before me, the subscriber _John Burkett_ _Sylvia J Burkett_

in and for the County and Commonwealth aforesaid, personally appeared _JOHN BURKETT_
and _SYLVIA J BURKETT_

who being duly sworn, according to law, doth depose and say _THAT I (WE) ARE GIVING_
THIS SWORN STATEMENT IN THE INTEREST OF JUSTICE
AND THAT I (WE) HAVE NOT BEEN PROMISED ANYTHING
FOR GIVING THIS STATEMENT NOR HAVE I (WE) BEEN
COERCED INTO GIVING IT. IF REQUIRED I (WE) WILL
GIVE THIS STATEMENT PERSONALLY BEFORE ANY
APPROPRIATE FEDERAL OR QUASI—FEDERAL BOARD.

To whom this statement may concern, I Sylvia J Burkett and John Burkett, were promised by Alonzo Canaday examiner from the F.D.I.C. that the statements we would make to convict Charles L. Solar and others, that if they were convicted we would get our money back.

Mr. Alonzo Canaday also told us he personally would see to it himself, that he would bring it up to the Board of Directors of F.D.I.C.

During the Court Trial I was asked by Defendants Attorney Alexander Cooper if we were promised our property back. I Sylvia J Burkett said no. But if Mr. Cooper would of asked me if we were promised anything. I would of answered him yes we were promised our money back.

We were told to study our statements and say nothing more by the Government Attorney. The statements we are referring too, were worded by Alonzo Canaday, and typed by Mr. Gardner from F.D.I.C. Corp.

Sylvia J Burkett
John Burkett
1039 Nelson Ave
Breckenridge, Pa

and further deponent saith not.

Sworn and subscribed before me this _20_

day of _January_ A. D. 19_62_

John D Magnison (SEAL)

John Burkett
Sylvia J Burkett

My Commission Expires _Dec 7-1963_

[15]

FORM NALY No. 169-L—Affidavit   For Sale by P. O. Naly Co., Law Blank Publishers, 414 Grant St., Pgh. 19, Pa.

Commonwealth of Pennsylvania,

County of Allegheny } **ss.**

Before me, the subscriber _____ a Notary Public _____

in and for the County and Commonwealth aforesaid, personally appeared **John Burkett**

of 1039 Nelson Avenue, Brackenbridge, Pa.

who being duly sworn, according to law, doth depose and say that I am giving this statement in the interests of justice and that I have not been promised anything for giving this statement nor have I been coerced into giving it. If required, I will give this statement personally before any Federal of Quasi-federal court.

The testimony I gave was false because we were promised we would get our money back by Alonzo Canady. The statement was worded by Mr. Canady and typed by Mr. Hardner. We were told to study our statements and say nothing more than what was on the statement by Mr. Harvin. These false statements were made at the trial of Charles Slater and others in Federal Court

and further deponent saith not.

Sworn and subscribed before me this 28th

day of June A. D. 19 62.

JULIUS N. SOPOLIGA, Notary Public
PITTSBURGH, ALLEGHENY COUNTY, PA.
MY COMMISSION EXPIRES
MARCH 5, 1965

My Commission Expires _____

John Burkett

[16]

Commonwealth of Pennsylvania,

County of .... ALLEGHENY ... } ss.

Before me, the subscriber ...... Helen D. Gillette, A Notary Public

in and for the County and Commonwealth aforesaid, personally appeared ...... LEO GALLAGHER &

..... Mrs. LEO GALLAGHER of R D #1 Natrona Hgts., Penna. ......

~~who being duly sworn, according to law, doth depose and say~~ that I (we) are giving this
~~sworn statement in the interest of justice and that I (we) have not~~
~~been promised anything for giving this statement nor have I (we) been~~
coerced into giving it. If required I (we) will give this statement
~~personally before any appropriate federal or quasi-federal board.~~

When we needed money to buy out our partner, Mr. Gross, and
to pay off a mortgage held by the First National Bank of Natrona, Pa.,
we tried to get loans from several banks, and also from a friend, a
farmer in Butler County. We were turned down. Later this friend
told us to try the Old Freeport Bank. The officers of the Old Freeport
Bank said they were unable to grant the loan because we had no perm-
anent water system, and that the bank could not use the liquor license
as security. They said we did not have enough security.

We knew Dr. Heineman and went to him and offered him $1000
as we had offered to other people, if he would put up security for us.
He put up $8000 in the form of a Certificate of Deposit, which was
assigned to the Old Freeport Bank as security.

We didn't pay on our loan at the bank for nine months,
because we were putting too much money into our business, improving
the property and furnishings. About a year later we were able to get
the money from another bank, because of these improvements which increased the value of our property.

In 1958 a Mr. Canaday, an F.D.I.C. agent, came to us and
said that if we would make a statement, we could get our $1000 back.
This $1000 involved a deal between us and the doctor concerning some
construction machinery which included a bulldozer. The government
agents kept coming to us until we got scared and did what the government men told us to do. We signed several statements written by them,
one being signed during the trial of Mr. Sober. Such a long time
had passed between the time we made the loan at the Old Freeport Bank
and these statements, that we may have said things at the trial that
weren't true. Also at the trial, when we were testifying, no one
questioned us or brought out the deal concerning the construction
machinery which involved the $2000. We never did know why we signed
so many statements

and further deponent saith not.

Sworn and subscribed before me this ...7th...

day of ...March... A. D. 19 62

...(signature)...
Notary Public
Natrona Hgts, Pa.

My Commission Expires ...... Feb 23, 1965

Leo Gallagher
Mrs. Leo Gallagher

[17]

FORM NALY No. 169-L—Affidavit   For Sale by P. O. Naly Co., Law Blank Publishers, 415 Grant St., Pgh. 19, Pa.

Commonwealth of ~~Pennsylvania~~ Ohio,
County of LAKE }ss.

Before me, the subscriber ~~Justice of Peace Maria Heyman~~ Michael D Coffey
in and for the County and Commonwealth aforesaid, personally appeared
Gustave C. & Maria Heyman
who being duly sworn, according to law, doth depose and say that ~~I~~ we are giving this statement in the interests of justice and that ~~I~~ we have not been promised
anything for giving this statement nor have ~~I~~ we been coerced into
giving it. If required, ~~I~~ we will give this statement personally before any Federal or quasi-federal board.

During late fall of 1957 when we were trying to
secure a loan to pay off the old Freeport Bank in
Freeport, Pa., and additional money to expand our business
we went to see Mr. Samuel Kauffman who was an
officer of the First National Bank of Freeport, Pa.
After hearing our story he told us he could not
handle our loan at this time. He told us that
Mr. C. S. Sober an officer of the old Freeport Bank
would not be there long as his (meaning Mr.
Kauffman) connections with Frank Irwin Jr a member
of the Federal reserve board and President of the
First National Bank of Tarentum, now known as
the Union Bank of Pgh., had connections and
political power with the controller of currency
who was a director in the federal deposit insurance corp, and also friend of Attorney Coburn
counsel for the federal deposit insurance corp were
going to get charges against C. S. Sober an officer
of the old Freeport Bank. C. S. Sober and others
were arrested in late 1958 and came to trial
in early 1959. I was a witness at the trial
and did not have the opportunity to explain the
answers I gave. Also my wife was never called to
testify at the trial. However my wife was called to the stand
at the hearing for a retrial, but again was not given chance
to testify before a jury. Also the court appointed lawyer that I
~~talked~~ ~~with~~ told me, that I should not change any thing I had said
at the ~~trial~~ and further deponent saith not.

Sworn and subscribed before me this 14
day of April A. D. 1962

Michael D Coffey
5940 Andover Road
Mentor, Ohio

My Commission Expires

MICHAEL D. COFFEY, Attorney
NOTARY PUBLIC—STATE OF OHIO
My commission has no expiration date.
Section 147.04 R. C.

Gustave C Heyman
Maria Heyman

6491 Iroquois Trail
Mentor, Ohio

Commonwealth of Pennsylvania,
County of...................................... } ss.

Before me, the subscriber...

in and for the County and Commonwealth aforesaid, personally appeared.................................

who being duly sworn, according to law, doth depose and say... that I am giving this statement in the interest of justice and that I have not been promised anything for giving this statement nor have I been coerced into giving it.
If required, I will give this statement personally before and Federal
or quasi-federal board.

During the examination of The Old Freeport Bank in 1958, I was
questioned by the F.B.I. on several occasions. When they would ask me
about a particular phase of the investigation, I told them all I knew
about it. They did not believe I was telling them everything or
was not telling the truth. After four Officers and Directors had
been arrested, I ask Mr. Higgins and Mr. Ludister of the F.B.I.
what my position was in relation to the investigation. They suggested
that if I wanted to know where I stood, that I should call
Mr. Sittelbaum, United States Attorney, and ask him. They did not
say that he wanted to see me.

At a re-hearing which took place in the Federal Building
in Pittsburgh after the trial, I met Mr. Sittelbaum in the hall.
He asked me why I was there as this hearing did not concern the
counts against me and then he said "I don't know why you're
involved in this thing anyway." In response to this, I said "It
wasn't my idea Mr. Sittelbaum, apparently it was yours". To this he
answered "You had your chance. If you would have come into
my office when you were invited, you wouldn't have been involved"

and further deponent saith not.

Sworn and subscribed before me this 4th

day of APRIL ....A. D. 1962

J. D. Maglisco ....(SEAL)

Jack C. Reese

My Commission Expires DEC 7 1963

JOHN D. MAGLISCO, NOTARY PUBLIC
NEW KENSINGTON, WESTMORELAND COUNTY
MY COMMISSION EXPIRES DECEMBER 7, 1963

[19]

Commonwealth of Pennsylvania,
County of WESTMORELAND } ss.

Before me, the subscriber _____ A NOTARY PUBLIC

in and for the County and Commonwealth aforesaid, personally appeared_____

JACK C. REESE

who being duly sworn, according to law, doth depose and say that during the examination of The Old Freeport Bank of Freeport, Pa. in 1958, the officers of the bank were told that some records of The Old Freeport Bank were being photostated at Edwards Studio in Tarentum, Pa. by an officer of The First National Bank of Tarentum, Pa. We were concerned and began trying to find out if this was true and how they were getting the records.

On Tuesday, Aug. 5, 1958, Ira L. Sober and I confronted Mr. John P. Brown, Chief Examiner of the F.D.I.C. in my office and questioned him about taking bank records out of the bank without notifying the officers of the bank. He admitted to us that records had been taken out of the bank and said "What did we do that was so bad." He also admitted at this time that the F.D.I.C. Examiners had had several meetings with Frank Irvine of The First National Bank of Tarentum, Pa.

On Saturday, Aug. 9, 1958, I went to see Mr. Schenk, the owner of Edwards Studio, however, I was unable to locate him at that time. At 8:30 the same evening, Leonard J. Rychlik, a Justice of the Peace in Lower Burrell Twp., Pa. and I went to Mr. Schenk's home and waited until 11:30 but he did not return home.

On Sunday, Aug. 10, 1958, I made three trips to Mr. Schenk's home and finally found him home on the third trip. I immediately returned to New Kensington to get Mr. Rychlik and went back to Mr. Schenk's home, hoping to get a sworn statement. Mr. Schenk admitted to Mr. Rychlik and myself that Frank Irvine, Jr. of The First Nat'l Bank of Tarentum, Pa. had come into his studio within the past ten days with another man whom he did not know (his description of the man fitted Mr. Canaday of the F.D.I.C.) to have records of The Old Freeport Bank photostated. He said that he did not know what records they were, but could identify them if he saw them. We asked him who paid the bill, and he stated that he had not yet been paid. He would not give us a sworn statement.

and further deponent saith not.

Sworn and subscribed before me this 12

day of MARCH _____ A. D. 1962

Donald H. Hunger (SEAL)

Jack C. Reese

DONALD H. HUNGER, Notary Public
Arnold, Westmoreland Co., Pa.
My Commission Expires_____ My Commission Expires
January 29, 1963

LAW OFFICES

MORRIS, SAFIER AND TEITELBAUM

1122 FRICK BUILDING

PITTSBURGH 19, PENNSYLVANIA

LEONARD M. S. MORRIS
MILTON SAFIER
HUBERT I. TEITELBAUM

TELEPHONE
ATLANTIC 1-2855

August 11, 1961

Mr. Charles Sober
Hotel Webster Hall
4415 Fifth Avenue
Pittsburgh 13, Pennsylvania

Dear Mr. Sober:

In accordance with our discussion, I met with the General Counsel of the Federal Deposit Insurance Corporation in Washington D. C. recently and discussed with him the possibility of your requalifying for employment in a bank insured by that corporation.

I was advised that the proper procedure is to request the appropriate form and data from the supervising examiner of the corporation, Mr. Mounts, at Columbus, Ohio. This form must be secured by the bank desiring to employ you. Generally the bank should submit that form through Mr. Mounts along with accompanying data, the nature of which Mr. Mounts will suggest.

Generally, the General Counsel suggested that along with a certified copy of the indictment and sentence of the court, information should be submitted from people who are knowledgable in the banking field. It was suggested that bankers in this general area would be best qualified to judge whether such re-employment would be advisable and the Board would give greater weight to letters from such individuals.

As I orally advised you the General Counsel suggested that such reinstatements are not generally considered favorably until a period of five years has elapsed so that rehabilitation can more effectively be determined.

I will be pleased to discuss this matter with you further at any time you may desire.

Very truly yours,

Hubert I. Teitelbaum

HIT/rmp

[21]

LAW OFFICES
MORRIS, SAFIER AND TEITELBAUM
1128 FRICK BUILDING
PITTSBURGH 19, PENNSYLVANIA

LEONARD M. S. MORRIS
MILTON SAFIER
HUBERT I. TEITELBAUM

October 19, 1961

To whom it may concern:

    I am writing on behalf of Charles L. Sober, Ira L. Sober and Jack Reese. All three were convicted for certain violations of federal law during the time when I was United States Attorney for the Western District of Pennsylvania and in charge of the prosecutions. The offenses which they committed were for violation of banking laws but to the best of my knowledge did not involve personal dishonesty since I do not believe that any of the three received any personal financial gain. Their violations were for a sort that involved breaches of regulations which had been codified into criminal offenses without involving any necessity of receiving moneys for their own benefits.

    I have since had frequent occasion to talk with Mr. Charles Sober, and I am personally convinced that his rehabilitation has been complete.

    The bank with whom they were connected prior to their convictions remained in excellent financial condition and was not in any way hurt by the offenses which they committed.

Very truly yours,

Hubert I. Teitelbaum

HIT:map

arole Ltr 6
r. May 1959)

United States Department of Justice
United States Board of Parole
Washington

FEBRUARY 1, 1962

Name   SOBER, CHARLES L.

Register Number   1985-AL

The records of this office indicate that you have completed the period of the Federal sentence on which you were released for supervision.

Sentence began   11-28-60

Supervision ended   11-27-61

Therefore, this letter is forwarded to you as evidence of your discharge from supervision.

Joseph N. Shore

Parole/~~Youth Division~~ Executive

1933

FEDERAL DEPOSIT INSURANCE CORPORATION

WASHINGTON

December 14, 1961

Mr. Charles L. Sober
Hotel Webster Hall
4415 Fifth Avenue
Pittsburgh 13, Pennsylvania

Dear Mr. Sober:

On December 4 you visited my office and informed
me that photostats of certain material relating to your
ambition to become a director of an insured bank had been
left in Chairman Cocke's office. I now have reviewed the
material and note that this does not constitute an application on the part of The Old Freeport Bank, Freeport,
Pennsylvania, or of any other bank and therefore we have
no occasion for taking action on the subject of your ambition.

I note also that your attorney, in a letter dated
August 11, 1961, advised you of the procedure whicn would
have to be pursued were any bank desirous of employing you
as either an officer, director, or employee and therefore it
will not be necessary for me to go into details as to the
requirements of Section 19 of the Federal Deposit Insurance
Act.

In the absence of further word from you we will
hold the photostatic material, which you left, in our general
files.

Sincerely yours,

Neil G. Greensides
Chief, Division of Examination

June 7, 1961

Chairman and Board of Directors
Federal Deposit Insurance Corporation
Washington, D. C.

Gentlemen:

We, being all of the directors of The Old Freeport
Bank of Freeport, Pennsylvania, wish to advise you that
we have full confidence in the honesty, integrity and
ability of Mr. C. L. Sober. In the best interests of
the Bank, we should like to utilize Mr. C. L. Sober's
ability in some capacity, where he can make his greatest
contribution to the future success of the Bank.

We are familiar with your regulations governing Mr.
C. L. Sober's position on account of his case in the
United States District Court for the Western District
of Pennsylvania. Under the circumstances, we realize
that we may not make any move to employ Mr. C. L. Sober
unless we obtain your permission and consent. It is
for this reason that we write this letter in the hope
that you may decide to set aside any restrictions that
you may have against Mr. C. L. Sober's association with
this Bank. We firmly believe that Mr. Sober is entitled
to consideration, and we definitely believe that if we
are permitted to have him associate with the Bank, that
it will be beneficial to the stockholders of the Bank.

Sincerely,

[signatures]

FEDERAL DEPOSIT INSURANCE CORPORATION

WASHINGTON

July 26, 1961

Mr. J. J. Sample, Jr.
R. D. No. 1
Freeport, Pennsylvania

Dear Mr. Sample:

Your letter of July 13, addressed to the
Corporation has been referred to me for attention and
reply.

You are advised that the Corporation has no
matter pending before it concerning the eligibility
of Mr. Sober to serve as an officer or director of an
insured bank. Mr. Sober has been fully advised as to
the procedures that should be pursued in the event
that any bank desires to make application for permission
for Mr. Sober to so serve.

Sincerely yours,

Royal L. Coburn
General Counsel

LAW OFFICES
J. ANTHONY MORAN
1701 "K" STREET, N. W.
WASHINGTON 6, D. C.
—
REPUBLIC 7-3650

April 16, 1962

Honorable Erle Cocke, Sr.
Chairman
Federal Deposit Insurance Corporation
Washington 25, D. C.

Re: Petition by Sober, Sober and Reese for Consent to
Serve as Employees of an Insured Bank, as Required
by Section 19, Federal Deposit Insurance Corporation

Dear Sir:

There are attached hereto petitions by the above named
parties that they be permitted to serve as employees of a
Federal Deposit Insurance Corporation insured bank known as
the Old Freeport Bank, Freeport, Pennsylvania.

This office is familiar with FDIC General Memorandum #13,
revised May 12, 1959, as pertains to Section 19 of the Act.
We have attempted to comply fully with the requirements of
this memorandum and have done so in the case of C. L. Sober.
However in the cases of Ira L. Sober and J. C. Reese we do
not have a clearly defined request from a bank for reasons
which are set forth in the attached petition and hereinbelow.

The attached petition contains evidence which alleges
collusion and misconduct by FDIC employees who were assigned
to the Columbus District and the Washington office. These
allegations, if substantiated, could subject the persons involved
to dismissal from the FDIC and possible criminal prosecution.

It also contains evidence to support allegations of
collusion and misconduct by certain officers and directors
of the First National Bank of Tarentum, Pennsylvania, now
known as Union National Bank of Pittsburgh.

There are also contained in said petition, allegations and
charges of misconduct by certain officers of the Old Freeport Bank

who are presently serving in that capacity. Some of these charges
of misconduct are alleged to have been discovered as recently as
the week of March 12. This discovery was made during an examination
by Mr. James Flannigan, a Bank Examiner for the Pennsylvania Department
of Banking, who recently conducted an examination of the subject Bank.

In view of this situation it is impossible to comply fully with
the procedures set forth in General Memorandum No. 13. If relief from
the alleged injustice and misuse of Federal authority were permitted to
continue because of non-compliance with the above mentioned
memorandum, then such procedures would constitute a bar to the
applicable provisions of the Act, and cause serious question as to
their constitutionality.

Because of the serious nature of this matter, it is felt that
this petition warrants special handling by the members of the Board
of the FDIC who, I am sure, would insist upon a fair and impartial
investigation of all the facts. Any FDIC employees who are alleged
to have been improperly involved in this matter should be disqualified
from any connection with a new investigation and hearing. In this
respect, it is requested that the FDIC reopen this matter and cause
a fair and impartial investigation to be made, and thereafter, a
hearing. If this request is not granted may we be advised if any
other administrative remedies are available.

It is further requested by the undersigned acting in behalf of
the Petitioners and in behalf of certain stockholders and directors
of the Old Freeport Bank, that a Conservator be appointed by the
FDIC to conduct and manage the business of said bank until a proper
investigation and determination in this matter can be accomplished.

This Counsel has advised the petitioners and other parties herein
of the serious nature of the allegations that have been made in said
petition and of the possible consequences thereof.

If you require any additional information, will you kindly contact
this office.

Sincerely,

J. ANTHONY MORAN

JAM:cb
Atts.

It is herein requested that the Federal Deposit Insurance Corporation
sent to permit Charles L. Sober, Ira L. Sober and Jack C. Reese of the
Freeport Bank of Freeport, Pennsylvania to be reinstated as employees
said bank in accordance with Section 19 of the Federal Deposit Insurance
. Because of the nature of the information contained in this petition,
is hereby respectfully submitted that the Members of the Board of
ectors of the Corporation examine, consider and decide this petition
waive those procedural requirements with which petitioners have
been able to comply, and disqualify from participation in any manner
ein those Corporation employees who may be guilty of misconduct in
nection with this matter.

A) The names of the persons involved are:

> Charles L. Sober
> Pittsburgh, Pennsylvania
>
> Ira L. Sober
> Vandergrift, Pennsylvania
>
> Jack C. Reese
> Arnold, Pennsylvania

B) Statement of Facts disclosing nature of offense:

The petitioner Charles L. Sober was the President of the Old
eport Bank of Freeport, Pennsylvania; the petitioner Ira L. Sober was
e-President; the petitioner Jack C. Reese was Cashier. The petitioners
own and have owned for several years approximately 30 percent of the
ck in the aforesaid bank. In 1958, an investigation based on reported
conduct of petitioners was conducted by duly authorized agents of the
poration, Alonzo Canaday and John Brown. (See Exhibits A, A-1 and A-2).
o involved in said investigation were certain members of the Federal
eau of Investigation. As a result of material allegedly uncovered
a questionable investigation, the petitioners were indicted on August 15,
8 for alleged violations of various sections of Title 18, U. S. Code,
set forth in a copy of the said indictments which are attached hereto.
hibits A and B.)

They were tried on two indictments containing multiple counts alleging
lations of Section 220 of Title 18 U.S.C., which forbids receipt by
h persons of gifts or commissions for procuring bank loans; 18 U.S.C.
tion 371, the conspiracy statute; 18 U.S.C. Section 656, governing the
ense of embezzlement by bank officials; and 18 U.S.C. Section 1005,
ining the offense of making false entries in books or records of insured
ks. At the close of the government's evidence, judgments of acquittal
e entered by the court on certain counts and the jury returned verdicts
not guilty on some of the others including all of the counts charging
ezzlement.

Charles L. Sober: Violation, 18 U.S.C. 220, 371, 1005; a sentence
one year and $500 on each count to run concurrently. He paid the fine,
ved approximately half of this sentence and was paroled on May 1, 1961.

Ira L. Sober: Violation 18, U.S.C. 1005 (five counts). His sentence
suspended and he was placed on probation for a period of three years
fined $2,500.00. The fine has been paid and the petitioner is
ng considered for removal from probation.

Jack C. Reese: Violation, 18 U.S. C. 1005 (3 counts). His sentence
suspended and he was placed on probation for a period of three years with
ine of $500 on each count to run concurrently. The fine is being paid
the petitioner is being removed from probation.

C) Notification of the Bank's Bonding Company: We have notified the Bonding Company of the Old Freeport Bank of this petition and, as yet, have not received a reply to such notification.

(D) Certified copy of the Indictment and Judgment on the Indictment: A photostatic copy of the Indictment and an extract of the Judgment entered on the Indictment are attached hereto. (Exhibits B and B-1)

(E) The Indictment does not reflect the purpose for the investigation or how the information, which was presented to the Grand Jury, was obtained. It is generally assumed that information obtained during an investigation by agents of the Federal Government is factual, impartial, and obtained in accordance with accepted investigatory methods. It is also generally accepted that Federal agents involved in an investigation conduct themselves with Professional propriety and dignity in the discharge of their duties. It is further generally accepted that agents of the Federal Government in the conduct of an investigation neither offer comfort to the parties they interview nor do they coerce, harass and intimidate parties into giving information which the parties do not believe to be true. It is further generally accepted that agents of the Federal government during the conduct of an investigation do not form an association or relationship with any person or individual who by reason of position, business or otherwise, may have a motive for personal gain, aggrandizement, or vindictiveness against the party or parties being investigated by such federal agents. It is generally assumed, and I am sure it was assumed by the Grand Jury who returned a True Bill in this matter, that the information presented to them by the United States Attorney, which had been obtained by authorized agents of the Federal Government, had been obtained in a generally accepted manner. Unfortunately, this does not appear to be the case in this matter.

Briefly, the Old Freeport Bank from the time of its establishment until the time set forth in this investigation, had been a progressive bank and had departed from the conventional, somewhat-outmoded customs usually employed by banks in small towns, insofar as pertains to the personal consideration of its depositors, loan applicants and other bank customers by the bank officials. This bank had steadily risen to a position of great competition to a competitor bank, the First National Bank of Tarentum, now known as the Union National Bank of Pittsburgh. It is natural to assume that the President of said competitor Bank, Frank Irvine, was quite disturbed by the amount of business the Old Freeport Bank was attracting away from his bank. When the Old Freeport Bank indicated its intention to open a branch office in the city of Lower Burrell, the said Mr. Irvine indicated his intention to somehow stop the petitioner, Mr. Charles L. Sober, from opening branch bank in Lower Burrell which would be in competition with his branch bank at the same place. (See Exhibit C). Mr. Irvine, who was reportedly "close to the Administration in Washington" stated that he would "fix Charley Sober," or words to that effect, and further that "Coburn (Royal L. Coburn) would know what to do" or words to that effect.

During the aforementioned trial, Mr. Alonzo Canaday testified under oath that he had been with Mr. Frank Irvine only one time when he was seeking investigative leads. A proper investigation would reveal that Mr. Canaday met with Mr. Irvine on several occasions and, as a matter of fact, a friendly relationship had apparently developed between the two and Mr. Irvine entertained Mr. Canaday at the Breckenridge Country Club and other places. (See Exhibits C, D, and E). During the investigation, Mr. Canaday obtained records of the Old Freeport Bank and, without the permission of any of the officials of said bank (See Exhibits C and D) removed them from the bank, took them to the competitor First National Bank of Tarentum. These records were turned over to Mr. Frank Irvine, Jr., an official of said competitor bank, who had them photostated and returned to Mr. Canaday. (See Exhibits C and D).

Thereafter, Mr. Canaday, along with John Brown, another agent of the Corporation, talked to many people who were customers of the Old Freeport Bank. Their tactics were such that complaints were registered by several people they visited (See Exhibits F, G, H, I, J, K, and L). However, by the methods used they were able to illegally obtain statements during the investigation prior to the trial and even during the actual trial from individuals who were used as complaining witnesses of the Government and actually were permitted to testify at the trial. The testimony of some of these witnesses was discredited during the trial. Other witnesses have

- 2 -

worn affidavits that their testimony was false and had been obtained from
hem by Mr. Canaday on the promise by him that they would have returned
o them certain monies or other property if their testimony was "colored"
o that it would convict the petitioners (Exhibits F, G, and H, and
upplemental Opinion and Order, Circuit Court of Appeals #13037 to 13041
nclusive).

It is alleged herein that if the Grand Jury had been made cognizant
f how the facts presented to them had been obtained and the real reason
nd purpose for subject investigation, it is very doubtful that they would
ave returned a True Bill. It is further alleged that the conduct of
essrs. Frank Irvine, Sr. and Jr. and Alonzo Canaday leaves them liable to
ndictment for the collusive and other illegal acts perpetrated by them.
t is further alleged that if the statements made by Mr. Irvine, Sr.
oncerning his relationship with Royal Coburn are found to be based in
act, then he may be a co-conspirator in this nefarious plot.

F) Mitigating Circumstances:
a) None of the petitioners herein had any kind of a criminal record
rior to alleged subject offense.

b) C. L. Sober was found guilty of two misdemeanors and a felony
hich is a statutory felony in the nature of a "malum prohibitum" rather
han a crime that is "malum per se." The Court, in its sentence of
. L. Sober, apparently recognized this situation and it was reflected
n his sentence of the party which did not exceed one year imprisonment.
urther, the Court recommended C. L. Sober be paroled after he had served
ne-third of his sentence.

c) The petitioners I.L. Sober and J. C. Reese were both found guilty
f violating Title 18, U. S. Code 1005 which also are violations of a
egulatory statute that have been interpreted as being a felony instead of a
isdemeanor.

d) It is pointed out that after a very exhaustive and intensive
nvestigation by agents of the FDIC and FBI there was never a shred of
vidence produced that any of the petitioners were guilty of any dishonesty
n connection with their operations in the Old Freeport Bank.

e) The indictments contain some 19 counts, the majority of which were
ither dismissed by the Court or by the Jury.

f) The testimony concerning the counts upon which the petitioners
ere found guilty has, in every instance, been repudiated by the witnesses
n sworn affidavits attached hereto as Exhibits F, G, and H. And said
itnesses swear under oath that they were definitely promised something of
alue by Mr. Canaday providing they "colored" their testimony in such a
ay as to convict the petitioners. Other witnesses swear in attached sworn
ffidavits, Exhibits C and D, of promises and threats of actions that would
e taken against them if they did not comply with the requests of Messrs.
anaday and Frank Irvine, Sr. This certainly indicates the real purpose
ehind this investigation and the manner in which it was carried out.

It is quite apparent from all the facts in this case that Mr. Frank
rvine, Sr., because of his concern of increased competition from the Old
reeport Bank, used the auspices of his former office and his self-alleged
connections" with certain personnel of the FDIC in Washington and the then
dministration officials as a means to eliminate competition to his banking
usiness. It certainly appears to be a travesty on justice whenever one
erson because of his alleged "connections" in business and politics uses
uch advantages to harm a competitor. There is no doubt the evidence
hich the petitioners can produce if given the opportunity which they seek
erein, will show the misconduct of government officials and collusion
etween government officials and private citizens.

[31]

- 3 -

g) It is stated by the U. S. Attorney, who so laboriously and tenaciously prosecuted this case in order to obtain a conviction, in a letter dated October 19, 1961, which is attached hereto as Exhibit "M," stated that "the offenses which they committed were the violation of banking laws, but, to the best of my knowledge, did not involve personal dishonesty, since I do not believe that any of the three received any personal financial gain. Their violations were for a sort that involved breaches of regulations which had been codified into criminal offenses without involving any necessity of receiving moneys for their own benefits........I have since had frequent occasion to talk with Mr. C. L. Sober and I am personally convinced that his rehabilitation has been complete."

Also, there are available upon request petitions that contain approximately 600 names which were signed by persons in the area of the Old Freeport Bank and its branch, which testifies to the general feeling in the community regarding the rehabilitation of the petitioners. Further, on December 27, 1960, a letter from the Honorable Judge John L. Miller, who tried this case (See attached Exhibit "N"), recommended to the Parole Board that they release the petitioner, C. L. Sober, immediately upon serving one-third of the sentence imposed. The Parole Board thereupon acted in the matter of C. L. Sober and he was released after serving approximately six months of his sentence. The action of the Court and the Parole Board would certainly reflect that in their judgment, Mr. C. L. Sober has rehabilitated himself.

h) In view of the circumstances outlined above and hereinbelow, a proper full field investigation should be made to enable an accurate determination of all the pertinent facts and circumstances, because it is certainly indicated that not only has rehabilitation occurred since the time of the offense, but such rehabilitation in this case may not be an issue to be considered by the Board.

i) None of the petitioners herein have had any kind of a criminal record, prior to this matter. Jack C. Reese is a life long resident of the State of Pennsylvania, an honorably discharged veteran of World War II, and has an excellent reputation in the community. Ira L. Sober, likewise, is a life long resident of the State of Pennsylvania, an honorably discharged veteran of World War II and has an excellent reputation in the community (See Exhibits T and U). Further, in a letter dated March 27 from two directors of the Old Freeport Bank and attached hereto as Exhibit S-1, this background is further substantiated.

Charles L. Sober also has an excellent reputation in the community, as evidenced by attached letters, Exhibits "O," "R," and "R-1" which support this claim. On June 7, 1961 the Board of Directors of the Old Freeport Bank requested that the Corporation reinstate said petitioner (See Exhibit S-3).

Since the time the action was taken by the Directors as evidenced by Exhibit S-3, it appears Herman Israel, who became President of the Bank when C. L. Sober was removed because of the actions set forth above, had a change of heart in connection with the reinstatement of the petitioners because the petitioners, Charles L. Sober and Ira L. Sober, refused to turn over to the said Mr. Israel voting rights to their stock. Further, the said Mr. Israel refused to honor an agreement he had made with petitioner Charles L. Sober to equally share certain other shares of stock in the Old Freeport Bank. This act made it necessary for petitioner to take legal action against said Mr. Israel. On Tuesday the 9th of January, 1962, notices of a Stockholders' Annual Meeting were sent out by the Old Freeport Bank. One of the purposes for this meeting was a further attempt to disenfranchise the petitioners and to prevent the Directors from continuing the request to the Corporation that said petitioners be reinstated as employees of the Bank. In an attempt to control the Annual Meeting, the said Mr. Israel had printed a Stockholders' Annual Meeting Notice which contained a proxy which purported to represent to said stockholders that proxies could be given to only three men: "H. J. Israel, A. Amerson Boyd, and W. R. Sutton." (See Exhibit V.) This situation has not yet been resolved and the matter is presently in a Pennsylvania State Court. Several of the Directors of the Bank have notified the Pennsylvania Department of Banking that said Bank under its present management is being mismanaged, and this office has been advised that the management of the bank is apparently in violation of the banking laws of the State of Pennsylvania and of the Federal Deposit Insurance Corporation. In view of these allegations it is suggested that a Conservator be appointed to manage the aforementioned bank until such time as a proper investigation of all the facts and circumstances involved herein can be properly investigated and a consideration made in this matter.

WHEREFORE, the petitioners Charles L. Sober, Ira L. Sober and Jack C. Reese respectfully request the Members of the Board of the Federal Deposit Insurance Corporation as follows:

1) That the Board Members order a full investigation of all the allegations concerning the facts and circumstances surrounding this matter from the date of origin.

2) That any employees of the Corporation who are alleged to be parties of interest in this matter be disqualified from any participation in this entire matter.

3) That after a full investigation has been conducted the Board have a hearing of all the facts and circumstances as hereinbefore presented, or

4) That the Board based on this petition and its supporting documents permit the petitioners to be reinstated as employees of the federally insured bank.

5) That the Board cause a Conservator to be appointed to manage the affairs of the Old Freeport Bank of Freeport, Pennsylvania until this matter is properly resolved.

6) For any and other administrative remedy and relief that the Board deems to be fair and just.

Respectfully submitted:

_____
J. Anthony Moran

Attorney for the Petitioners
1701 K Street, N. W.
Washington 6, D. C.

March 27, 1962

J. Anthony Moran, Att'y at Law
1701 "K" St., N. W.
Washington 6, D. C.

Mr. Moran,

We as directors of The Old Freeport Bank wish to make the
following statement:

During the time C. L. Sober was in prison, we thought it
would be nice to have Ira L. Sober and Jack C. Reese reinstated in the Old Freeport Bank. Mr. Wm. Dobkin contacte
Mr. G. E. Mounts of the F.D.I.C. and Mr. Fred Wigfield of
the State Banking Dept. and arranged for a meeting in
Pittsburgh with Ira L. Sober. This meeting took place in
the early part of 1961. At this meeting, they explained
the procedure that had to be followed.

When C. L. Sober was released in May 1961, Mr. Herman
Israel, President of The Old Freeport Bank, agreed to hire
C. L. Sober, Ira L. Sober, and Jack C. Reese and send the
necessary papers to the F.D.I.C. At the regular monthly
meeting of The Board of Directors, Mr. Israel made a statement to the effect that he would make arrangements to hire
C. L. Sober, Ira L. Sober, and Jack C. Reese providing the
stock owned by C. L. Sober and Ira L. Sober be put in a
voting trust with him having the voting rights.

Sincerely yours,

Wm. Dobkin
Director, Old Freeport Ban

Alphonse J. Gelorme
Director, Old Freeport Ban

[34]

May 16, 1962

Mr. Charles L. Sober
Hotel Webster Hall
4415 5th Avenue
Pittsburgh 13, Pennsylvania

Dear Charlie:

Received your letter of May 14.

Please be advised that your friends at the Old Freeport Bank pulled a fast one on us of which we had no knowledge at the time we prepared and filed the presentation for your reinstatement. In a letter dated August 25, 1961, a majority of the Directors withdrew their signatures and rescinded the action of June 7, 1961. As you recall, we submitted a photostat of that letter as an exhibit to the petition.

In view of the above, the FDIC has raised a technical question concerning that technicality which I hope we can overcome. However, if it is possible for you to obtain a request for yourself and the other petitioners from any other bank in any other capacity, I would suggest that you do so and let me know as soon as possible.

Sincerely,

J. ANTHONY MORAN

JAM:cm

THE NEW CHES-A-RENA, INC. *Pennsylvania's Finest*

ROUTE 28 · · PHONE BRoad 4-8181
CHESWICK, PENNSYLVANIA

December 22, 1961

Charles Sober
℅ Webster Hall Hotel
4415 Fifth Avenue
Pittsburgh, Penna.

Dear Charlie,

I have been doing a lot of thinking since I was with you last night to see Mr. Maurice Spitalny the orchestra leader in his apartment in the Penn Sheraton Hotel in Pittsburgh.

The big question is why your attorney Mr. Cooper did not do something about this. I think when Mr. Spitalny was nice enough to tell Mr. Cooper about picking up one of the jury women who told Mr. Spitalny to leave her off near the Federal Building as she and the other jury members were going to send the bankers from the Old Freeport Bank to jail.

I believe this was enough to get you a new trial but I am not an attorney therefore I think you should do something about this, see another attorney or some one.

your friend,

Christopher J. Dattola

Commonwealth of Pennsylvania, }ss.
County of Allegheny

Before me, the subscriber _____ Marie McFarlane

in and for the County and Commonwealth aforesaid, personally appeared ___ Jack Devereaux

who being duly sworn, according to law, doth depose and say :— am giving this sworn statement in the interest of justice and that I have not been promised anything for giving this statement, nor, have I been coterced into giving it. If requested I will give this statement, personally, — before any appropiate judicial or quasi-federal board.

As I had, had several business dealing with the Old Freeport Band and with Mr. Chas. Sober, I was interested when I heard from a friend of mine that Sam Kaufman of the First National Bank of Freeport Pa. was trying to get an investigation started against the Old Freeport Bank in general and against Chas. Sober in particular on his banking practices as I had, had several dealings with Mr. Sober — I knew that such an investigation would be started from a Jalousy standpoint as the Competitors of the Old Freeport Bank were not very happy about losing business to the Old Freeport Bank — not because of any mis practice of Banking laws — but because of Superior Service. Shortly after hearing about such an investigation a Mr. Anaday, of the Federal Deposit Insurance Corp. who was completing an audit of the Old Freeport Bank — called at my home and asked me if I would be willing to submit a statement against

and further deponent saith not.

Sworn and subscribed before me this 24th

day of April A. D. 19 62

Marie M. Farlane (SEAL)

Jack Devereaux
115 4TH. ST.
FREEPORT, PA.

My Commission Expires _____
MARIE McFARLANE, NOTARY PUBLIC
PITTSBURGH, ALLEGHENY COUNTY
MY COMMISSION EXPIRES NOVEMBER 29, 1965

[37]

Commonwealth of Pennsylvania, } ss.
County of......Allegheny......

Before me, the subscriber......................................Marie McFarlane......

in and for the County and Commonwealth aforesaid, personally appeared....Jack Devereaux............

who being duly sworn, according to law, doth depose and say......................

the banking practices of Chas F. Sober Fra J Sober and Jack Reese

As I had nothing to complain about I told Mr. Canaday that I didnt feel that a statement from me would be helpful to Sam Kaufmann's cause, as I felt that the things that Mr. Sober was doing were very helpful to the people of Freeport. After a lengthy conversation Mr Canaday seemed to think that he had convinced me of some sort of wrong doing in the business transactions of Mr. Sober. As I knew he was completly in error — I stopped to inform Mr. Sober of the things that I had heard about an investigation. As Mr. Sober probably felt that he was not guilty of any wrong doing — he didnt seem at all concerned about any investigation.

Later I was approached by two men from the F B I and asked if I would give a statement, I told them that no one had done anything detremental to me and that I wouldn't give any statements. They entered into and enlongated sermon of my duty as a good citizen to help in such an investigation and assure me that regardless of what I thought

and further deponent saith not.

Sworn *and subscribed before me this* 24th

day of.... April ....*A. D. 19* 62

Marie McFarlane (SEAL)

Jack Devereaux

115 4TH. ST.
FREEPORT, PA.

MARIE McFARLANE, NOTARY PUBLIC
My Commission Expires...... PITTSBURGH, ALLEGHENY COUNTY ......
MY COMMISSION EXPIRES NOVEMBER 29, 1965

[38]

FORM NALY No. 169-L—Affidavit   For Sale by P. O. Naly Co., Law Blank Publishers, 415 Grant St., Pgh. 19, Pa.

Commonwealth of Pennsylvania,

County of Allegheny } ss.

Before me, the subscriber Marie McFarlane

in and for the County and Commonwealth aforesaid, personally appeared Jack Devereaux

who being duly sworn, according to law, doth depose and say

that these were crimes involved in the business transactions of the Old Freeport Bank — so I gave them an account of the business deal that they seemed so interested in.

I didnt feel then and I dont feel now that there were any bad banking practices involved in any of my transaction with either Mr. Pobers or the Old Freeport Bank I was later called to testify at the trial of these men. Again I just stated the points of the deal that I had with Mr. Stingman. I feel now, as most of the Freeport people that these men were guilty of nothing more than superior service to the people and the victims of jealous competitors – using departments of the United States Government to accomplish their purpose of removing these men from the Banking Business

As this case was finally thrown out of court – apparently, I was right in feeling that there wasent any mis practices involved. Again I feel that as Mr. Kaufman – Mr. Canaday and the others committed a grave injustice in this matter. Mr. Pobers' and Mr. Geese should surely be reinstated by the Federal Deposit Insurance Corporation

and further deponent saith not.

Sworn and subscribed before me this 24th

day of April A. D. 1962

Marie McFarlane (SEAL)

Jack Devereaux

115 4TH. ST.
FREEPORT, PA.

My Commission Expires MARIE McFARLANE, NOTARY PUBLIC
PITTSBURGH, ALLEGHENY COUNTY
MY COMMISSION EXPIRES NOVEMBER 29, 1965

[39]

R. S. WILDER and J. M. LONDINO
Certified Public Accountants
521 FIRST AVENUE
AC. 4-6687   TARENTUM, PA.   ED. 5-9261

April 2, 1962

To.Whom It May Concern:

I have known Mr. Charles L. Sober for several years since
we were engaged as Auditors for the Old Freeport Bank of Freeport with which Mr. Sober was connected for a long period of time.
We have continued to make independent audits of the Bank since
Mr. Sober was forced to leave and we have not found any irregularities
that have arisen because of Mr. Sober's activities as head of the
bank.

I have also filed Income Tax Returns for Mr. Sober since the
time that I met him and to my best knowledge He hâs always been
honest in his dealings with me in every way and he has never asked
me to do anything wrong.

I would recommend that Mr. Charles Sober be given a chance
to participate in normal business activites again and that any
stigma against his name be removed.

Respectfully submitted,
R. S. Wilder C.P.A.
R.S.Wilder,C.P.A.

Petition

TO: THE HONORABLE ROBERT F. KENNEDY, ATTORNEY GENERAL OF THE UNITED STATES; THE FEDERAL DEPOSIT INSURANCE CORPORATION; THE PENNSYLVANIA DEPARTMENT OF BANKING; U.S. CONGRESSMAN JOHN DENT; U.S. CONGRESSMAN JOHN P. SAYLOR; STATE SENATOR ALBERT R. PECHAN.

We, the undersigned, being residents of Freeport, Armstrong County, Pennsylvania, and surrounding territories, state that we have known Mr. Charles L. Sober for many years both personally and in his capacity as an officer of The Old Freeport Bank. We also know his family and are familiar with his past life, particularly with the fine civic and communal contributions that he has made in the communities in which we live. We are aware of the fact that he had a case in the Federal Court in Pittsburgh, but we believe in his honesty and in his integrity, and we further believe that he should be given an opportunity to engage in the business of banking where he has made such a tremendous contribution to the success of The Old Freeport Bank, as well as the community in which it is located. On the basis of his past record and accomplishments, and believing that he is a fine, upstanding, and upright citizen, we petition your honorable Board to reinstate him to his rights and privileges to engage in the banking business.

In the following pages are reproduced only a small portion of hundreds and hundreds of signatures collected by petition.

	Name	Address	Occupation	Date
1	Elmer (signature)	356 Leesburg Rd. Greensburg, PA	Salesman	8/8/61
2	John J. Hughes	2613 Market St. McKeesport Pa	Uniformer	8/8/61
3	Martin Kolb	2102 Forbert Rd. McKeesport PA	Tavern owner	8/8/61
4	Shirley Calderone	152 Vandergrift Pa Bermudsville	Fireside Cat.	8/11/61
5	Arthur P. Blumenfeld	644 Pierce Pl. PP Greensburg Pa	Mill Worker	8/14/61
6	Larry E. Graham	642 Sunset St. Greensburg Pa Vandergrift	Boltman	8/11/61
7	Lawrence Calderone	324 Morrison Ave Vandergrift Pa	Service Station	8/12/61
8	(signature) Gould	161 Columbia Ave Vandergrift Pa	Merchant	8/12/61
9	(signature)	517 Franklin St Vandergrift Pa	Merchant	8/12/61
10	Joseph F. Bacco	225 Longfellow Greensburg Pa	Merchant	8-13-61
11	Leonard J. Copart	354 2nd Ave Vandergrift Pa	Glass Worker	8-12-61
12	Kenneth (signature)	973 Vandergrift Pa	Glass Worker	8-12-61

No.	Name	Address	Occupation	Date
86	James R Mobley			9566 8-24-61
87	R R Rodgers	218 2nd St Freeport Pa	chief of Police	8/23/61
88	Dorothy Stutzman	Sarver Pa	Housewife	5/24/61
89	Clyde Richard	Sarver Pa	Housewife	5/24/61
90		Box 277 Freeport Pa	Bar work	Elec 5/61
91	Robert M Fiss	111 West Alm Freeport Pa	Mechanic	8/26/61
92	Donald H VanPyke	55 ½ Franklin Ave Freeport Pa	Merchant	8/26/61
93	Otto S Welch	120 Butler Road	Meat Market	8/24/61
94	Mark R Reft	430 Old Pike Road	Truck Driver	8/26/61
95	Audrey Fretzel	" "	Housewife	8/26/61
96	Frank L Kepler	273 Old Pike Rd Freeport Pa	Farmer	8/26/61
97	Mrs Arthur Knox	RD #2 Sarver Pa	Painting	8/26/61
98	Margaret Treppan	Cabot PA	Housewife	8/26/61
99	Lydia Luggini	Cabot Pa	Housewife	8/24/61
100	Sidney J Lyman	R K #4 Saver Pa	Contractor	5/24/61

Name	Address	Occupation	Date
86. Hazel W. Roenigk	Box 310 R.O.#1 Cabot Pa	Tax Collector	Aug 7, 1961
87. Paul R. Roenigk	Box 310 Cabot R.O. Pa	Farmer	Aug 7, 1961
88. Arthur H. Roenigk	Box 310 Cabot R	Store Mgr	Aug 7, 1961
89. Victor Kunkel	Cabot 171 1/2	Farmer	Aug 7, 1961
90. Wayne M. Sell	Sarver Pa R.O.#2	Trucker	Aug 7, 1961
91. E. T. Macurdy	Sarver Pa R.O.#1	Proprietor	Aug 7, 1961
92. Harry H. Cooper Jr	977 Leys Freeport Pa	R.R.	Aug 10, 1961
93. William H. Macurdy	334 Sixth St W Freeport Pa	businessman	Aug 10, 1961
94. John Knoblock	R.O. 1 Box 251 Freeport Pa	RR Foreman	Aug 11, 1961
95. M. R. Rau/in	313 - 2nd St.	Salesman	Aug 11 - 61
96. Ralph Shreck	R.D.#1 Freeport Pa	Ass't. Foreman Corporation	Aug 11, 61
97. Emma Jane Grube	R.D.#1 Box 91 Freeport Pa	Housewife	Aug 11, 61
98. John R. Klym	R.O.#1 Freeport Pa.	Funnel Operator	Aug 11, 61

No.	Name	Address	Occupation	Date
52	S.R. Belcar	143 Walnut St Freeport PA	1 Rs	7-28-61
53	Thos. Dougherty	Freeport R.D. #1/4P	Wool Mill	7-29-61
54	Richard R. Curran	324 Second St Freeport	Bricklayer	7-29-61
55	James S. Her	115 4th St Freeport PA	Tool Scr	7-29-61
56	A.R. Montgomery	Sarver, Pa	Farmer	7-29-61
57	Ken Christie	Freeport PA RD 1	truck & Coal	7-29-61
58	Lloyd Stotz	RD #1 Freeport	P.R.R.	7-29-61
59	Miles W Barnett	116 Steward St Freeport	Ret P.R.R.	7-29-61
60	Blanche W Jones	597 Mill St Freeport	displ welder	7-31-61
61	___ Murdock	109 Market Schoenburg Pa	Merchant	8-1-61
62	Fred Wilson	RD #2 Sarver Pa	C.P.R.	8-1-61
63	___ Stukea	R.D. #2 Sarver Pa	self employed	8-1-61
64	Myrtle Mead	RD #2 Sarver Pa	Housewife	8-1-61
65	Wilbur Mead	Box 123	Labor	8-1-61
66	Alfred L Snow	123 CAB 7P	Brakeman	8-1-61

#	Name	Address	Occupation	Date
1	Mrs Lue Lewis	116 Buffalo St	Housewife	Aug 4, 1961
2	Anthony Katchi	217 High St Lake Freeport PA	Welder	Aug 5th
3	George Zapulich	RD #1 Sarver PA	Electrician	Aug 5th
4	Dora G Moudering	Box 205 Freeport PA	Foreman	Aug 5th
5	Harry H Hoak	#1 Freeport PA	Labor	Aug 5th
6	Ray Hoak	" " "	"	"
7	Betty Hoak	" " "	"	"
8	Ferguson Balline	RD #1 Freeport PA	Housewife	Aug 5
9	William Balline	" " PA	George	"
10	Emma Murphy	RD1 Sarver, Pa.	"	Aug 7
11	Ralph McDermott	1246 Butler Rd Freeport PA	Labor	Aug 8
12	Martin T Porter	358 Freeport RD PA	Labor	Aug 12
13	Edward Vilotti	318 Freeport Rd PA	Labor	Aug 12
14	Herman Stilliams	321 Freeport PA	Labor	Aug 12

32	Andrew Feng	R.D.#1 Cabot Pa	Retired	8/14/61
33	Edward Long	N.2 #1 Cabot Pa	Farmer	8/14/61
34	Thomas Long	RD #1 Cabot Pa	Wife	8/14/61
35	Ernest & amy	RD#1 Saxonburg Pa		
36	Ralph Althouse	Mabel R 1 PA		
37	Mrs. Balsam	Saxonburg PA		9/12/61
38	Buff Buckman	Saxonburg PA	Retired	9-12-16
39	Mrs. J. Tuckman	Saxonburg PA	Wife	9-12-61
40	Bernard Laake	Saxonburg PA		9-12-61
41	William Laake	Saxonburg PA	Wife	9-12-61
42	Mabel J Cypher	RD#1 Cabot Pa	wife	9-13-61
43	Wm M Cypher	RD#1 Cabot Pa	Milkman	9-13-61
44	Joseph Balch	Saxonburg PA	Brown	9-16-61
45	Clyde Peck	Cabot PA	Shiller	9-16-61
46	R.M. Pennington	Saxonburg PA	Tabor	9-16-61

#	Name	Address	Occupation	Date
17	C. F. Beard	1417 5th Ave [illegible]	Carrierman	8-28-61
18	Howard Delp Solomon	308 E 9th Ave Twin Falls	Millworker	8-28-61
19	Betty J. Solomon	308 E 9th Ave Twin Falls	Housewife	7-8-61
20	James R. Clark Jr.	1433 5th Avenue Nat'l Hghts	Clerk	8-28-61
21	Wilbur R. Burns	1431 Sixth Ave Nat'l Hghts	Millworker	8-28-61
22	Mabel L. Burns	1431 Sixth Ave Nat'l Hghts	Housewife	7-28-61
23	Charles W. Carney	1005 Idaho Ave Nat'l Hghts	Merchant	8-28-61
24	Mrs. Charles W. Carney	1005 Idaho Ave, Twin Falls	Clerk	8-28-61
25	A. J. Veurther	416 Milbourn St [illegible]	M. H. Agent	[illegible]
26	Frank Navetti	R#1 Buhl, Ida	Auto Dealer	8-29-61
27	George Ann	1133-7½ Ave E City	Auto Salesman	[illegible]
28	Willan D. Shields	309 Bailey Rd Grichts	Salesman	Aug 29 1961
29	[illegible]	R. Castleford Twin Falls	Contr Dealer	[illegible]
30	[illegible]	Box X 130 RD #1 [illegible] Burns	[illegible]	8-23-61

No.	Name	Address	Occupation	Date
17	Edna A. Rhodes	Box 388 RD#2 Leechburg Pa	Housewife	7/19/61
18	Bertha A. Rhodes	Box 388 RD#2 Leechburg Pa	Housewife	7/19/61
19	Donald H. Rose	323 Wilmer Ave. Kensington Pa	Truck Driver	7/19/61
20	Frances H. Rose	383 Wilmer Ave. New Kensington Pa	Clerk	7-12-61
21	Shirl Rothenmich	730 Glassboro New Kensington Pa	Contractor	7-19-61
22	Beulah Fryfoebner	250 Clendon Ave New Kensington Pa	Housewife	7-19-61
23	Harry Bechras	1439 5th St the row	Housewife	1-2-61
24	Jacob ... neskuch	R D #1 Apollo	Housewife	8-2-61
25	Jack Mugglecee	R D #1 Apollo 780 Tenth St	Military	8-2-61
26	Walter L. Ludwick	Oakmont Pa 233rd Street Butler Pa	Research Engr.	8-2-61
27	John E. Carpentry		Mgr	8-8-61
28	Irwin Woodenberg	Pa	Reginal Technican	S.S.61
29	Carl Marachi	Vandergrift Pa	Machine	8/8/61
30	Louis Orche	R.D. 1 Gilbert Pa	Machinist	8/8/61
31	Louis W. Orche Jr	R#D, Gilbert Pa	Housewife	8/8/61

Name	Address	Occupation	Date
52	Jean Bachman	R.D. #3 - Butler Pa	Housewife	8-31-61
53	Stephen Strotz	R.D. #3 Butler Pa	Housewife	8-31-61
54	Edward Pietschman	R.D. #3 Butler Pa	Housewife	8-31-61
55	Ralph Bachman	R.D. #3 Butler Pa	Farmer	8-31-61
56	Maria Carufm	MR 1 Laurence PR Freeport Pa	Pipe Fitter	8-31-61
57	Laurence C Wetzel	431 old P.K. Rd	Truck Driver	8-31-61
58	Mrs. Lee Wetzel	431 Old Gerald - Freeport Pa	Housewife	8-31-61
59	Mrs Clarence Price	428 Violet Dr Freeport Pa	Housewife	8-31-61
60	Candy B Burke	4-1) Box 271 New Kensington Pa	Merger	8-31-61
61	Richard F Baff	2898 Leechburg Rd Lower Burrell Pa. PR	Self-Employed Insurance Agent Notary Public	8-31-61
62	Arthur C Beale	R.D. #7 Freeport, Pa	Self-Employed Service Station	8-31-61
63	Thomas R Burke	572 Lambhurst Freeport	Retired	9-1-61
64	Henry J Murphy	231 Mill Export Pa	Plumber Production	9-1-61

No.	Name	Address	Occupation	Date
32	Rosella C. Elliott	1067 McIntyre Lane	Housewife	7-28-1961
33	Mrs. ___ Bessemer		Merchant	1-25-61
34	___ Bessemer	162 ___		1-25-61
35	Mrs. Al. ___	R.F.D 1 Fairport, Pa.	Laborer	1-25-41
36	C. ___ Buford	1687 McIntyre Lane		1-25-61
37	Mrs. ___	Box 13 Russellton PA	Factory Worker	1-25-61
38	___ Wilma Rogers	R.D 1 ___ PA	Housewife	7-28-61
39	Joseph ___	82 ___	___	7-28-61
40	William D. Rhodes	113 South ___	___	7/28/61
41	Paul A. Wright	31 Cherry St.	Mechanic Co.	7/28/61
42	Coach Brighton	320 Clubhouse	Contractors	7/29/61
43	Patricia L. Wood	Oakridge Dr.	Secretary	7/29/61
44	Frank ___	252 ___	___	7/29/61
45	Thomas B. Kibbe	427 Hilltop Dr.	___	7/29/61
46	___	530 ___	___	7-29-61
47	___	Bessemer Park		7/31/61

Name	Address		Date
52	Mrs. Ethel Cypher	Fenelton, Pa.	Housewife	Aug 22-61
53	Mrs. Mary Ann Logue	R.D. 1 - Cabot, Pa.	Housewife	Aug. 29, 1961
54	Mrs. Jennie French	R.D. 1, Cabot, Pa.	Housewife	Aug 29, 1961
55	Bob Zona Jr	R.D., Cabot Pa	Labor	Aug 30, 1961
56	Lucile Zona	R.D. 1 Cabot Pa	Housewife	Aug 30, 1961
57	John F. Kampf	RD 1 Cabot Pa	Labor	Sept 2, 1961
58	Richard M. Williams	Sarpenburg Pa	Millwright	Sept 27, 1961
59	Kathryn J. Montgomery	P.O.# Sarver Pa	Bookkeeper	Sept 27, 1961
60	Mrs. Leland Montgomery	R.D.# Sarver Pa	Housewife	Sept 29 61
61	Leland R. Kampf	P.O.# Sarver Pa	Engineering Tech P.C.M	Oct 2-61
62	J. J. Dasher	R.D. # Sarver Pa	Inspector	Oct 3-61
63	E. P. Parmer	R.D. 1 Cabot PA	Farmer	Oct 3-61
64	Carl M. Parker	Sarver Pa	Mechanic	Oct 3-61

No.	Name	P.O.	Occupation	Date
66	James W. Neely			
67	John Loughlewrty	93 Manchiterpoost Pa	Retired	8-18-61
68	William Seeley	R.D. #1 Sarvel Pa	Service Worker	8-18-61
69	Thomas Brake	Saxont Pa	Mechanic Locomotive Engineer	8-18-61
70	Virla J. Outhrah	215 Riverside Saxont Pa		8-19-61
71	Walter J. Turner	RD #1 Huntington Pa	Neeley	8-19-61
72	Paul Thomas	Saxonburg Pa	Merchant	8-21-61
73	J. Browning	1801 Freeport Rd Natrgta	Merchant	8-21-61
74	Clarence Fair	R.D. 1 Saxont Pa	Carrier	8-22-61
75	John E. Wyffard	RD #1 Bowers Pa	Railroad	8-22-61
76	Walter W. Hoffman	Box #4 Saxonborg Pa	Self Employed Dry Cleaner	8/25/61
77	Wood T. Snover	Saxonburg Pa	Self Employed	8/22/61
78	Rudolph Parisi	RP #4 Butler Pa	Merchant	8/22-61
79	Helen Parisi	RD #4 Butler Pa	Merchant	8/22/61
80	A.H. Manhart	RD #1 Saxonburg Pa	Farmer	8/22/61

Name	Address	Occupation	Date
17	R # 2 Sarver Pa	Clerk	8-1-61
18	R.D. #1 Cabot Pa	Merchant	7-26-61
19 Charles & Rush	R.D. # Cabot Pa	Merchant	7/24/61
20 Ernest F. Schott	Sarverburg Pa	Merchant	7/26/61
21 Louis Renn	Freeport Pa	merchant	7/26/61
22 Roger Luppenlespu	Freeport Pa	Burgess Chairman	7/26/61
23 A. M. Letchild	Freeport Pa	mill man	7/24/61
24 James W. Seibel	Freeport PA	carpenter	7/26/61
25 Raymond Summers	R.D. # 1 Box 332 Sarver	Labor	7/26/61
26 Robert A. Dalmane	423 W. 8th Ave Tarentam	USED CAR DEALER	7-27-61
27 Fred W. Young		Salesman	7/27/61
28 August J. Schipman		Coin deal	7/27/61
29 L. C. Elliott	R.d. 1 Freeport Pa	Engineer Ore. B & RR.	7-27-61

No.	Name	Address		Date
66	Mary Doloty	Rd #1 Boswell Pa	Agnes W. [?]	9-1-61
67	Mrs. Ella Bolz			
68	Frank W. Hoover	Box 16 Somerset Pa	Bond Buyer	9-1-61
69	Florence & Harry Sarver	Pa	Housewife	9-1-61
70	Robert E. Shuee	Ferndale Pa	Laborer	9-1-61
71	Lyle Shuee	New Kensington Pa 996 Willard	Buccaneer	9-2-61
72	J. Konieski	160 Willow [?]	Carpenter Ret	9-2-61
73	J. Frueligan	219 N. Mill St.	Baker	9-2-61
74	S. Davis	222 Seymour [?]	Artist	9-12-61
75	Ng. Ackman	546 Franklin St	Railroader	9-2-61
76	E. Darrow	514 Ripon Dr. New Kensington Pa	Dry Shopper	
77	Frank Mrazik	RD 2 Box 410 Pa	Machinist	9-6-61
78	Vito J. Mrazik	RD #2 Box 410 Pa	Housewife	9-6-61
79	Ernest Helmick	Shelton Park National Life	Salesman	9-6-61
80	Melvin Earley	527 North St Freeport Pa	Census [?] P.P. Ry	9-6-61

Name	Address	Occupation	Date
17 Esther E. Bibr	Box 352 Russell, Pa.	House Wife	11/27/61
18 William W. Palmer	Russellton, Pa.	Pharmacist	11/27/61
19 P. Montgomery	Russellton, Pa.	P. E. Broken	11/27/61
20 Susan E. Munson	Susan E. R.	Dr. Bohn	11/27/61
21 Howard A. Munson	Russellton, Pa.	Teacher	11/20/61
22 Clayton J. Saul	R.D. #1 Spiceburg Pa.	Truck Driver	11/29/61
23 Ernest J. Walsh	Box 95 Centerville, Pa.	Office Manager	11/29/61
24 Hugh A. Frick	Box 123 R D 1 Cheswick Pa.	Brakeman	11/30/61
25 Ryburn M. Frick	1214 Box 123 Cheswick Pa.	Engineer	11/30/61
26 Catherine M. Murray	Russellton, Pa.	Housewife	12/1/61
27 Ralph Burres	357-3rd Pa.	Carpenter	12-2-61
28 W. K. Clayton	Di Worthington, Pa R D 1 Pa.	Clerk	12-2-61
29	552 Franklin Pa. R D 1 Pa.	Supervisor	12-2-61

Name	Address		Date
1	Jesse C. McKee	400 Market St Freeport Pa 80 yrs shoe	Retired	7-18-61
2	Floss J. Stewart	507 Market St Freeport Pa	P.R.R. Brakeman	7/8/61
3	Wilbur Stewart	507 Market St Freeport Pa		7-15-61
4	Mary M. Marcables	507 Market St Freeport Pa	Housewife	
5	Charles W. Burford	309-4 St Freeport Pa	Merchant	7/19/61
6	Mrs E Howze III	302 4th St Freeport Pa	Housewife Merchant	7/19/61
7	Joseph Ricker	224 Fifth St Freeport Pa	Jeweler	7/19/61
8	Robert Powell Jr	256 Freeport Pa	Mill Worker Restaurant Operator	7/14/61
9	Bertha Kamer	223 - 5 St Freeport Pa		7/19/61
10	Mrs K Kamer	223 - 5 St Freeport Pa	" "	7/19/61
11	Pearl Klingay	509 Market St Freeport Pa	Freeport	7/19/61
12	George Klingay	509 Market St Freeport Pa	Freeport	7/19/61
13	Naomi Douglass	336 Second St Freeport Pa		7/19/61

#	Name	Address		Date
17	Stanley Karpyak	CITY OF LOWER BURRELL PA 1116 Hydevand	Laborer	8-4-61
18	William Clatt	498 Craigdell Rd NEW KENSINGTON PA	"	"
19	Samuel Kiral	R D #3 Leechburg PA NEW KENSINGTON PA	Truck Driver	8/4/61
20	Lewis L Hulbert	3172 Orchard Dr CITY OF LOWER BARRELL PA	Route Salesman	8/4/61
21	Dorothy Platt	207 Marlborough Dr	Clerk woman	8-5-61
22	Joseph Midas	237 Bellat Springdale PA	Carpenter	8-5-61
23	Wm C Foster	136 Reed New Ken PA	Carpenter	8-5-61
24	E L Harris	656 Kimball " " PA	Carpenter	8-5-61
25	Charles Hulgin	85-9 3rd Ave NEW KENSINGTON PA	Constable	8-5-61
26	E Van Horne	1707 Woodmont ave NEW KENSINGTON PA	Mechanic	8-5-61
27	Robert L Greer	291 Ky Drive CITY OF LOWER BURRELL PA	Laborer	8-5-61
28	Loretta Haген	" "	Housewife	8-5-61
29	Charles Carroll	200 Cherrywood NEW KENSINGTON PA	Barber	8-5-61
30	Robert H Canfield	21-11th Cap NEW KENSINGTON PA	Mechanic	8-5-61

#	Name	Address	Occupation	Date
		3088 Bailey St	Glassboro	8-6-61
31	H. J. Hewitt			
32	William Fawcett	3c1 6th St, New Kensington Pa		8-8-61
33	Hugo Declemente	1600 3th Ave, New Kensington Pa		8/2/61
34	Angel Santalici	214 Morgan St, New Kensington Pa	Shoe Repair	6/6/61
35	Ernest Ewing	2617 Kenneth Ave, City of Lower Burrell Pa	Bank Clerk	8/8/61
36	Felicia Spiro	125 Willow Dr, New Kensington Pa	Housewife	Aug 31 1961
37	John Scott Spiro	2783 Grant St, New Ken Pa	Construction Estimator	Aug 31, 1961
38	John Spiro	125 Willow Drive, City of Lower Burrell Pa	Contractor	Aug. 31, 1961
39	Sara E. Spiro	2783 Grant St, City of Lower Burrell Pa	Housewife	Aug 31, 1961
40	Helen Gebhart	5308 Middle Rd, Freeport Pa	Saleslawn	Sept 1, 1961
41	Miss Richard Knoble			Sept 1, 1961
42	Mr. Richard Knoble		Mechanic	Sept. 1, 1961
43	Dolores Greer	1318 Butler Rd, Freeport Pa	Housewife	Sept. 1, 1961
44	Dolores Cupp	548 Wall St, Freeport Pa	Housewife	Sept 1, 1961
45	Harry Herman	Sarver R.D. 1 Pa	Tube	Sept 9, 1961

	Name	Address	Occupation	Date
1	Louis S. Karly	6631 Shetland Dr	Pgh. 6-Pa	7-17-61
2	Peter O'Karly	6631 Shetland Dr	Pgh 6 Pa	7-17-61
3	John Burkett	1039 Nelson Ave	Brackenridge Pa	7/17/61
4	Sylvia J Burkett	1039 Nelson Ave	Brackenridge	7/17/61
5	John J. Spence	1205 Spring Hill Rd	Natrona Hts	7/22/61
6	Gustave C. Heyman	RD #2 Iroquois Trail	Beaver, Pa	7/19/61
7	Maria Heyman	6491 Iroquois Trail RD #2 Beaver	Beaver, Pa	7/19/61
8	James H. Smith	RD 1 Saxonburg Pa	miner	7/21/61
9	Anna T. Smith	RD 1 Saxonburg Pa	Housewife	7/21/61
10	L. Arthur Spencer	1205 Spring Hill Rd	housewife	7/22/61
11	James A. Bartoll	3950 Bakerstown Rd	Gibsonia Pa	7/22/61
12	Helen A. Bartoll	3950 Bakerstown Rd	Y'housew Pa	7-22-61
13	Pauline Nickels	P.O. Box 503	foreman housewife	7/26/61